Contents

Foreword

Delegates at the 2006 Community and Youth Workers' Union (CYWU) national conference stood in silent respect and sadness at the death of our dear friend and lifelong active member, Jeremy Brent. We also celebrated his life and appreciated his magnificent contribution to youth work practice and theory and to trade unionism.

Nationally, CYWU is greatly indebted to his consistent, reliable, good-natured and influential contribution. Of course, our Bristol members have lost a wonderful friend and comrade, and like us all, will always remember him with affection. Bristol Youth Service has lost one of its most talented and respected workers.

Jeremy was a very complete person and a professional; he recognised that thought without action leads nowhere and action without thought is useless. Consequently, he combined his great commitment to young people with a commitment to other youth workers. By helping to get youth workers organised to defend themselves and improve their position and improve society's view of them, Jeremy recognised that individual youth workers would be stronger. He consequently gave freely and generously of his time to be an active trade unionist in the Bristol Branch of CYWU. He was always there, wisely, quietly and modestly giving support and encouragement to collective work.

No person or youth centre is an island; we all exist in a wider landscape, and Jeremy was always aware that unless we considered the wider picture, our little worlds would be less colourful and less protected. He believed that we cannot really achieve fairness for young people and a better deal for them, unless, as professional workers, we can achieve justice and respect for ourselves. That is why his trade unionism was an integral part of his youth work.

It was the same with his youth work practice. He always put daily occurrences into context. From the minutely observed events of life for young people in Southmead to the closely considered interventions of himself and colleague youth workers, Jeremy reflected deeply and shared his thoughts for the benefit of others in some eloquent and moving articles that we will, as a union and a profession, republish. Because his work was grounded in real life and practice, Jeremy was able to say more effectively and powerfully in a few pages what many more theoretical writers take chapters to say. His writings should inspire all youth workers to write more about the simple everyday things that are so full of interest and insight to our shared humanity.

These are dangerous times. As mighty world powers strut the globe destroying young lives, Jeremy's life and work remind us of the virtues of the local, the peaceful and the carefully crafted. Global powers like to move people from country to country, destabilise local communities or tell workers that they must be infinitely flexible on the labour market and change from job to job and career to career, being Jacks and Jills of all trades. Jeremy's commitment to one community and one skilled profession demonstrates the virtues of stability and perfection of a craft. By being rooted, confident, knowledgeable and committed, he was able to fly and take many young people with him.

He did not want promotion out of face-to-face work. He wanted to be alongside young people as they became more creative, more responsible, more ambitious, more caring and more able to enjoy each moment as it flies by in this wonderful human world.

Jeremy's work demonstrates the vital importance of youth work within the spectrum of learning. Through youth work, informal learning takes place. From the voluntary relationship established with young people, a dialogue begins that develops through trust and mutuality to professional friendship and accompaniment. In such a journey, the rights of young people and their voice are primary. Youth workers have built a unique public service, always difficult for the state to contain and appreciate, that has some of the most lastingly positive effects. Jeremy reminds us of the subtlety of this work and its great political significance; we express through youth work deep commitment to others and through this commitment to individuals a universal commitment to a transformed society that will put people, not profit, at the centre of economic and political aspiration.

Some people have lofty monuments built in their name. Jeremy was worth far more than such superficial things. He left a living real legacy of values and styles of work that will never be extinguished and will unobtrusively influence generations to come. We all owe Jeremy and his family a great deal

Doug Nicholls, National Secretary
Community and Youth Workers' & Not for Profit sector of Unite the Union

Notes on the author

Jeremy Brent was born in Buenos Aires, Argentina in 1950 and moved to Bedford, England when he was five. After studying at Bedford School and working on building sites in Notting Hill and Shepherd's Bush, he went to Oxford University where he developed his already keen interest in anarchist politics. On graduating, he founded and ran the South Oxford Adventure Playground. He started working at the adventure playground on the Southmead Estate in Bristol in 1975, before moving on to the youth centre in 1978; he was to carry on working there for the rest of his life. He took a Masters degree in Cultural Studies at Birmingham University in 1992, and went on to complete a PhD at the University of the West of England, Bristol in 2000. He published a number of articles in youth work and community development books and journals. He died in 2006 after a short illness. He is survived by his partner, Meg, and his two sons, Trevor and Colin.

After his death, many of those who had been close to Jeremy expressed their desire to see his thoughtful and inspiring works published. In this book, we have brought together his PhD thesis and the article 'Communicating what youth work achieves: the smile and the arch', first published in the journal *Youth and Policy* in 2004. These are accompanied by a foreword by Doug Nicholls, National Secretary of the Community and Youth Workers' Union, and an introduction by Richard Johnson. In the Epilogue, three of the main 'characters' of the work and Jeremy's son, Colin, update the reader on the situation in Southmead in 2008. Marj Mayo then reflects on the relevance of Jeremy's work today. Jeremy's work, both academic and at Southmead, was guided by critical self-reflection and conducted with intellectual, political and professional integrity. We hope the publication of this book will provide tools to those looking to sustain and build on these principles.

Trevor and Colin Brent

Introduction

No easy answers: Jeremy Brent, Southmead and 'community'

When this volume was first proposed, I said I would like to comment on the PhD thesis on which it is, in part, based and for which I was one of the academic advisers. In preparation for my contribution, I re-read the thesis, an experience that combined the contradictory feelings of sadness and of delight. My sadness stemmed from the loss of a good and kind man, a brave, thoughtful and effective professional, and a friend with whom I had shared a close intellectual and political dialogue for several years. The delight lay in recovering qualities in his work that I had admired in reading his earlier drafts – a subtle, self-reflective, ruminative wisdom, often delicious writing, an intense engagement with issues of everyday practice and with the people he worked with, and an ability to expose many different sides of the same question. There is satisfaction, too, in realising that his work remains relevant for today and so can serve as one memorial to a life of sustained human solidarity. In what follows, I want to try to specify these impressions without, I hope, losing the emotional threads that unite them.

Southmead, Birmingham, Bristol

One way of seeing *Searching for community* is as a story of three places (though I am sure there were more). Central, of course, was Southmead, the North Bristol housing estate where Jeremy Brent worked from 1975, first for an adventure playground, then running Southmead Youth Centre. As John Westcott puts it in the booklet produced for Jeremy's Memorial Day on 2 September 2006, 'no one had ever worked at Southmead for so long ... it turned out to be his life work'. As Jeremy himself put it, with typical honesty about his ambivalences:

> This quarter of a century's involvement of mine with Southmead puzzles me. It was not my intention to stay so long when I first took work there on a six-month contract. Staying that long does indicate a strong attachment to ... something. This something has not always been Southmead itself, with which I have a love–hate relationship, but the continual feeling I have of unfinished business with the

place and the people, like a familial relationship. (Chapter One, this volume, pages 16-17)

In 1991-92, however, he took time out to study on the MA programme at Birmingham University's Department of Cultural Studies and Sociology, the renamed and expanded Centre for Contemporary Cultural Studies (CCCS) that was founded in the mid-1960s. This was where we first met, and there are, in retrospect, some parallels in our two stories, stories that touched for a time in the UK's second city. In the year that Jeremy first arrived in Southmead, I was appointed to teach a new MA course in Birmingham. CCCS wasn't exactly a community organisation, but it was an unusual academic collective, influenced by 1960s' ideas of participatory democracy, and with a strong shared sense of the social and political significance of knowledge and of the way in which it was produced. Typically, the intellectual work of CCCS was organised in small collectives. An historian by background, I was originally hired to teach cultural history on the MA programme, while Stuart Hall, who was Director of CCCS until 1979, taught theories and approaches to culture. In the early 1990s when Jeremy came to Birmingham, I was still teaching on this Masters programme (now a Masters in Social Science), responsible for a core element on 'frameworks of culture and power' – a broadly historical account of the different ways in which cultural questions have been seen as having political significance. I also led a research and reading group on approaches to identity. Residues of the earlier idea of research sub-groups remained in a range of more specialised options. I remember that Jeremy worked on racism and anti-racism, and wrote an excellent dissertation entitled 'The battle of Golden Hill', about an environmental struggle he was involved in and wanted to record and assess. It was a continuing feature of the educational philosophy of what had come to be called 'the Birmingham School' that people were encouraged to work on the issues that most concerned them.

I remember Jeremy as a creative and supportive 'student' and a deeply thoughtful man, both in the discussion of complex ideas and in the evaluation of political and educational issues. He clearly enjoyed the freedom of sustained thinking and, perhaps, some release from his demanding work at Southmead. Yet I can remember few students who have been so thoughtful and well informed about the nexus between theory and practice (or, as I prefer to say theory, research and other practices). This relationship was at the centre of his work and he typically refused easy answers. He refused to subordinate critical thinking to pragmatic decision making, but he was also sceptical about much academic knowledge. Later, back at Southmead, immersed again in everyday conflicts and rewards and keeping a diary for his PhD research at the University of West of England (UWE) in Bristol, he wrote a striking passage that sums up many of his themes and sounds the keynotes for this introduction. He was reflecting on the experience of having physically to eject a young man from Southmead Youth Centre:

> At the time of the most interesting events I am so involved in what is going on, uncertain of it and myself, and tired – difficult then to write it all down.
>
> Also difficult to make it an academic exercise for analysis. Maybe it should be though. At present I feel sceptical about academic knowledge.
>
> There is a kind of optimism about ideas, a playfulness, a feeling of power as they are understood and manipulated.
>
> There is a pessimism and depression when confronted by angry and violent young people – a feeling of powerlessness, of feeling unable to cope, of not being able to take on all the implications.
>
> Ideas can give you the run of the world – action is limited.
> (page 64)

There's certainly a (justified) irritation here with (some?) academic knowledge. There is a sense of its incapacity when faced with hard choices and impossible situations. Yet there is also an exhilaration about ideas and their possible power – an intellectual excitement that I also remember in the author as a person, and that as a teacher of critical ideas, I naturally share.

So I was pleased when, with the historian Jeffrey Weeks and the sociologist Jon Bird, I was asked to be one of Jeremy's advisers when he registered for a PhD at UWE. UWE, it seemed to me, provided the intellectual space and academic recognition that was vital for Jeremy's type of local, community-based research. The four of us sometimes met at UWE as a panel and sometimes Jeremy and I met, one to one, at my house in Leicester. I remember that during an early crisis concerning Jeremy's health, I went to visit him and his partner Meg at home in Bristol. On this visit – or perhaps it was another – Jeremy showed me round the Southmead estate and the youth centre, giving me a glimpse of two important spaces in his life.

I didn't hear that he had died until I was asked to write this introduction, and the first thing I remembered was how supportive

Jeremy (and other students at Birmingham) had been when my wife, Jill, died suddenly in January 1992. Although I managed to keep on teaching, this must have been only four months into Jeremy's experience of the Birmingham course.

The thesis

Jeremy described his research as 'a search for a way to understand and engage with community, both in general, and specifically in Southmead' (page 11). His method is complex, with different layers. He was concerned with what he called 'settings' and these included the wider material and cultural contexts within which Southmead as an estate was placed. These contexts included its positioning in a global political economy (for example, the employment situation, the arrival of a supermarket and the involvement of businesses in community provision), the ways in which it figured in city politics and policies and the way in which it had been publicly represented – often, he argued, with a false 'objectivity' – as a 'difficult housing estate'. This, in itself, distinguishes his approach from a tradition of community studies much preoccupied with the internal relations and 'unique' character of a locality. Also distinctive was the way Jeremy moved all the time from recording detailed case studies – often of events in which he himself was involved – to mapping not just spaces or places, but also relevant arguments and ideas. Indeed, one of his key 'settings' is 'the vast amount of thinking, talking and writing that exists about community'. As he put it, with his careful, undismissive but sceptical eye (page 21):

> Community as an issue also infiltrates much everyday thought and action, and is bandied about in local and national politics and policy making as well as being the subject of a wide range of academic discourse. As such a ubiquitous term, however, it does have to be given a health warning – 'handle with care'.

At the centre of the thesis on which this book is based are particular moments in the construction of forms of community or collective identity by adults and young people, always with this human agency in the intimate foreground. He typically steps back a pace, however, to reflect on these happenings in order to understand them. Understanding, here, involves both seeing the logics and the sense of people's meanings and (sometimes bizarre) actions, and recognising fully the participant-observer's own complicity in both the situation and the judgements about it. This did not mean, however, that he held back from evaluation. A key question indeed is how far a particular community practice opens possibilities or closes them down – and for whom.

Jeremy was also, I think, interested in *explanation* and this involved drawing on a wide range of ideas that he also explicitly grasps and describes. These ideas may be about the standpoint or point of view of participants (including researchers), about pleasure and aesthetic value in communal forms, or, very richly, about the uses and effects of language, or narrative or media representation, and especially, of course, about the lives and collective actions of young people, and about the construction – and the deconstruction – of forms of 'community'. There is not enough space in this introduction to explore all these themes, themselves only a selection of those covered in the book. It is in any case much better to read Jeremy's own version. But I do want to comment briefly on his basic arguments about community as a form of collective identity before turning to their significance for today.

Community as constructed

Jeremy rejects cut-and-dried definitions of community, partly because they often act normatively to exclude and discipline, or alternatively to romanticise and set the romance in stone. As we shall see later, he was critical of both these approaches, especially perhaps the first. Rather, community is best understood in terms of the processes by which it comes about. Community isn't something that is given or can be relied on. Rather, the idea of community is attached to different forms of collective identity that have actually to be created. Community in this sense is always fragile and fractured, always takes variable forms and always involves particular kinds of power. It includes, embraces and empowers, but it also excludes.

There are many particular 'moments' of community explored in the book. Sometimes, especially in the case of young people, these take the form of ephemeral carnivals, testing the law or moral conventions or the normal boundaries of space – for example, building a wall from paving slabs, taking over a local wood, joyriding. Sometimes the construction of community is explicit in particular media or forms of representation – a visual art project and exhibition, a community play, a local radio station. The more enduring constructions of community take the form of community organisations. Four main examples are explored in some detail: a drugs project with an emphasis on counselling users; a development trust providing training and leisure activities; a group of mothers running activities for children; and a campaign targeting drug dealers and providing sporting opportunities for young people. Each of these differ – and sometimes compete – in the social groups they mainly activate, in the leaderships thrown up, in the typical modes of action, and in the version of 'Southmead as community' that they produce. Crucial in this view of community, of course, is the phenomenon of group action. Actions may carry their own symbolical meanings embedded in the site or form of activity, or, in the case of the more stable organisations and the art, drama or local radio, they may articulate a more elaborate programme or version.

It is important to stress the distinctiveness of this view of community and what is being argued *against*. Three views of community are usefully mapped in Chapter Eight. These are common in the academic literature and they also inform policies and everyday common sense. First, and critically, community (and 'communitarianism') is sometimes seen as an illusion. It has 'magical' properties. It hides or mystifies more important issues. It ignores global forces; it masks or distorts recognition of inequalities of class, gender or race. It ignores both the cross-border flows and the constraining structures that feature in modernity. Community – and an emphasis on locality in general – is at best a vain attempt to check these global processes. At worst, it is allied to racist and other exclusions or serves narrow political or commercial advantage. A second view is that community is 'an organic form'. It is 'the life world' of everyday existence, never wholly colonised by 'the systems of politics and economics'. Community in this sense is often seen as having a superior reality: it is 'real life', 'real people', spontaneity rather than artificiality, a space of authenticity and natural human relations. This strongly positive view of community is often allied to a third: a straightforward identification of a community with a place. Southmead, then, is simply 'a community'.

Jeremy agrees with the first view of community in its opposition to romanticisation and in its focus on global–local relationships, but he does not in any way dismiss local collective action, under the banner of community, as illusory or false. Structural realities and cross-community flows of messages, power and people do not cancel out the validity of locally based communal actions, although they certainly complicate them. Jeremy is also very sharp with action programmes like the Bristol Social Project of 1952-63, in which areas like Southmead are presented as 'trouble spots' with which only professional intervention can deal:

> The act of telling people that the understanding on which
> they base their activity is illusory perpetuates the relationship
> of the superior role of the social scientists to unknowing

participants that we first encountered in the work of the Bristol Social Project. (page 212, this volume)

He considers it defeatist to see community activity always as a means of social control.

> Community activities are messy and conflictual, the opposite of the stasis and pacification that would exist only if there were quiescent resignation to the forces around rather than mobilisations. These community activities [his four case studies above] were not defensive, but made offensive claims on the wider world. They were ways by which people entered the maelstrom rather than succumb to it. (page 212)

Far from being static, he sees community activity, and the collective actions of young people especially, as themselves 'a maelstrom, all about movement, with its young people [like capital] even unleashing their own forces of creative destruction' (page 212). It follows from this view that arguments about 'political worth' cannot be generalised. The value of an action depends on 'the focus that it is built around, and the issues that it confronts' (page 212) and also, as the analysis is followed through, its effects. As to the relationship with global forces and the possibility of broader alliances for change, it is only when local community action is seen as 'simple' or is essentialised that it is necessarily opposed to 'global community' or, to use the current rather individualising keyword, 'global citizenship'. From this point of view, 'neither local nor global community is sufficient without the other' (page 213). Both can be 'humanising (if illusory) constraint[s]' on the flows and divisions that threaten people's control over their own lives (page 213).

It is worth adding, at least for an academic readership, that this view of community politics draws heavily on contemporary theories and researches into questions of identity, the collective identity of nation, ethnic group or tradition, for instance. There is the same 'constructivist' move – communities like nations or ethnic identities do not arise primordially but are historically produced. There is a fascination with the means of construction that takes the author, in a typical cultural-studies move, into the territories of the literary, the artistic, aesthetics, rhetorics and language more generally. There is also the parallel or interrupting deconstructive move, drawing explicitly on theorists like Jacques Derrida, Michel Foucault and Mikhail Bakhtin. Community is not fixed but moving, not essential or singular but multiple, never finished as a process, always deferred, not to be judged in general but only in its specific effects. It is, in my view, this second deconstructive move that helps this book to avoid the tyrannical choice of having to embrace 'community' or dismiss it, applaud it as progressive or criticise it in totality – and to come up with something much more interesting and useful.

To put it another way, it helps the author to clarify his own standpoint and role in relation to Southmead and its different forms of collective action, including, of course, the presence that is often half hidden or at least has a low profile in the story – Southmead Youth Centre itself. 'Standpoint', or point of view, and the criticism of standpoint theory are a crucial part of *Searching for community*. Broadly, standpoint theory, which first came out of one kind of Marxism and was subsequently developed by sections of the Women's Movement in the 1980s, insists on the truth-producing potential of subordinated social groups. The powerful are not necessarily all-seeing and those with less power may have a sharper sense of how power and knowledge interact. Standpoint theory informs the discussion of insider and outsider views of Southmead and the need for Southmeaders to resist external representations with positive pictures of the estate. It also informs the recognition of the gap between youth and adult perceptions of issues in the area and the way in which adult versions of community may often be defined against 'the youth'. Above all, perhaps, it informs the author's search – most evident in Chapter Five – to understand his own position as a middle-class professional and 'coaxer', who works on a working-class estate. The sense of emotional identification here is very strong, but the difference is not forgotten – or allowed to be forgotten, one suspects, from the vivid accounts of confrontation. Yet it is not surprising that in reflecting on theories of standpoint, the author rejects any automatic identification of social position – especially class position – with superior or inferior knowledge or with 'right-on' or 'right-off' politics. Standpoint theory informs his own rejection of 'the master's view' – the superior, objectifying gaze on people as problems. It informs his strong support for, and participation in, community arts. But this is a *critical* theory of standpoint, in which subordinated groups or their points of view do not always produce truer insights or better actions, and may be self-destructive or self-defeating, or usually, perhaps, a mixture of all these. So the author's attachment to the people of Southmead leaves plenty of space for critical awareness of 'self' and 'others' and for pondering the nature of this relationship. He understands very well, for instance, the response to external criticism (of which he may be the bearer) that 'takes the form of a kind of humanising nationalism' (page 124). He also grasps the ironic truth that this resistance can 'subjugate and silence the diversity that is within the area' (page 124) and so close down its possibilities.

Relevance today

Searching for community is very much a product of its time, both of the mid- to late 1990s and the longer post-1960s trajectory of (especially) New Left thinking. While community and participation – and, more broadly, an emphasis on popular agency – were strong legacies of (and to) the New Left and the new social movements of the 1960s and 1970s, the devastating experiences of Thatcherite individualism, the intellectual revival of neoliberal theories and the real erosion of social solidarities, placed the traditions of thinking about community in a new light. The take-up of various aspects of communitarianism in New Labour's 'Third Way' phase, before and after (but mainly before) 1997, was part of the ubiquity of 'community' that the author charts more fully in the opening parts of the book.

There are three main ways in which it seems to me that this study remains highly relevant today, although I know these do not exhaust its usefulness.

The first concerns the crisis in working-class representation, which is in large part a consequence of the particular destructive political work of Blairite New Labour. It is because the language of class has almost disappeared from mainstream political repertoires that 'community' has become a kind of metaphor for class (and for many other social divisions, especially ethnicity and race). So a study that recognises the continued reality of class as well as the fact that class solidarities must be constructed, may take different and surprising forms, and must still be evaluated and self-assessed carefully, seems to me of key importance.

The second key significance is best drawn out in the supplementary essay that does not appear in the thesis, but is published in Chapter Ten and is referred to as 'The smile and the arch'. One of the things the author and I argued about was how far, or how explicitly, he should draw out the implications of his study for professional practice, and for public policy. I read 'The smile and arch', rather self-centredly perhaps, as an answer to my request that he should do more. The essay draws out more of the implications of his analysis for youth work.

What is especially interesting to me now, however, is that the author's own practice is juxtaposed to the imposed models of youth work that have emerged under New Labour, and represent the regulative, disciplinary side of its adoption of individualising market relationships.

Perhaps it was this growing contrast that enabled him to articulate his own version more clearly. He juxtaposes a 'messy', open-ended, coaxing of self-agency from young people – a learning about themselves 'by physical action as much as by talking' (page 267) – alongside the contemporary emphasis on 'predetermined targets'. His version is for young people 'to learn about creation and transformation', by being 'coaxed' and resourced in different kinds of activity, from arts to sports. This has implications for the professional, not all of them easy. Being untargeted does not mean being disorganised, or unprofessional. As he puts it in a beautiful insight about the professional self, 'ironically, to be non-managerial with others takes a much greater depth of management of self' (page 267). In this context, as regulative mechanisms squeeze and constrain, and young people must deal with what is often a fearsomely hostile world, the role of youth worker is – a formulation I love – 'a kind of kink in the chain of command' (page 268).

The third and most important reason why Jeremy's life and work is relevant today concerns personal and social ethics and what is taught in the actual living of a life. 'Community', of course, also signals an ethic of this kind and is often contrasted to the dominant individualism of our times. This individualism and the competitiveness that often accompanies it is not – like community – something that is simply found in human nature. It has been worked for politically in a wide range of managed social practices, including new forms of education and youth work. It also has its heroes and exemplary types. By contrast, Jeremy's life and work, for reasons that he admitted to finding 'puzzling', focused on helping young people to find some agency of their own. It was a model or example of *social solidarity*. Like all such embodiments, it taught a practical lesson as well as, more directly, 'getting things done'. No one's life has one message alone, but Jeremy's work was in part about our need for help and also our need to give it – in short, about our social dependence – and it was a message that was lived through to the end.

Richard Johnson

ONE

Four settings: contexts and questions

Introduction

This book is a search for a way to understand and engage with community, both in general, and specifically in Southmead, a housing estate in north Bristol. This search has grown out of four settings, which together provide the book with its context, its subject matter and its concerns. The settings run as themes throughout the narrative, each with its own relevance, and are as follows: Southmead itself, a place where discourses of community run strong; my own long-term involvement as a youth worker in the area; young people in Southmead; and ideas of community, all sorts of ideas of community, popular, professional and theoretical. These settings form the basis of the book, interweaving with each other in its descriptions, analyses and findings.

First, I have to make a statement as to what the book is *not*. It is not a judgement on Southmead, or on the people that live there. The importance I attach to this statement, and why I feel it is so necessary to make it, will become increasingly apparent as the book continues. For now, I will leave it to the words of local activist, Les Palmer:

> For years and years we have had people coming in from outside to find out what's wrong with us, how we live, and what makes us so criminal.[1]

I do not intend my approach to Southmead to be that of the urban planner visiting a shanty town in Patrick Chamoiseau's novel, *Texaco* – 'this strange visitor was coming to question the usefulness of our insalubrious existence'[2] – a phrase that captures the tone of enquiry from which people in poor areas all over the world, including Southmead, suffer. A major part of the book will be taken up with looking at such enquiries, the writings and surveys that Les Palmer

---

[1] Radio Southmead, 12 August 1994
[2] Chamoiseau, 1997: 11

was referring to that share that tone, and the questions they raise of the way they represent and problematise Southmead.

My concern about my approach is, of course, meaningless to those who have no knowledge of Southmead or its 'reputation', so before going on to look at what the book *is* about, let me first flesh out those four settings and the relationships between them, to give some idea of the issues involved.

The four settings

Southmead

No thumbnail sketch can do Southmead justice, but to start somewhere, and to give a preview of the questions that will follow, here are some of the most used representations and statistics – the very ones that will be the subject of greater critique in later chapters. The housing estate that is Southmead (as distinct from the hospital of the same name, which is adjacent, and not part of this study) is in north Bristol, with a population of over 10,000 counted in the 1991 Census.[3] The estate was 'primarily developed over a twenty five year period between 1930 and 1955' with later infill. The housing is 'low density' – the vast majority comprising three-bedroom houses with gardens. There are no tower blocks.[4]

Ever since Southmead was built, it has had a reputation for trouble and poverty. It was the subject of a major action research study by the Bristol Social Project in the 1950s, and in one of the papers from that project, tellingly entitled *Difficult housing estates*, it is described as 'containing areas of bad reputation which caused the whole neighbourhood to be held in low esteem'.[5]

Three decades later, a survey stated that:

> Throughout its history, Southmead has received attention in the media as a problem estate where crime, lawlessness and anti-social behaviour are rife. *Riots* [in italics in original] and fire bombings in the early and late 1980s and the problem of joyriding, which recently received national coverage, have all seemed to firmly establish Southmead as 'Bristol's trouble-plagued estate'.[6]

---

[3] Bristol City Council, 1996a
[4] Bristol City Council, 1983
[5] Wilson, 1963: 3
[6] Safe Neighbourhoods Unit, 1991: 7

In the 1999 *Audit of crime and disorder in Bristol*, Southmead was named as a major 'crime hot spot' in the city, the only area with as many entries (five) in the eight police priority categories.[7] The 'problem' tag therefore has a long history – from at least 1952, when the Bristol Social Project research was set up, until at least the end of the 1990s.

Southmead has also always featured as one of the poorest areas in the city in the *Poverty in Bristol* reports that Bristol City Council issued from 1985, with the 1996 report in this series stating that the estate falls within the 'highest' fifth of the five indicators used to measure deprivation in Bristol.[8] To add to this gloom, the Southmead ward (which, because of the arbitrary nature of ward boundaries, also contains one affluent area that is not part of the estate) was, in 1998, scored as having the third worst quality of life out of 34 Bristol wards.[9]

The difficulty of the area is further indicated and compounded by the closure of the local secondary school in 2000[10], despite local opposition, following years of damning inspection reports, bad press (in the words of the local newspaper, the school 'was branded a failure by Government inspectors' in November 1997[11]) and subsequent reduction in pupil intake.

All this information, all these 'facts', lead to Southmead becoming laden with a number of official and popular notions and discourses of crime, deprivation, place and community, and (as with other similar areas) being the subject of persistent moral and political questions to and by politicians, policy makers, local professionals and residents.

Southmead is not alone as an area with such statistics. There are some 2000 such estates throughout Britain, the main feature of Southmead being size – it is four to nine times larger than the '20 of the most difficult' that were surveyed in a Joseph Rowntree Foundation study.[12] Both poverty and disorder are endemic in such areas.[13]

Naming Southmead as an area of problems should not be the same as blaming it, although, as Les Palmer felt in his Radio Southmead interview, that has always been the case. The word 'Southmead' is often used in Bristol as a kind of code word for trouble, intoned as a mantra with the names of other areas (in Bristol, these being Hartcliffe, Knowle West and St Paul's) – a metonym for disrepute that stirs great emotions.

---

[7] Bristol Community Safety Partnership, 1999a: 31
[8] Bristol City Council, 1996a: 53
[9] Bristol City Council, 1999: 36
[10] *Bristol Observer*, 14 April 2000
[11] *Bristol Evening Post*, 8 September 1998
[12] Power and Tunstall, 1995: 7, 12
[13] Campbell, 1993; Power and Tunstall, 1997; Coles et al, 1999

These two views from the comment book of an exhibition of art by young people from Southmead held at Bristol City Museum and Art Gallery in 1996 show some of the feelings involved:

> This makes a change – youth in Southmead usually burn down churches. This Exhibition is a huge waste of space. These same people will be stealing your car next week.

> Wicked and wild. It's about time more creativity happened in Southmead rather than slagging the place off.

Although most of the comments about the exhibition were favourable, none missed the import of it being young people from Southmead, from the wild margins of the city, who were exhibiting in such a central venue, in such a proper art gallery.[14] All cities have such notional disreputable areas, with some of their names graduating to become national code words (Brixton, Moss Side, Toxteth, Meadowell) – words that, to borrow a phrase from Wittgenstein, '[strike] a note on the keyboard of the imagination'.[15] This 'imagining' of Southmead is one of the factors the book will be looking at as an ingredient in its existence.

Naming Southmead in this study, therefore, is not altogether comfortable. It already carries an almost unbearable weight of inquiry and social meaning, to which a further study, whatever its approach, can only add. However, I have used the name for three reasons. First, any disguise would be impossible to maintain. I have already referred to a major study of the area in the 1950s, which was carried out by the Bristol Social Project. That research team, too, was aware of the 'general dislike' of the publicity its presence caused, and in its report 'concealed the identity of people and places by pseudonyms'.[16] Southmead was called Upfield. However, that Upfield was actually Southmead was common knowledge in the area when I first arrived there in 1975 – the mask was ineffective – and this can be substantiated from other writings about Southmead that refer to the Bristol Social Project.[17] Any attempt by me to create a camouflage would need such an immense amount of subterfuge as to be hilarious, diverting readers into becoming

---

[14] This exhibition is discussed further in Chapter Four.

[15] Wittgenstein, 1976: 4

[16] Spencer et al, 1964: ix, 34

[17] Benjamin, 1966, 1974. These books contain passages that describe how Southmead Adventure Playground was set up by the project, and tallies with accounts of the project in Wilson (1963) and Spencer et al (1964).

sleuths as they are tempted to break the disguise. Second, it is important for the book that the voices of people from Southmead, including their public statements, are heard and properly attributed (as with any quotations), and these voices, of course, both state the name and have different points of view from official representations, as in the song Southmead, Glorious Southmead from the Southmead Community Play.[18] Hiding the name would mean silencing these important voices and their views, which are the subject matter of one chapter, and appear throughout the book. Third, naming the place grounds the book. While theory is used as an intrinsic part of the book, this is always in relation to a peopled, material space. As with Manuel Castells, I use empirical analysis both as a communication device, 'and as a way of disciplining my theoretical discourse, of making it difficult, if not impossible, to say something that observed collective action rejects in practice'.[19] Much writing on space and community is infuriatingly abstract. The French geographer Henri Lefebvre writes of Michel Foucault, who, he says, even as he extols the importance of space:

> ... never explains what space he is referring to, nor how it bridges the gap between the theoretical (epistemological) realm and the practical one, between mental and social, between the space of philosophers and the space of people who deal with material things.[20]

Southmead for me is both a practical space full of people and a realm of theory and knowledge. In order not to lose that connection, I feel it necessary to keep the name, not to relegate Southmead to being just a 'case' that can be studied, hidden behind a pretended identity. Southmead is not a pretence.

This naming of Southmead does create difficulties. Naming the place puts the burden of responsibility on to me of being totally scrupulous – no hiding behind fictions, no blurring of the data. There are, however, some pieces of 'evidence' that cannot withstand such openness. Certain local conflicts have been excised from the narrative, as any but the blandest accounts would open troublesome wounds and create further conflict. There are incidents I have felt it necessary to disguise. Where I have obtained information through my privileged position as participant in the area, or where what was said or done

---

[18] Beddow, 1994
[19] Castells, 1997: 3
[20] Lefebvre, 1991: 4

was private, I will conceal the names so as not to unfairly expose the individuals involved.

The final problem with naming Southmead is the problem of voyeurism, of turning the area into a spectacle. People do already tour Southmead to see what it is 'really' like. I myself have escorted journalists, film crews, business people, trustees of charities, students and representatives of government and other agencies around the area (there is a certain art to being such a local guide).[21] Most of these tours are instrumental – they bring in funds. What would tours by social theorists bring?

With all these difficulties, I do have to make a case as to why, and how, I am writing about Southmead at all. This problem of writing 'about' Southmead will be tackled in much more detail in the next chapter, and the way Southmead is represented is a major preoccupation of the book.

My involvement

I started work in Southmead in 1975, and working with young people in the area has been my full-time occupation ever since, first on the adventure playground (one of the projects started by the Bristol Social Project), and then as youth worker, running the local youth centre, detached youth work, and a wide variety of different projects for young people (sports, arts, health, and so on). This is not the place to describe that work, although examples from it will appear in the book, showing both difficulties and quandaries as well as successes. There is a book, a 'people's history', about the youth centre, and a documentary video, as well as the cornucopia of reports, strategies, business plans, photographs, music, films, paintings and so on that such an operation inevitably produces for its own particular audiences.[22]

This quarter of a century's involvement of mine with Southmead puzzles me. It was not my intention to stay so long when I first took work there on a six-month contract. Staying that long does indicate a strong attachment to ... something. This something has not always been Southmead itself, with which I have a love–hate relationship, but the continual feeling I have of unfinished business with the place and the people, like a familial relationship.

---

[21] For example, a group of business executives on a Seeing is Believing visit in June 1996.

[22] Truman and Brent, 1995; Southmead Slamming, 1999. Other material is listed in the References.

The longevity of the relationship means that Southmead has become an important part of me, which could be seen as either a strength or an encumbrance to this research. So while the relationship is the reason that I wanted to undertake the research, there are strong arguments that such a close relationship makes any research suspect. I am close, physically and emotionally, to what I am studying, a criticism that has been made of other writers of community studies.[23] I am not an 'unencumbered self', independent and unfettered. However, there is a strong countervailing argument that such a position would anyway be an impossibility, certainly according to the communitarians in the debate that is raging, mainly in North America, between themselves and liberals.[24] While the ideal of the unencumbered self may be one free of all ties, the communitarian argument is that ties do not necessarily bind, but are the relationships that enable thought and action. Although not being unencumbered, however, neither do I feel I am a 'situated self', the communitarian idea of self that is criticised in its turn.[25] Situatedness posits far too static a description of the relationships that I am in, and would imply that my thoughts and actions are determined entirely by my situation, which would indeed bind me down. My own preference for self-description would be that of being a 'relational self', as espoused by feminist critics of both the communitarian and liberal positions.[26] I am in a relationship of interdependence with Southmead. The point here is not to argue through all the myriad of positions in these debates in abstract, but to indicate that any discussion of the 'we' or 'they' of community also cannot avoid discussion of the 'I'. Hopefully the tension between the two is a tension that is in the words of one communitarian, 'creative'.[27]

One of the reasons for this research is to explore the questions that arise from that relationship. The research did not start from an academic intent, even though I use academic tools, but from personal, professional and political concerns. Mine is the analysis of a participant, one who wants to 'participate *properly*', through maintaining a critical position.[28] This concern is not merely due to self-absorption. The type of relationship I have with Southmead is replicated throughout the country by people carrying out some form of 'service to the community'. This relationship is problematic and often criticised as

---

[23] Bell and Newby, 1971: 55

[24] Avineri and de-Shalit, 1992; Sandel, 1992; Bauman, 1993: 40

[25] Phillips, 1993: 181; Bauman, 1993: 41

[26] Frazer and Lacey, 1993: 178

[27] Etzioni, 1988: 8

[28] Derrida, 1995: 4

being 'a form of dominating' people[29], and as class-based. Raymond Williams writes of two interpretations of community:

> ... the idea of service, and the idea of solidarity. These have in the main been developed by the middle class and working class respectively....The idea of service, ultimately, is no substitute for the idea of active mutual responsibility, which is the other idea of community.[30]

That was written well before the growth of the current plethora of community professionals, but the role of 'professionals' in Southmead contains just that conflict, involving questions as to *who* is being 'served', and how, with all the power dynamics and conflicting solidarities involved. The stresses and ambivalences of such a position, however, do provide a position of knowledge. I am in Southmead for over 200 days a year, a much closer involvement than any outside researcher, and have both a particular view, and considerable personal and professional knowledge. While the whole book draws on that knowledge, one chapter will be dedicated to a greater exploration of its strengths and problems.

Young people

A major part of my professional knowledge concerns the position of young people in the area, and the politics surrounding them. There are two polarities of view that initially shout out from the literature. The first is the long-standing, in effect orthodox, view that young people are trouble. The second is a counter-orthodoxy that they are not listened to or respected enough.

Without fail, all the various official surveys of Southmead cast young people as a, even *the*, major problem of the area. That very first research by the Bristol Social Project was set up because of the problem of young people: 'Juvenile delinquency was the initial problem and starting point for the project'.[31] At the risk of being repetitive, but to show how strong a motif this is, here are excerpts from later reports that continually reiterate that theme. Out of the blue, with no lead-up of argument or evidence, a 1983 report states that 'youth problems [are]

---

[29] Corlett, 1989: 7
[30] Williams, 1958: 315, 317
[31] Spencer et al, 1964: 24

a major factor in Southmead'.[32] A report written in 1991 is full of disparaging references to young people, including the one that: 'There was almost universal agreement that those largely responsible for crime in Southmead are young people'.[33] The final sentence in the section on Southmead in the 1996 poverty report, again after no previous discussion of, or data on, young people, and with no reference to the relevance to a poverty analysis, states: 'The area is *dominated* by young people and families with dependent children living in local authority housing'.[34] The 1999 *Audit of crime and disorder in Bristol* gives as one of the reasons for Southmead being a priority ward for crime and disorder that there are more than 25% young people in the population.[35] The local media can be, of course, even less restrained in some of their headlines, although when young people do well (in approved ways) the media do (contrary to local myth) report that too.

An opposite view comes, understandably, from young people themselves. In the *Young People's Survey of Southmead 1998* there is a strong feeling that adults do not listen to them – especially those with authority: 'There would be co-operation with young adults (sic) if people actually listen to us and see our point of view for a change (17 year old girl)'[36], and evidence from the survey suggests that, far from being community wreckers, young people actually care deeply about, and want to be involved in, improving their local area.[37] This survey was the first one to ask them their thoughts on a range of issues, rather than, as with other reports, asking about their criminal behaviour or drug taking, and was greeted with great enthusiasm by all the young people that took part, who devised the questions, disseminated the questionnaire, filled in the forms, analysed the data, and took part in follow-up discussions. It was the first survey to treat them as local residents, with a stake in the area. Despite the fact that there are large numbers of young people living on social housing estates, they are somehow not seen as part of them, as researchers in other areas have found:

> To many of our interviewees 'residents' were simply 'tenants' thus ignoring the fact that young people were also 'residents', albeit residents with distinctive needs. Rather

---

[32] Bristol City Council, 1983, section 2.3.13

[33] Safe Neighbourhoods Unit, 1991: 46

[34] Bristol City Council, 1996a: 54 (emphasis added)

[35] Bristol Community Safety Partnership, 1999a: 28

[36] Kimberlee, 1998: 5, 15

[37] Kimberlee, 1998: 11

young people were often defined as an uncontrolled nuisance and a danger to the community.[38]

The issue thus far seems to be clear-cut – that there is malign labelling of young people, and the projection on to them of all of the woes of the area, which is unfair and needs to be reversed. I partly agree with this position, except that the relationship between young people, an area and the idea of 'community' is rather more complex. For instance, some young people do commit crimes that are destructive to the lives of both young people and adults. But young people also create their own collective life. One of the features of the social life of young people in Southmead is the way certain sites – street corners, park areas, shops – by some mysterious way suddenly become the place where crowds of young people congregate and socialise. These places become young people's space for a time, with their own shorthand titles (including, over the years, 'Greystoke', 'the woods', 'the bollards' and so on), until eventually the police are called, and the crowds are dispersed until, a few weeks or months later, a new site emerges as that place to be. One area, 'the green', was used so often as a gathering place and centre of joyriding and battles with the police, that in 1996 it was built on. 'They've taken *our* green away', I was told by young people at the time.[39] Three months later the crowds met up again at 'the woods', until they were moved off. These gatherings could perhaps be described by the concept of 'neo-tribes'. Neo-tribes have been characterised as 'recently invented communities involving some membership choice' that occur in '"wild zones" ... where aesthetic and other resources are thin on the ground'.[40] They are arguably a modern version of 'community' in a mass society, with young people in Southmead being active and creative inventors of their own such tribes, their own unstable and 'effervescent' communities[41], a challenge to the nostalgic idea of community as 'warm togetherness'.[42] These ideas, so baldly stated here, will be explored further in a chapter on young people and community.

---

[38] Coles et al, 1999: 44

[39] Diary notes, February 1996

[40] Lash and Urry, 1994: 318

[41] Maffesoli, 1996: 66

[42] Bellah, 1997: 388

Newman University
Library
Tel: 0121 476 1181 ext 1208

Borrowed Items 18/05/2017 12:00
XXXX2218

Item Title	Due Date
* Managing and leading in inter-agency settings	08/06/2017 23:59
* Searching for community : representation, power and action on an urban estat	25/05/2017 23:59
* Partnership working	08/06/2017 23:59
* Partnership working in health and social care	08/06/2017 23:59
* big society : the anatomy of the new politics	08/06/2017 23:59
* Community development : a critical approach	25/05/2017 23:59
* Partnership working in health and social care : what is integrated care and	08/06/2017 23:59
* Understanding community : politics, policy and practice	08/06/2017 23:59
* Coordinating services for included children : joined up action	25/05/2017 23:59

* Indicates items borrowed today
Thankyou for using Newman Library
www.newman.ac.uk/library
library@newman.ac.uk

Ideas of community

The concept of neo-tribes is one of the many ideas in the vast amount of thinking, talking and writing that exists about community within the history of sociology and its grappling with modernity. Community as an issue also infiltrates much everyday thought and action, and is bandied about in local and national politics and policy making as well as being the subject of a wide range of academic discourse. As such a ubiquitous term, however, it does have to be given a health warning: 'handle with care'. How could one otherwise use a term that has been claimed by such a wide variety of people as in the following examples?:

• fascists – much of the social rhetoric of the German Third Reich was that of promoting 'folk community', a 'constantly used slogan' of the Nazis[43];
• anarchists, both pacifists and supporters of the police-hating paper *Class War*, which calls for something called 'community justice'[44];
• the police themselves, who, in a publicity leaflet in circulation during 1995, stated that: 'Community relations is at the heart of policing in the Southmead District';
• business executives, whose organisation, Business in the Community, visited Southmead in 1996.

Community has a long history as an idea used across the ideological spectrum, not just in this random selection, but also by Marxists, conservatives, and supporters of the liberal-social democrat tradition, each with different conceptions of and claims to it.

So when *lack* of community is continually used as a reason for the woes of Southmead, care is called for; there are certain versions of community that one hopes are not the ones being evoked, and the writings do not make it clear what they would mean by the *presence* of community, other than that people would behave more responsibly, as defined by the researchers. This assertion of a lack of community is a major theme in all the more official writings, with only the researchers of the Bristol Social Project being sceptical about the good of community as a concept, which they saw as outdated, even though the original project proposal was to encourage community.[45] By the end

---

[43] Grunberger, 1974: 36
[44] Issue 50, no date
[45] The proposal, from Spencer et al (1964: 3), is quoted in Chapter Three. Community as an idea has made a comeback since that work was written.

of the project, its team had reached different views about community. Two of the major mainstays of so many concepts of community, neighbourhood and local power were seen as either irrelevant in the modern world, or lacking:

> What stood out from this work was how little the estate neighbours could actively contribute to the leadership required, and the consequent unreality of any expectation that ... there could be any substantial "degree of responsibility for their community".[46]

This lack of ability to build community is often seen as one of the deficiencies of poor areas. The Bristol Social Project did call for the creation of a new type of worker, the 'community organiser', not to build community, already dismissed as impossible in the modern city, but instead to do almost the opposite – to help people 'cross the boundaries of their immediate locality and thus to extend the range and scope of their social relationships'.[47] The project wanted people to look outward, not to be bound by their neighbourhood. This is the only report on Southmead in which the lack of community is not identified as a problem to be rectified by official action.

From that report onwards, most of the official views of the actual existence of community in Southmead have been similarly negative, although its existence in later reports does seem to be *desired*. All the reports have that low estimation of the ability of people in Southmead to run their community affairs. The 1983 *Southmead Report* stated that:

> The real problem is likely to have stemmed from a lack of community involvement in the first instance. Over the years this attitude has resulted in the present situation where there is very little community action or leadership.[48]

The 1991 survey called for 'a coherent community safety strategy', to be led by local government and the police because of low resident confidence and involvement.[49] Official agencies are seen as having to take the burden that, for whatever reason, local people are not able or

---

[46] Spencer et al, 1964: 38

[47] Spencer et al, 1964: 309

[48] Bristol City Council, 1983, para. v

[49] Safe Neighbourhoods Unit, 1991: 7, 64

willing to take for themselves – a contentious view that will be further discussed as this book progresses.

This official view of the lack of community in Southmead is severely contested by many who live there, who have very different ideas about what community means. Community is an idea as used in everyday life as it is in official circles, and an example of its vernacular use is given in the next section of this chapter. Many people in Southmead are proud of their community life. In 1999, a short film, Rush, was made at Southmead Youth Centre.[50] The story is about running, and the buzz it gives. The main protagonist discovers this buzz when he urgently needs to draw some cash, so has to run from Southmead, where there are no cashpoints, to the neighbouring middle-class area, Westbury-on-Trym, where there are several. Apart from the absence and presence of cash machines being major markers of the difference between the two areas, the Southmead participants wanted to show a difference in community feeling. While the protagonist ran through Southmead, there would be people socialising on the streets who were interested in and hailed the runner. When he reached Westbury, he would be on his own, ignored by the 'snobby' people there who would be too bound up with their own lives to be concerned with his. In that Southmead version of community, it is Westbury that is the area with no community life. Unfortunately, in the edit suite most of the 'community' scenes were cut – they were complicated to shoot, and took the film well over its six-minute time limit.

Throughout the area's history, there have been groups using the term community in Southmead (an example being the Community Council, set up, ironically, by the Bristol Social Project), and a range of activities promoting the concept (such as the Southmead Festival), though maybe not doing what was officially expected of them. Then, dramatically, in the 1990s there was a massive increase in activity that claimed community as its basis. Behind all these groups and activities there were strong, often highly conflicting, ideas of what community is about that the book will explore in depth.

There is the temptation, in these circumstances of conflicting meanings and claims of community, to try to come up with a definition against which these claims can be verified. This is the approach of some writers – either to have a definition against which to test whether or not community has ever existed[51] or to distinguish between 'genuine'

---

[50] Directed by Rob Mitchell. My knowledge comes from being co-producer.
[51] Phillips, 1993 (his answer is no).

and 'counterfeit' communities.[52] That type of approach has, however, been criticised as being virtually useless, as, because of its nature, the term community is never used in a neutral fashion.[53] This is the reason why *ideas* of community come to occupy such an important part of this book. While the book is written in a way similar to an ethnography, exploring social phenomena rather than testing them against a hypothesis or claim (an example could be 'Does community exist in Southmead?')[54], this approach is not enough, in itself, without being strongly aware of the ideas involved. *Ideas* are an integral part of community practice, which is not simply an object based on *fact*.[55] As Walter Benjamin put it, 'someone who wishes to decide "on the basis of the facts" will find no basis in the facts'[56]; all facts are mediated by the ideas through which they are viewed. So to be aware of my own and other people's ideas on community, I have read widely within the various literatures on the topic, and to lead me through the empirical evidence of, and the ideas about, community, I use a range of theoretical approaches as critical tools.

I use the plural, literatures, advisedly, because there is no single body of literature on the subject of community. Instead, there are a number of strangely unrelated literatures, each containing its own set of arguments, that do not engage with each other or progress in the same direction, but operate on completely different planes. Part of the difference between them is that they come from within different national debates and preoccupations. For example, Jean-Luc Nancy (French) criticises Habermas (German) and Rorty (US) of being intolerant of the 'modern French work' that radically challenges their notions of consensus and communication[57], but then for his part does not mention the work of North American communitarians. Part of the difference comes from the discussion taking place within different academic disciplines. For example, A.P. Cohen, an anthropologist, supports what he sees as an empirical phenomenon, 'people's attachment to community'[58], with many examples; his insights, which highlight the importance of symbols in community construction, are totally ignored by communitarian writers, who, despite their enthusiasm for promoting the good of community, manage to '[maintain] their arguments at a high level

---

[52] Freie, 1998

[53] Plant, 1978

[54] Atkinson and Hammersley, 1994: 248

[55] Plant, 1974: 4

[56] Benjamin, 1997: 177-8

[57] Nancy, 1991: 155

[58] Cohen, 1985: 38

of abstraction' with a lack of substantive argument.[59] There is very little dialogue between different disciplines, particularly those that see themselves as empirically based, and those that are theory led, a divide that this book aims to cross.

Within the different literatures are a number of arguments about community. Here is my personal and incomplete list of authors and their (oversimplified and overlapping) positions within the arguments (remembering that the authors who share the same brackets almost certainly do not share all the same views). Communities do exist (Alinsky, Braden, A.P. Cohen, Etzioni, Gates, Gusfield, Kelly, Maffesoli, Nancy, Rajan, Sandel, Weeks); should exist (D. Atkinson, Bellah, Boswell, Marx and Engels, Mouffe, Taylor, Walzer); do not or cannot exist (Bauman, Harvey, Peet and Thrift, Zukin); exist in impossible ways (Castells); are false, even dangerous (P. Cohen, Touraine, Sennett); are necessary (Hall, hooks, West); pose dilemmas (Bhabha, Brown, Corlett, Dominelli, Frazer and Lacey, Gilroy, Mayo, Unger, R. Williams, Young, plus most of the other authors listed); are female (Benjamin, Bornat, Campbell, Dominelli); are modern inventions (Bauman); are outdated (Cooke). Among all these positions are very different concepts of what it is that is being discussed, and the communities under discussion, though mostly communities of geographically fixed place, include translocal communities of race, gender and sexuality. It is difficult, given these differences, to trace all the many debates about community, and such an exercise serves no purpose in the development of this book, which is concerned with ideas in, and not separated from, action. The different arguments and approaches will not be ignored, but will be used throughout the book in dialogue with the other settings.

While ideas of community (vernacular, official and academic) is one of the settings of this book, it is not necessarily from direct writings on community that the most interesting or useful thoughts and insights have come. The References section contains many other authors whose ideas help formulate the angle from which I am viewing the settings – a process that Slavoj Zizek calls 'looking awry' – writers whose ideas help me 'render visible aspects that would otherwise remain unnoticed' that help me 'stage' my ideas.[60] These include novelists, a poet, art critics and literary theorists, as well as the more expected sociologists, anthropologists and geographers. And behind much of my thinking is the uneasy awareness of the spectral presence (spectral partly because of *their* levels of high abstraction) of Jacques Derrida, Jürgen Habermas

---

[59] Frazer and Lacey, 1993: 137
[60] Zizek, 1991a: 3

and Michel Foucault, who hang in my subconscious like three rather ghostly lodestones pointing in different directions. What follows is an atrociously brief glimpse at those directions, not a summary of all their thought.

Derrida is not well disposed to the '*archaic*' concept of community, that '*primitive conceptual phantasm*'[61], but his conception of *différence*, 'the name we might give to the "active" moving discord of different forces'[62], provides two ideas that can help conceptualise community: the idea of meaning being created through difference (communities formed by people thinking themselves into difference[63]) and the idea of meaning being constantly deferred ('incompletion' as a principle of community[64]). Community maybe can be seen as an example of an 'impossible presence'[65], an idea bound up with notions of continually unsatisfied desire. This opens up the possibility of thinking of community as something desired but never attained, but no less potent for that. Derrida is used extensively in my discussions on communication, difference and the impossibility of defining community.

Habermas is more interested in forms of reason than desire, with an argument for *diremptive* as opposed to *exclusive* reason, which 'distinguishes solidary social practice as the locus of historically situated reason'.[66] From his idea, it could be argued that it is the practice of solidarity at the heart of many ideas of community that produces what he calls communicative reason, through processes of intersubjective recognition. Knowledge thus created has a 'glimmer of symmetrical relations marked by free, reciprocal recognition'[67], an idea that captures the utopian ideal of many communitarians. For Habermas, that glimmer helps us cope with social complexity: 'Communicative reason is of course a rocking hull ... even if shuddering in high seas is the only mode in which it "copes"'.[68] Community as a coping mechanism in the maelstrom of modernity is a recurring trope in writings on community. However, the main question Habermas poses for me is whether meaning is created not through difference, but through recognition, with community as a form of this recognition. Mikhail

---

[61] Derrida, 1994: 82 (emphasis in original)
[62] Derrida, 1982: 18
[63] Cohen, 1985: 117
[64] Nancy, 1991: 35
[65] Derrida, 1982: 19
[66] Habermas, 1987: 306
[67] Habermas, 1992: 145
[68] Habermas, 1992: 144

Bakhtin, Jessica Benjamin and Charles Taylor also emphasise the idea of recognition, and play their own parts in this discussion.

While Foucault does have ideas of community[69], it is his ideas of power that continually question the concept of community. His ideas of relationships are suffused with themes of asymmetry rather than symmetry, with power rather than reciprocity as their basis. Foucault's insistent idea of power being 'everywhere'[70] is an antidote to community writings, which have been well criticised for lacking a theory of power[71], and the 'myth of egalitarianism' perpetrated by so many community studies.[72] This idea of power is that it is dynamic rather than static, 'exercised rather than possessed'[73], similar to Kobena Mercer's idea of community, which 'could be said to be a verb not a noun – something you do rather than something you own'.[74] Foucault's ideas of discourses of power are more dynamic than ideas of power as structure. Within his ideas, power is not only negative, but also productive: 'it produces reality'[75], for example, the idea that the reality of Southmead is created by power relations. These ideas of power as being both relational and creative pose several questions: are communities an effect of power relations or are they a field of power, with power relations acting *within* community – the 'microphysics of power', and if power is built up from the micro level, are community politics therefore *worthwhile*? For Foucault writes that power 'comes from below'[76], an idea that can give hope of possible resistance to places such as Southmead, where people can and do feel without power.

This book is not an exposition of the ideas of these three thinkers, and certainly not an attempt to adjudicate between them, but makes use of these ideas of *différence*, recognition and relations of power in its dissections of community.

---

[69] Explored in Rajchman, 1991

[70] Foucault, 1979: 93

[71] Frazer and Lacey, 1993: 161

[72] Cohen, 1985: 33

[73] Foucault, 1977a: 26

[74] Mercer, 1995: 14

[75] Foucault, 1977a: 194

[76] Foucault, 1979: 94

Interrelating the four settings: one sunny afternoon in Southmead ...

I want to show now how Southmead, my own relationship to it, young people and ideas of community weave together. The following is an account of an incident that took place in the summer of 1998.[77]

> *I was at work on a sunny afternoon, sorting through old photographs for a display at a community fun day. Out of the window I saw three teenage boys I know stealing bicycles from a delivery van. I ran out to find them unpacking the bikes just by the Youth Centre. I asked them to return them, but was told to 'fuck off' as they rode off. I talked to the police, who gave chase. They returned empty handed, and requested a statement from me. I asked for time, and went looking for the boys. I found one of them, together with a group of friends, and told him that if the bicycles were returned I would not give a statement to the police. The group was angry and threatening. One said: "What do you think you are, a fucking hero of the community?". Another: "You don't come from Southmead. It's none of your business".*
>
> *Later that day, as no bikes were returned, I did give my statement to the police. Over the next few days I was physically threatened and publicly abused as a 'grass' by a large number of people not directly involved with the incident for breaking the communal taboo of 'no grassing'. My own bicycle was trashed.*
>
> *The fun day took place several days later, and was successful and friendly, with people continually saying 'this is what community is about' to each other, to me and to anyone else who was listening. People loved the photographs, there was much laughter as they recognised young versions of themselves and their friends, and remembered the occasions when the photos were taken. The event itself went on long into the night, with people drinking in a marquee. I was told afterwards by one of those present that there had been discussion about the bicycle incident, with the men there talking with the boys about my role in the community (including my length of 'service'), and finally supporting my action. From then on the abuse I received fizzled out. Despite that support, several people felt I had been foolish to report the boys, because*

---

[77] This account is taken from diary entries written at the time. Throughout the book extracts from my diary are reproduced in italics, to distinguish them both from quotations and the main body of the text.

> *I knew what would happen. The boys all went to court, pleaded guilty, and were fined.*

This small incident connects to four of the book's settings, and opens up discussion of their interrelation.

First, the incident took place in Southmead. Although it could have happened anywhere, it was not a hypothetical incident, and displays both 'negative' and 'positive' aspects of the area. Southmead is the area in which those young people were trying to exercise their power, the area where the adults at the fun day had spent most of their lives. It is a (minute) part of the history of the place. The story does show how hard it is to blame people if they do not report crime (a frequent accusation directed at people in poor areas), and this was only a minor offence carried out by 14-year-olds, not, for example, major heroin dealing. I was given institutional and financial support from the police and my employers, and could go home, away from the area, so the consequences for me were very different than they would have been if I lived there, which questions my relationship to the area.

Second, my own involvement is obvious. I saw, I acted, I was acted on. I already knew the people involved, and knew about the boys' previous involvement in causing damage in the area. I was angry with them for putting me in a position where I would either have to collude with their actions or report them. My actions were not the 'action' part of 'action research', to see what would happen next; they were the actions of a participant. The incident opens up questions of knowledge and power; possession of knowledge compromised my neutrality, knowledge was not purely neutral information, and no act could have been neutral. Its use depended on whose 'side' I was on. I did try to be open with what I knew, but would personally have been better off if I had not seen the incident – ignorant of the theft, neutral and unhassled. Finally, because of the knowledge people had *of* me, I was supported. Knowledge is not a one-way process – not only researchers possess knowledge.

Third, young people (specifically boys) were involved, in a collective action both at the time and afterwards. They were busy, and had their own collective understanding. The incident concerned the relationship between young people and adults in the community.

Finally, ideas of community were used by all of the participants, and these were intimately connected with practice:

- community as shared history, both through the photographs, and as the reason for the support given me;

- community as a *desire* for and celebration of togetherness – the fun day itself;
- community as *territory* and *difference* – "you're not from round here";
- community as *morality*, on two fronts – either I was taking a moral stand as a 'hero of the community' or I had no right to breach the morality of 'no grassing';
- community as boundary enforcement – was I to be forced *out*, or be allowed to stay *in*, eventually decided by the *power* of the male adult group;
- community as a locale of face-to-face resolution of problems – part of *solidary social practice*;
- community as *gendered*, with men taking a powerful role;
- young people as *destructive* of community, but with their own collective grouping.

All these vernacular ideas and practices have a counterpart in the literatures – it is maybe due to my reading that I glimpse them – although it would be pedantic to tick off which resonates with which author.

The story starts to show the range of inquiry that arises from the intertwining of the four settings – the ambiguities within the 'reality' of Southmead, the ambivalences of involvement, the challenge of young people and the multifaceted nature of ideas of community. It is now time to formulate some questions for that inquiry, the questions thrown up by the settings.

The concerns and structure of the book

The first, and major, concern of the book is that of representation: how Southmead is represented, what effects this has, how representation is an arena of conflict, and how representation is closely connected to relations of power. The book looks both at who is producing representations of Southmead and the cultural forms involved.

The second concern is what is community? What sort of phenomena are we talking about when we name Southmead as a place, and community as a social form, or as actions, desire and so on? If these are not simple objects or forms susceptible to easy definition, what manner of phenomena are they, or, maybe more meaningfully, what are their '*possibilities*' as phenomena?[78] Community is a notoriously

---

[78] Wittgenstein, 1976: 42

difficult concept to pin down (a point made in much that is written on the subject), and is rather like Derrida's Specter:

> *It is* something that one does not know, precisely, and one does not know if precisely it *is*, if it exists, if it responds to a name and corresponds to an essence.[79]

Before getting carried away by the possibilities of community just because community is the subject matter of this book, it is necessary to ask if it is the right focus. Community could be a completely spurious social idea that masks much more important forces in people's lives, for example class, race, gender or globalisation. So the concern is not just about the *existence* of community, but also about its *value*.

The book's third concern is that of involvement with community. What do participation and community action mean? What is the role of 'service to the community'? Are there any practical lessons to be learnt from a theoretical understanding of community?

By the end of the book, I hope to have made clear the issues raised by representation, have gained some idea of what community is, have discussed action and participation by young people and adults, and explored problems of engagement.

To approach these questions, the book will be arranged as follows. As the book is itself a representation, so Chapter Two will look at major problems of writing about, and representation of, not only Southmead, but poor areas and subjugated groups in general. The chapter will look at the problems of what material to use as data with which to represent Southmead. Writing itself is a form of participation with the area, so those concerns of involvement with community begin to play a major role. Chapter Two argues for a method of approach to the topic best described as *bricolage*.

The next three chapters will examine different types of epistemological approaches to Southmead. Chapter Three will look at the outsider's view: the different surveys, maps and media coverage of the area. Chapter Four will examine representations from within, insider knowledge as shown through different forms of community expression, both formal and informal. Chapter Five will look in greater depth at participant knowledge, the strengths and flaws of an outsider-within position. These chapters pose questions of objectivity, knowability and representation that impinge on the issues of power and action.

---

[79] Derrida, 1994: 6

Using the caution that these chapters will provide, the book then moves from issues of representation to issues of behaviour and action. Chapter Six will concern itself with the behaviour of young people and its relationship to community, both their own collective formations and their effects on adults, and the challenge these pose to conceptions of community. Chapter Seven will look at a number of different forms of adult community action.

By then I should be ready to look at the question of the existence, possibilities and significance of community. There will be two concluding chapters. Chapter Eight will discuss different conceptions of community and place, and through long discussion will formulate an idea of community that acknowledges the ambiguities encountered through the book's investigations.

Chapter Nine will look at the implications of these arguments for action. Having criticised community writing for being too abstract, it seems incumbent on me to come up with some solid conclusions, but this is an incumbency I will shy away from. The book will not present a blueprint. Much of the book's argument is against managerial and technical 'solutions' to the 'problem' of Southmead. No previous blueprints have either been put fully into effect or have ever 'worked'. While there is a place for action planning on a small scale by participants, this is always based on contingency – local or national policies, availability of money, the local support any particular initiative can attract – and often achieves different results than those envisaged. The use of this book for action lies in its awareness of the relationships within which action takes place, the relationships of power and representation that pervade its explorations.

TWO

Researching Southmead: problems of representation and participation

Introduction

In Chapter One, I referred to how the intended representation of Southmead in the film Rush changed through the filming and editing process, with the community-oriented street scenes not reaching the final cut. While the film started off as a community film project, in its final version it is a celebration of individualism. The publicity blurb states: 'At night a proud young man sits on the estate. He doesn't need to follow the crowd ...'.[1] The making of this film shows how the desire to create a coherent and intelligible story for an audience changed the depiction of the area in the final work. The editorial argument was that 'the street scenes did not work cinematically'.

Writing as a method of representation also carries with it the desire of the author to create an intelligible and coherent text. It, too, transforms its material as it turns it into words on a page, which is what gives writing its excitement, just as film making is exciting. It is important to be aware that this transformation is not neutral, and there are three particular reasons why I consider the question of writing, or any form of representation, to be so important to this book. First, there is a battle of representation, which plays a crucial role in the history of Southmead. Southmead and its young people are the subject of a range of contested representations, with representations themselves becoming major areas of conflict. 'Outsider' representations of Southmead, for example in the press, or 'insider' representations, as in the community play of 1994, have all been the subject of strong feelings and fierce debate. Outsider representation is often perceived as one of the oppressions from which its inhabitants suffer, a subject I will return to in the next two

---

[1] In the programme Brief Encounters: The Bristol Short Film Festival 1999. This individualism, incidentally, is entirely fictional; at least 50 people, plus infrastructures of finance, equipment and skills, were involved in bringing this film to the screen.

chapters, when I look at the issues of the external gaze and community expression, and this recurrent insider/outsider motif.

The second reason for being concerned about the representation 'of' Southmead is the way that such representations channel the direction of enquiry. Most representations, in delineating problems that can be attached to the geographical area of Southmead, cast Southmead itself as a problem, and there are many examples of this approach. However, in these representations what Southmead *is* as a phenomenon is never considered. What sort of phenomenon we are talking about is an important point of discussion, and I want to be careful that the mechanics of representation do not, as in the film, unwittingly determine an outcome.

The final reason for examining representation of Southmead is that writing this representation involves myself, as writer, with the area. This issue of involvement has already been highlighted as one of the major settings of the book. Writing may be a very different form of active participation from, say, running a local football team, but still involves a strong, not to say complex and ambiguous, relationship with the area. Writing is an activity both in *intimate* relationship with its subject matter, and profoundly *distant* from it.

The passion that the representation of Southmead arouses was brought home to me by an incident in April 1997, when The Place We're In: A Multimedia Exhibition Done by Southmeaders opened at the Watershed Media Centre in the centre of Bristol. The exhibition, consisting of large photographs, computer-manipulated images and stories, taped conversations, digital projections and a website, was produced with young people by two artists. The material was controversial, including, among other topics, the young people's own images and discussions of joyriding and drug taking. On its first day, I took a colleague to the exhibition. As we approached the gallery, we could hear a family from Southmead yelling angrily at the images, disconcerting the gallery staff, who had never before witnessed such rage at an art exhibition. The family told us they had come to visit from loyalty, but were furious that this was what the 'art' was – pictures of activities and people that they hated, that were not beautiful, that should not be on display. My colleague is a skilled peacemaker, and the exhibition was unscathed. There was still a deep, if less dramatic, concern at the official opening a few days later. The occasion was packed with people from Southmead who had come to check how 'their' area was being represented – was it fair, did it portray the right image? The press coverage was checked, and people were pleased that it was not negative. The general feelings about the exhibition were ambivalent – the exhibition gave a problematic view of Southmead, not easily categorisable within a good/bad binary; nor easily categorisable as being either an insider or an outsider representation. The version of Southmead the exhibition portrayed was recognisably the work of young people, but it was being shown in a public place outside the area. Its approach was respected for the way young people had been given cameras to take the photographs, but there was discomfort with the resulting images, for example, the one of a stolen car surrounded by a group of young people.[2]

This book is yet another representation of Southmead, part of a long chain of representations. It is not exempt from the questions that will be being asked of all the other representations that I will be looking at, be they neatly, if problematically, categorised as coming from inside or outside. Knowledge of these other representations, of course, profoundly affects this one. Michel de Certeau writes: 'We never really write on a blank page, but always one that has been written on'.[3]

To put these issues into a wider context, I first look at different genres of writings about poor areas, and show the way these implicate both the writer and the reader in a relationship with the subject. From the analysis of these arises the challenge of how I, or anyone, can write about any subaltern group, a challenge to the role of the writer that has been of continuing concern to radical social theorists.

Writing on poor areas

This book could be seen as yet another investigation of a poor area. All over the world poor areas suffer from strange visitors, who come, as the novelist Patrick Chamoiseau writes from a shanty town in Martinique, 'to question the insalubriousness of our existence'.[4] There are some very particular ways that poor areas are written about, different to portrayals of other geographies – writings that fascinate with their narrative and works that transfix with figures. I want to look at examples of these writings, to examine the way poverty is represented and the effect this has.

In their book *The politics and poetics of transgression*, Peter Stallybrass and Allon White write about 19th-century investigations into slums by

---

[2] I was one of the organisers of the project that lead to the exhibition, and had to deal with the 'problematic' nature of the exhibition both with the press, and at the opening ceremony, when I was cheered when I said that Southmead is not a zoo. This account is taken from diary notes taken at the time.

[3] de Certeau, 1984: xviii

[4] Chamoiseau, 1997: 11

a wide variety of writers (there are famous accounts, for example, by Henry Mayhew, Edwin Chadwick, Karl Marx and Friedrich Engels). They discern the psychic fascination, for these writers and their readers, with that 'other' (in this case, slums and poverty) that is constructed as low, so much fascination, in fact, that 'the city's low becomes a site of obsessive preoccupation'.[5] Their argument is that these writings (which were extremely popular) were read not just out of social concern, but as part of the material used for the construction of the psychic identity of the bourgeoisie – an obsession with the grotesqueness of poverty to contrast with and legitimate the normality and propriety of their own lives. The writers recreated the poor 'for the bourgeois study and drawing room as much as for the urban council chamber'[6], and by using *writing* shielded the readers from the danger of *actual* contact. In the 1880s:

> There was a flood of writing *about* the slums which could be consumed within the safe confines of the home. Writing, then, made the grotesque *visible* whilst keeping it at an *untouchable* distance.[7]

Not only did this writing confirm the self-identity of the readers as being not grotesque, it was also supposed to be good for the poor themselves:

> The 'labouring' and 'dangerous' classes would be transformed, it was implied, once they became visible. On the one hand, there would be surveillance by *policing*; on the other, the inculcation of *politeness* through the benign gaze of the bourgeoisie.[8]

Although these writings are over a century old, they remain influential; Mayhew is quoted extensively by one of the contemporary works looked at below[9], and many of the ideas remain current. Making visible is still a tool of control of the despised low, or 'other', as the rash of surveillance cameras installed in many areas, including Southmead, in the second half of the 1990s bears witness to. Being surveyed as

---

[5] Stallybrass and White, 1986: 145
[6] Stallybrass and White, 1986: 125–6
[7] Stallybrass and White, 1986: 139 (emphasis in original)
[8] Stallybrass and White, 1986:135 (emphasis in original)
[9] Davies, 1998

an aid to behaviour is now a common experience – what Foucault calls Panopticism, 'a mechanism of power reduced to its ideal form'.[10] People should think that they are being watched, to make them automatically behave without need for any other form of external discipline. This ideal is not necessarily *achieved*, but that is an argument separate from whether it is *desired*. Young people in Southmead gain a lot of enjoyment from running up the supermarket roof and showing their bottoms to the security cameras.[11] Being surveyed is a common experience of poor people and poor areas. In terms of *writing*, there is a corpus of works about poverty and disorder in Britain today. While these works differ in many ways from those of the 19th century (smell and sewerage are not such prominent themes, for example), they are still about the authors making visible 'other' worlds that are hidden within the dominant prosperity, of a hidden country 'nestling within the country of the affluent, but utterly different in its way of life'.[12] These writings are supplemented by television documentaries, such as Eyes of a Child[13], which brought vivid scenes of squalor, violence and neglect into the living room via the safety of the TV screen.

There are three books in this genre that I want to look at; their emotionally charged titles and dramatic covers reveal part of the plot: *Goliath: Britain's dangerous places* (Campbell, 1993); *Danziger's Britain: A journey to the edge* (Danziger, 1997); *Dark heart: The shocking truth about hidden Britain* (Davies, 1998). They are all fine books, written by well-known journalists, and, leaving aside their superior writing skills, are similar to books that I could write about Southmead. The vivid descriptions of scenes of joyriding in Oxford (Campbell), of the (lost) battle against drug bullies in Leeds (Davies) and of depression in Leicester (Danziger), and the stories of heroism in adversity, are full of familiarity. I have my own fund of matching stories (so many that I am often told to write about them in a book). What I am not sure of is how these stories can be told without being exploitative of other people's experiences, and without getting carried away by their entertainment value. The stated intentions of these authors are not to entertain, but to reveal these other worlds to those too smug to look outside of their own comfort, and to call for action (Davies), to share

---

[10] Foucault, 1977a: 205

[11] In Chapter Eight, there is an account of how one person at least feels about these cameras.

[12] Davies, 1998: viii

[13] Televised on BBC One, 10 September 1999

the despair (Danziger), to question community, support women and castigate the theories of the New Right (Campbell).

However, although the stories are sincere, the writing good and the intentions benevolent, there is a deep ambiguity within this writing. There are problems that I want to highlight: the role of the writer as the bringer of truth; the aestheticisation of poverty; the implicit construction of normality; and the dangers of moralism.

All three are travel books. Danziger is a praised writer of journeys in foreign lands; his is a travel book ('I began my journey at the beginning of June 1994 ...'[14]), set in the United Kingdom, drawing parallels with travelling in the shanty towns of the Third World. Davies writes of crossing an invisible frontier to visit the country of the poor: 'I set out to explore this place ... trying to record everything like some Victorian explorer penetrating a distant jungle'.[15] Both are saying that this country is not how it seems on the surface, and problems are *here*, not elsewhere. Campbell's book visits Cardiff, Oxford and Tyneside, places where there were riots in 1991, on a quest 'to know what the future holds'.[16] This travelogue genre is not a method confined to journalists, but is also part of the practice of many of the ethnographic accounts of sociologists and anthropologists, in which academic researchers recount their immersion in different places. The immersion is physical, mental and emotional, and is commonly written of as a journey, as Paul Atkinson has shown in his book on the ethnographic imagination: '[The ethnographer's journey] has features of a *quest* – a sort of voyage of search, adventure and exploration'.[17] The personal journey of the author, it is argued, strengthens the 'authenticity' of the account.[18] To the reader, interest in the travel lies in its tinge of excitement and risk – to the edge, the dark heart, the dangerous places – which has the effect of making the traveller a hero, the person who returns from this risky and exotic other world, having been face to face with otherness, bearing gifts of tales to those back home. Davies makes this connection with adventure and 'darkness' very plain as he quotes from both a 19th-century explorer of Africa, and Joseph Conrad's *Heart of darkness*, giving his work a disquieting colonialist flavour. Their heroism keeps the reader, whom the books assume are not part of the otherness, safe; they do not have to travel the same dangerous journey. The writer's

---

[14] Danziger, 1997: 8
[15] Davies, 1998: viii
[16] Campbell, 1993: xii
[17] Atkinson, 1990: 106 (emphasis in original)
[18] Atkinson, 1990: 110

experiences and stories can become more important than the world being described, appropriating this world of the poor for their narrative. Though they relay the words of the people that they meet, the words are selected and owned by the writer. The 'personal narrative' of the poor becomes part of their 'expert's narrative'[19], the experts being bearers of otherwise hidden truths.

The stories in these books are *good to read*. They contain tragedies, bleak humour, drama, heroic deeds. The travelling itself provides a good narrative hook, and the 'secrecy' that the authors are unveiling gives added excitement. But without poverty and despair, *these stories would not exist*. The stories succeed, in the way that Walter Benjamin described certain photography, 'in turning abject poverty itself, by handling it in a modish, technically perfect way, into an object of enjoyment'[20] – a charge that can also be levelled at the very lively and human photos in Danziger's book. The attempts at grim realism become transformed into texts that in their effect are anti-realist.[21] Poverty is turned into stories and pictures.

Implicit in these books is the idea that the authors are travelling from a 'normal' world to one that is abnormal and 'other', be it exotic or sordid. It is on the abnormality and grotesqueness of poverty that the gaze is focused. The writers and their own world are not examined; despite the experiences of their encounters being central to the books, they themselves remain strangely anonymous. As in most documentaries, in the programme on child poverty the TV crew was not visible. The children in front of the camera speak in answer to interrogation from the reporters behind the camera. They do not interrogate back, which implies that it is only the children, not the reporters, that are aberrant and need investigation.

This assumption that the world from which the traveller leaves is so normal that it does not have to be explained constructs poverty as deviant:

> By constructing poverty and deprivation in this way, as rooted in the characteristics of specific people and places and as only found in a few 'deviant' communities, mainstream society is assumed to be functioning properly.... blame

---

19 Plummer, 1995: 60
20 Benjamin, 1973: 95
21 Compare Walkerdine, 1997: 47, 50

is centred on the victims of poverty, rather than on the conditions of a wider society.[22]

Although the stated aim of all three authors is *not* to blame the poor, and in all three the mainstream is itself seen as flawed, the effect of bringing home the stories is to reinforce the norms of what civilised living is considered to be, with these norms, as Foucault reminds us, being an instrument of power.[23] The ambiguity in these works is that their challenge ends up reinforcing the very norms that create other people's lives as aberrations. Derrida has identified the issue of the researcher writing about the other as a problem at the heart of enquiry in the human sciences: 'The ethnologist accepts into his discourse the premises of ethnocentrism at the very moment he denounces them'.[24] These words about anthropologists who visit distant 'tribes' stand true for those that carry out this similar exercise 'in our midst'. They come from the (ethno)centre to visit the margins.

Finally, all three books concentrate on the *behaviour* of the poor (for example, Danziger and Campbell relate the breakdown of community to the behaviour of young men) so that the horror of poverty appears to be a behavioural rather than a resource or distribution problem. Davies does explain the detrimental effect of social benefit changes on people's lives, and all three books acknowledge the background of declining industries, but it is behaviour that gives the stories their dramatic content in a way that an account of structure could not. Although Campbell criticises communitarian writers for blaming the *morals* of poor people, rather than their *economy*, for creating community crisis[25], and Davies in his book attacks those who think that the poor are to blame for their poverty, the ambiguity inherent in the method of their accounts results in the reinforcement of such views. In the TV documentary, neglect and drug use were the highlighted issues, with only a presumed connection of these behaviours to poverty or inequality, which seemed to be considered wrong only because of their effects on behaviour. In these portrayals, there is a disjunction between the narrative pull of the storytelling, and the political conclusions of the authors, a chasm of meaning that lies within the writing.

There has been no such high-class journalism written about Southmead, though there have been shocking stories in the local press

---

[22] Goodwin, 1995: 79
[23] Foucault, 1977a: 184
[24] Derrida, 1978: 282
[25] Campbell, 1995: 56

that, in a cruder fashion, 'reveal' life in the area, with drug use as the main horror, as in a major spread entitled 'The lost generation. Children turn to crime to satisfy cravings for hard drugs'.[26] The article recounted individual tales of young drug users, and reproduced dramatically squalid photographs of drug use juxtaposed with images of 'normal' street scenes. The themes are not unlike those in the books. The paper called for more volunteers to help with the local drug project, justifying its investigation with a benign intent. These articles caused great upset in Southmead. I was told by people how much they resented being teased at their workplaces for living in such a terrible place.[27] Their own normality was turned into melodramatic otherness.

To counter the emotionalism of this type of storytelling, an alternative would appear to be to produce very exact and objective documentation of poverty. There is an abundance of literature on this topic, with Bristol City Council producing the *Poverty in Bristol* reports[28], and other examples such as studies for the Rowntree Foundation[29] and overviews of the social geography of poverty.[30] The typical layout of these reports is a large number of maps, tables, bar charts and pie charts, with some commentary. They are variable in their quality, but they, too, are full of representational pitfalls, of which their anonymous authors seem unaware. The narrative effect of their argument is to reify social processes, turning poverty into a static, spatially bounded aberration; there is a problematic relationship of the authors being the possessors of 'truth' about poor areas, and the result of the approach is to objectify people, reducing social actors to statistical lists.

The effect of the narrative of the reports (statistics, tables and graphs are, after all, a method of narrativising information[31]) is very similar to that of more descriptive accounts: poverty is portrayed as a local and spatial phenomenon. The way the figures are presented exaggerates this portrayal. The main dramatic turn of the *Poverty in Bristol* reports is to identify the areas that make up the poorest fifth of Bristol: 'This report should shock Bristol.... It reveals that one person in five in Bristol lives within an area of deprivation'.[32] A fuller analysis of the figures show that more people are poor outside of those areas than within them, although the reports make their poverty seem less important. To illustrate this

---

[26] *Bristol Evening Post*, 11 March 1997
[27] From my notes of a Voice of Southmead meeting, 12 March 1997.
[28] Bristol City Council, 1985, 1988, 1994, 1996a
[29] Power and Tunstall, 1995
[30] Philo, 1995
[31] See Plummer, 1995: 19
[32] Bristol City Council, 1985: 2

exaggeration, the difference in the percentage of households in receipt of council tax benefit (a strong indicator of poverty) between an area that makes it into this worst fifth and an area that does not is only that between 35.6% and 35.5%. There is a much starker difference between the 'worst' area (64.5% in receipt of benefit) and the 'best' (4.9%)[33], but this 'best' area is part of the Southmead ward. It is not its geographical location that makes it so relatively prosperous, but the economic position of its residents. Goodwin argues that the implications of an area approach to poverty 'implies that ... poverty is spatially bounded and restricted to isolated pockets of deprivation'[34], but:

> The spatial concentration of poverty is relatively low, and ... we should reject any conclusions which casually draw a link between certain types of urban locality ... and high concentrations of poverty.... the evidence points to a social, rather than a spatial, concentration of deprivation.[35]

This identification of poor areas, which are then highlighted (in the *Poverty in Bristol* reports the areas designated as poor each have individual profiles, while wealthy areas are subject to no analysis at all), makes it look as if it is the areas themselves that are the problem, and does not mention the role of wider economic forces. The way the data are represented pre-empts any discussion as to the relationship between places and social and economic forces. Castells stated the conundrum that 'people live in spaces, power rules through flows'[36]; the representational methods of the surveys only show places, they do not show flows. Poverty becomes a static classification, not a part of a dynamic relationship with wealth. In a similar way, the number of black and minority ethnic residents is given in these reports only for areas where they make up a higher than average proportion of the population. This has the effect of highlighting 'them' as if a problem of those areas, rather than showing how much more likely black people are to be poor, and throws little light on the workings of racism.[37]

---

[33] Bristol City Council, 1996a: 12-13
[34] Bristol City Council, 1996a: 79
[35] Goodwin, 1995: 68
[36] Castells, 1989: 349. This discussion is followed in Chapter Eight.
[37] Bristol City Council, 1991, 1996a: 40; Bristol Community Safety Partnership, 1999a

The importance here is to realise how the *method of representation* of information can affect the way the issues involved are thought about, or can even conceal those issues.

The second problem of these writings is in their hiding of authorship. The writers of the *Poverty in Bristol* reports are anonymous, as if the reports have not been humanly produced. This anonymity is part of the rhetoric of objectivity that permeates these reports, a representational way of increasing the status of the reports as objective accounts. As such, they are reifications, and claim an ontological and total status for something that is actually humanly produced, mirroring the way that they reify poverty.[38] Jessica Benjamin, writing about the idea of objectivity, argues that, while 'denying invisibility to nature', the contemporary scientist 'maintains the invisibility of his personal authorship, protecting his autonomy behind a screen of objectivity'.[39] These contemporary *social* scientists deny invisibility to poor areas, but likewise disavow their own presence. While in the travel books the author was always present, if never under question, in these reports the authors are absent, and are not there to be questioned at all. They are depersonalised and disconnected, a performance of the ideal of the unencumbered self.

This depersonalisation of the authors does not exempt the works from possessing a psychic dimension. Benjamin has no doubts that there is an element of fantasy associated with a desire for impersonal knowledge, and compares this desire with the desire to rape and dominate, a useful, if dramatic, analogy:

> We may note that this image of the scientist as an impersonal knower who 'tears the veil' from nature's body is reminiscent of the master in the fantasy of erotic domination, and his quest for knowledge parallels the rational violation in which the subject is always in control.[40]

The application of psychoanalytic ideas of fantasy/phantasy in this context is worth a short explanation. Juliet Mitchell defines this concept as used by Melanie Klein: 'phantasy emanates from within and imagines what is without'.[41] She explains that 'the "ph" spelling

---

[38] Berger and Luckman, 1967: 108
[39] Benjamin, 1990: 189
[40] Benjamin, 1990: 189-90
[41] Mitchell, 1986: 23

is used to indicate that the process is unconscious'.[42] In Benjamin's idea of this particular knowledge fantasy (she uses the 'f' version), the outside world is imagined as an object, an inanimate object to be discovered by the subject, the scientist. The objectification of the outside world confirms their own role as subjects, *who* know, rather than objects, *which* are known (note the change from the personal to the impersonal pronoun), in the way that the othering of the low confirmed the status of the bourgeoisie. The subject and the object are imagined as distinct and *different* from each other: the poor are different. Thus, the seemingly non-fantastical method used in these reports is as much part of psychic identity formation as the fascination with the other described by Stallybrass and White. Benjamin argues that this relationship of difference affects the understanding of the outside world: 'In the radical separation of subject and object we perceive ... the inability to grasp the *aliveness of the other*'.[43]

This is a major problem of the more statistical approach: in objectifying people into tables and graphs, it diminishes their lives. It gives an arid view of social existence, and ignores what Corlett calls the extravagance of life:

> There exist totalities of facts – for example, those accumulated by social science ... that can be studied 'objectively', but in principle there is always an excess which cannot.[44]

Those parts of life that cannot be turned into figures are ignored. Instead, the people surveyed become in these writings '*mute objects, brute things*, that do not reveal themselves in words, that do not *comment upon themselves*'.[45] The battle *against* such objectification is often a starting point of community mobilisation, as resistance to what Habermas calls 'objectifying descriptions of society'[46], with people demanding the right to be social actors. As we shall see in Chapter Four, much of the force behind community expression is an opposition to the way people are written about, an insistence that they are worth something as social actors in their own right. In the photograph of the car scene, the central figure looks out of the photograph defying the gaze of the spectator.

---

[42] Mitchell, 1986: 22

[43] Benjamin, 1990: 190 (emphasis added)

[44] Corlett, 1989: 177

[45] Bakhtin, 1981: 351 (emphasis in original)

[46] Habermas, 1992: 141

Campbell wrote of boys like him that they 'defied the definition of the passive underclass: these young men weren't *under* anyone'.[47]

As a contrast to these writings on poor places, I want to briefly mention another form of writing about place. There is a palpable excitement in much academic writing about cities, and the possibilities life in the city offers. These writings never, however, write about the city living of housing estate dwellers; it is as if they do not live in the cities so evocatively described by these dealing with grander themes. Thus, Richard Sennett introduces his book *Flesh and stone* as:

> A history of the city told through people's bodily experiences: how women and men moved, what they saw and heard, the smells that assailed their noses, where they ate, how they dressed, when they bathed, how they made love in cities from ancient Athens to modern New York.[48]

On this romantic quest, he passes through the major centres of Venice, Rome, Paris (repeatedly) and London. Marshall Berman, in his 'experience of modernity', writes of Baudelaire's Paris, Petersburg and, again, New York.[49] Walter Benjamin writes of Naples, Moscow, Marseilles and Baudelaire's Paris.[50] David Harvey writes about modernism and cities, all his examples being European and American metropolises (Paris features again as an archetype), and postmodernism in relation to (of course) New York.[51] Edward Soja, writing about postmodern geographies, depicts Los Angeles as 'the place where "it all comes together"', which has, more than any other place, 'become the paradigmatic window through which to see the last half of the twentieth century'.[52] In all these writings (and there are plenty more), cities are centres of excitement.

The writings about poor places, on the other hand, constantly remind us that the housing estate, as Marc Augé puts it in his book on non-places, 'is never situated at the centre of anything'.[53] They are not written about because of their architecture, art, café life, literature or sexual practices (although these are all there), but because of their

---

[47] Campbell, 1993: 29, (emphasis in original)

[48] Sennett, 1994: 15

[49] Berman, 1983

[50] Benjamin, 1969, 1997

[51] Harvey, 1990

[52] Soja, 1989: 191, 221

[53] Augé, 1995: 107-8

crime and poverty. They are demoted to being a site of investigation rather than of enjoyment.

The challenge

It is much easier to criticise representations of poor areas than to write one. The act of trying to capture any description or meaning is an agonising process, especially when I have set myself the task of conveying a sense of dynamic relationships rather than static position, pursuing Foucault's point that geographical space is not 'the dead, the fixed, the undialectic, the immobile'.[54]

Places always will be represented, and representing Southmead in reports and argument is a large part of my professional life. Data and explanation have to be continually presented for projects for young people to take place: of the two mentioned so far, neither the film Rush nor the exhibition The Place We're In would have happened without first a written case convincing people of how they were possible in Southmead, and the same goes for a wide variety of other work. The task of representation is unavoidable in any active relationship with the area. The challenge brings questions of *how* it is to be met; about what the data is, and how to use it; and about the productive, if highly ambiguous, possibilities writing gives for discovery. The approach outlined below is the method used for this book; it is not a claim that this is *the* way to do it, but an explanation of the way it is used here.

Bricolage

I have shown how the data of travellers' stories and the data of statistics affect the representation of poor areas. However, both are important sources of evidence, not to be discarded; there is no magic third type of data in their place, without drawback, that would lead us straight to a 'correct' representation. Eric Hobsbawm writes that, for grassroots history (which bears a resemblance to this enquiry in that it is about the 'common people' who do not make up the ruling classes[55]), there is no ready-made body of material available. New types of enquiry uncover new sources of material, and without there being ready-made data, he says that: 'We cannot be positivists, believing that the questions

---

[54] Foucault, 1980: 70

[55] Community expression is even more 'from below'. The ideas of knowledge from above and below, or from inside and outside, are discussed further in Chapters Three and Four.

---

and the answers arise naturally out of the study of *the* material'.[56] In studying Southmead, there is no single, known and contained body of material that leads to questions and answers. In its place, though, there is a mass of material of different types there to be found and gathered. Southmead is not hidden, unexplored, devoid of data, but is abundantly well documented; the 'hidden' nature of poor areas is a literary conceit of those who write to 'uncover' them rather than a reflection on the availability of information. In the face of this mass of material, the approach has to be one of pragmatism – to use what there is to be used, to use what can be used. The best description of this approach is *bricolage*, with myself in this instance acting as the *bricoleur*:

> The *bricoleur*, says Lévi-Strauss, is someone who uses the 'means at hand', that is, the instruments he finds at his disposition around him, those who are already there, which had not been especially conceived with an eye for the operation for which they are to be used and to which one tries by trial and error to adapt them, not hesitating to change them whenever appears necessary, or to try several of them at once, even if their form and their origin are heterogeneous – and so forth.[57]

Already the text of this book so far illustrates my approach as a *bricoleur*. I have used a variety of sources, and a variety of ways to interpret them, as *bricolage* applies not only to data, but also to the use of theories, to be used, so Gilles Deleuze put it in an interview with Foucault, as 'a box of tools'.[58] The writings of Derrida, for example, are one of the instruments at my disposal. As well as this being a pragmatic approach – what else can one do except use the means at hand? – there are more positive advantages to using it in relation to the world being studied, as pointed out by de Certeau:

> Statistical investigation grasps the material of these [everyday] practices, but not their *form*; it determines the elements used, but not the 'phrasing' produced by the *bricolage* (the artisan like inventiveness) and the discursiveness that combine

---

[56] Hobsbawm, 1998: 271 (emphasis added)

[57] Derrida, 1978: 285. Lévi-Strauss's description of the *bricoleur* is in *The savage mind* (1966). His use of the idea is not connected to research methods, but is about how people live.

[58] Foucault, 1977b: 208. In a book on feminist research, the metaphor used is one of recipe (Stanley, 1990: 41).

these elements, which are all in general circulation and rather drab.[59]

In de Certeau's view, *bricolage* is how life is lived, an inventive *tactic* as opposed to *strategy*, which is a model of imposition used both by power and by political, economic and scientific rationality.[60] Life, however, is irreducible to any single reading using any single imposed strategy. *Bricolage* as a research method is a conscious move in what Ian Parker calls the 'retreat to any set "methods" [which] will restrict our understanding of the complexity and multiplicity of meaning'[61], in order to match the polymorphous nature of the power, representations and actions of community, and the *bricolage* of life.

Janet Abu-Lughod, in her account of research in the East Village of Manhattan, emphasises the point that multiple methods are essential to a community study, and takes this one step further by arguing that 'community study requires more than a single ethnographer', because all the different groups mean that there is 'no single authorial [authoritative] image of the neighbourhood'.[62] I hope to show a multiplicity of images of Southmead, in compensation for this book being written by a single author.

Just claiming that *bricolage* is an acceptable method because weighty names say so is insufficient justification for a technique that, in a standard French–English dictionary, is translated as do-it-yourself (DIY), with *bricoleur* meaning handyman. DIY can go disastrously wrong. To prevent such catastrophe, and show my method of *bricolage*, I want to go through the processes used in this book in more detail. Transparency of process is necessary for the credence of *bricolage*; to see both its strengths and its shortcomings in its challenge to the claims of other methods, it should not overstate its own case. These processes can be arranged under the four headings of: accumulation, reading, re-presenting and writing, which I shall go through in turn. Interspersed with these, I outline the difficulties of participant research, and of translating and/or communicating between different social worlds and languages, both of which raise major issues for the book.

---

[59] de Certeau, 1984: xviii (emphasis in original)
[60] de Certeau, 1984: xix
[61] Parker, 1999: 2
[62] Abu-Lughod, 1994: 3 (brackets in original)

Accumulation

In preparing this book, I have accumulated a range of very different types of material, the 'elements' of *bricolage*. The range includes:

- Statistics and maps that refer to Southmead – census analyses, poverty reports, crime figures and so on – what are known as hard data. I have collected reports published from 1981 to 1999. These types of reports are starting to use a much greater diversity of source material themselves. Poverty on its own is seen as a narrow category. Since 1995, Bristol City Council has produced a series of reports on the quality of life that use a much wider breadth of information, although this information is still presented as area-based statistics. These can be seen as either widening the focus on what makes up the quality of life, or losing the focus on inequality and unfairness.
- Books, surveys, articles and reports on, or that mention, Southmead. Although I have not done any survey work for this book, I collect the surveys that have been done by others. These range from full-scale works to small-scale documents produced for particular purposes. The first of these was published in 1963, with data collected in the period 1952-58, the latest in 1999. There is a gap in my collection of any cyclostyled reports that may have been produced in the 1970s. Printed reports only started to appear in the mid-1980s.
- Media coverage – news items and articles in local and national newspapers, and reports on TV and radio. I collected any media material I found that mentioned Southmead in the period 1993 to 1999 – news reports, photographs, editorials, reviews and letters – on 'soft' as well as 'hard' topics, unlike the library of the University of the West of England, which only keeps press cuttings on Southmead relating to economic and planning issues.
- Cultural material produced in or from Southmead in the period 1986 to 1999 – books, a play script, poems, videos, music, photographs, posters, leaflets, community newspapers, radio transmissions, paintings, exhibitions and handbooks. A few of these are documentary, but most are not, and were never intended to be. Some are directly about Southmead, the rest are from it but not about it.
- My own diary notes and observations, kept from 1993 to 2000, of incidents and conversations encountered in my daily work in Southmead. These were usually noted down contemporaneously, or within a few days of them taking place. The practice of this recording is not easy, which I explain further in the next section. As these accounts appear in the text, they are usually edited into a readable

version, as my contemporaneous notes tend to be messy, long and disjointed. These observations are central to the book; they make clear my own relationship to the area and the subject, as well as my own role as both participant and observer, and they show examples of the issues that arise from engagement with community.

- My own background knowledge, which is less easy to use and attribute properly. If I record an account from someone else relaying their background knowledge, that becomes 'evidence', in the way that I am approached as a source by other people doing research (Southmead is a favourite location to send students to carry out 'community profiles'), who record and reproduce what I say as their evidence. This whole book is my evidence, and is inevitably informed by my experience of the area since 1975, although I will not assert that I simply 'know' something without giving reasons why.
- A small selection of reports and writings on other areas, for comparison.
- A collection of theoretical and other writings (as explained in Chapter One) to be my toolbox. This book is concerned with theoretical understandings of community, and although it is empirically based, it is also a critique of much of the writing on community. A critical approach through theory is a major part of the book.

All the publicly available material has been listed in the References at the end of the book. The accumulation of publicly available material poses the problem of keeping an archive, but could be done by anyone. The collection of material that concerns my own involvement with the area, that unique angle that I bring to the research, is far more problematic. To give some illustration of why, here are two examples of the problems encountered in practice.

Problems of participant research

A major problem of being both participant and researcher is that of conflict between the two roles. The most interesting moments, when there is a lot of material to record, are also the moments of the greatest participation in the action, giving little time to research. When there is conflict between researching and participating, the participation usually wins out, under the pressure of events. The conflict between the roles can be dramatic.

On 2 May 1997, there was a public meeting in Southmead called by the campaign group Voice of Southmead to protest against drug dealing in the area. There was a big publicity build-up to the meeting, with a dramatic poster and groups of 'about 40 men, and a dozen women' leafleting every house in the area.[63] There was intense interest in the local media. For the two weeks leading up to the meeting, there were a number of articles in the press, including questions about whether the group leafleting was a vigilante tactic. This was denied vehemently by the group, whose leaflet said: 'We are not vigilantes and do not belong to any political organisation'.[64] The group was supported publicly by the local vicar and the local police.[65] Two days before the meeting, there was regional television coverage of the mass leafleting in all its drama, and moving interviews with one of the main activists, the mother of a heroin addict, and her son, on television and local radio.

When I arrived at the meeting there was a long queue waiting to get in. The hall was full, with people standing at the back. There were about 500 people there. On the platform were the Labour MP for Bristol North West (elected the day before), local councillors, the local police superintendent and other officers, managers from local authority services, speakers from drug agencies and members of Voice. I was at the back, scribbling down everything I could see and hear as fast as I could into my notebook as a *researcher*, when a row broke out about the role of the youth centre in the battle against drugs, and the state of its facilities: "It's like a pigsty, not a place to be the centre of young people's lives. It needs a complete revamp". There were angry demands from the floor for me to answer for my actions as a youth *worker*: "Jerry, *you* get up there". *At this point my notes stop.* My research was completely overtaken by the aliveness of the other. From then on, I was fighting against being made a scapegoat for drug taking among young people. A year later, the youth centre did get a complete revamp, and many of its fiercest critics became its fiercest supporters, but only through very active participation on my part, not through research activities.[66]

Mostly the conflict was not so dramatic – just a battle for energy. My diary is full of comments about how tired I was being both participant and researcher.

The second major concern about collecting material is the feeling of being a spy who is taking people's words and transposing them for the sake of a different system of thought. The writer bell hooks

---

[63] *Western Daily Press*, 16 April 1997

[64] *Bristol Evening Post*, 16 April 1997

[65] *Bristol Evening Post*, 17 April 1997

[66] This account is distilled from diary notes and press reports. There is a fuller account of the Voice of Southmead in Chapter Seven.

warns against informers, 'those folks who appear to be allied with the disadvantaged, the oppressed, who are either spies or there to mediate between the forces of domination and its victims'.[67] This collection of information, says Said, so easily leads to control:

> Knowledge of subject races ... is what makes their management easy and profitable; knowledge gives power, more power requires more knowledge, and so on in an increasingly profitable dialectic of information and control.[68]

Patrick Chamoiseau's novel *Solibo Magnificent* is about the death of a Creole storyteller in Martinique. The story of his death, 'throat snickt by the word'[69], is the story of the death of an oral tradition and language, taken over by the written, colonising, French word. Chamoiseau casts himself as an ethnographer trying to capture the words of Solibo the story teller: 'I called myself a "word scratcher", a pathetic gatherer of elusive things'.[70] He calls his written version of the story ersatz[71], and felt it was a betrayal to write the words down. When I have been in a similar situation of recording stories, I, too, have felt this sense of betrayal, as if stealing the words of others.

In July 1995, there was a public meeting to discuss the future of the local scouts' hut, which at the time was being badly vandalised. Here is an extract from my record of that event[72]:

> *The local leaders were asked to speak first. They all used stories to explain the situation. They were well aware that they were doing this – they kept saying, "I'll tell you a story" or "There are lots of stories". The stories were about decline, combined with stories of loyalty and commitment. Funny stories – the cups being stolen during jumble sales....*
>
> *I wanted to take down these stories verbatim, even reached for my pad, but felt that this would have been intrusive, exploitative, and spoilt my own enjoyment in listening. If I had, would I have been able to show their richness, the powerful aesthetic in their*

---

[67] hooks, 1991: 9
[68] Said, 1978: 36
[69] Chamoiseau, 1999: 8
[70] Chamoiseau, 1999: 158
[71] Chamoiseau, 1999: 159
[72] Diary notes, 3 July 1995

> *construction?... They were also about being heard – several times*
> *it was said, "We don't feel so alone now".*

Apart from breaking down the feelings of isolation, these stories were calls for help and action (which a book does not provide). They were stories that challenged the purpose of my involvement in the area, raising Raymond Williams' question of different interpretations of community.[73] While stories are important in constructing versions of community in Southmead[74], accumulating them just as data is insulting, and questions the role of research without participation.

Problems of accumulation

At very first glance, the list of material accumulated looks as if it could enable me to reach what Marc Augé calls the 'ideal of exhaustive interpretation', and that it is therefore possible to succumb to the 'totality temptation'[75], and produce a complete representation of Southmead. That glance, however, is soon overtaken by a deeper understanding of this accumulation.

First, just in the listing of sources comes the realisation that there are so many voices, or sources, involved, and in such different forms, that they are irreducible to a single incontestable, or total, view. Not only are there different viewpoints, but they are expressed in different, even incommensurable, languages. How can one connect together material as diverse, for example, as housing statistics and an animated film made by young people that includes a fish-headed person and dinosaurs that metamorphose into fluffy balls.[76] There can be no attempt in this book to subsume all these differing viewpoints into one 'master' interpretation.

Second, there is the realisation that information is never collectable in totality; every day there are thousands of conversations, actions and transactions in and affecting Southmead; each week there are statistics gathered and reports filed; each month there are new policies and meetings and decisions. 'There is too much, more than one can say.'[77] The collection is limited by being my collection; there are other sources not used at all, of the sort beloved of grassroots historians, who can

---

[73] See Chapter One.

[74] For a 'sociology of stories', see Plummer (1995), whose work is crucial in the further discussion of this point in Chapter Four.

[75] Augé, 1995: 48

[76] Bristol City Council Housing Services, 1994; Hot and Twitchy, 1993

[77] Derrida, 1978: 289

extract major insights from parish records, health records, planning documents, school reports and so on. I could have created even more information by carrying out an original survey, but did not. The questions of the book are not ones that can be answered by collecting people's opinions on them; and, while I want to know people's idea of community, I wanted to see how this plays out in everyday situations, without the artificial prompting that questions provide. For example, if 60% of respondents told me that Southmead is a community, and 40% said it is not, this would not show that Southmead, on a majority vote, is a community.[78]

Third, the material does not have a simple temporal rationale. There is no single original point from which the existence of Southmead started (the first inhabitant? the first house? the first plan? the idea of buying fields to build a housing estate?), and its existence is ongoing, not complete. The material starts and finishes on dates convenient for this book (any choice of dates would be arbitrary), although it is a period in which historical change can be seen.

Fourth, all these sources are themselves representations, not components that can be constructed back into a replica Southmead. There is a myth, particularly prevalent in the area of multimedia, that by having several sources of information you can reconstruct the original. One of the artists involved with The Place We're In, when interviewed on the radio, listed all the different types of information that made up the exhibition, and said that 'we have been able to create a virtual Southmead', which people could 'visit' on its website.[79] This confuses a complex *representation* of Southmead with its *re-creation*.

Fifth, a question arising from these first four, is whether the variation of the material shows that Southmead, and its existence as a 'community', is ever, even as an abstract ideal, finalised and complete. Is it that it is always 'in play' because it actually has no foundation or centre, no beginning or end?[80] That there is always something that is missing is possibly not just a deficiency of the research process, but because there is no kernel there to be found. *Bricolage* raises the question that totalisation and finality of interpretation is impossible because the phenomenon that is Southmead itself excludes totalisation and finality. As an approach, *bricolage* helps us to break out of the habits of thought that lead to the essentialising of any single foundation of social

---

[78] In Chapter Three, there is discussion about poor use of survey material from Southmead.

[79] BBC Radio Bristol, 30 April 1997

[80] See Derrida, 1978: 289

relationships as being the source of a single and objective social reality, habits that construct the job of the radical social theorist as being that of discoverer of this foundation, exposing it in order to then transform social relations, rather than understanding that there is no foundation outside of those relations.

Sixth, it has to be made clear that *bricolage* is not the same as triangulation, by which data, particularly statistical data, are checked for credence by using different measures. It is multi-perspectival, so 'provides the potential for stronger (that is, more many-sided, illuminating, and critical) readings'[81], but it does not add up to any proof; if anything, it emphasises a complexity that belies proof.

Finally, looking at piles of files and notebooks and video cassettes, comes the very obvious realisation that the accumulation of material of itself is a meaningless activity. This material does not make sense unmediated by reading and analysis.

Reading

Having gathered the material, the first process to put it through is reading it to subject it to analysis, although there is 'continuous interplay between analysis and data collection'.[82] The approach I use is discourse analysis. What is written, or said, and the way it is expressed, is as important as events and facts themselves, and becomes a fact in itself. All the evidence listed above comes in the form of a variety of different systems of knowledge about Southmead, and it is for their value as different discourses that they are read. The role of discourse analysts as described by Ian Parker is that of 'continually putting what they read into quotation marks'[83], and that is what this process of reading all this evidence entails, including the evidence of my own observations. I have already shown this process through analysing the way that various writings portray poverty in a manner that constructs it as a spatial and behavioural issue. They became texts with effects, to be analysed as such, rather than unmediated sources of information.

Discourses therefore are not just simple descriptions of the world. Parker defines them thus: 'A good working definition of a discourse should be that it is *a system of statements which constructs an object*'.[84] So I am not reading the various pieces of data just for descriptions and

---

[81] Kellner 1997: 110. See also Johnson, 1987
[82] Strauss and Corbin, 1994: 273
[83] Parker, 1992: 4
[84] Parker, 1992: 5

facts; I am also reading them as statements forming the discourses that construct Southmead as an 'object'. These statements all have certain effects (some, of course, more powerful than others), and can well be in conflict with each other – the battle of representation that recurs as a theme throughout the book. The effects of how Southmead is comprehended as a phenomenon are important to understand, as different comprehensions lead to different actions, and in turn to a different reality. If Southmead is comprehended as a high crime area[85], the focus of action is on crime prevention, or as a poor area[86], the focus is on anti-poverty policies, and so on. The differing politics of these comprehensions are central to the very construction of Southmead as a place, as will be displayed in greater depth through the book.

The reading of the various material collected as discourses re-emphasises the incommensurability of the different material, and how this makes the collection of words an insufficient process.

First, and most easily overlooked, is how to understand silences, although they are, as Foucault has pointed out, 'an integral part of the strategies that permeate and underlie discourses'.[87] In looking for community, my eyes and ears become attuned to any mention of the term; it is a keyword in my mental filing system. However, I can exaggerate its importance if I am not also aware of all the occasions when it is *not* mentioned. What meaning, for example, should I give to the fact that in 17 editions of *Southmead Writers*, which explains itself as 'a collection of poems and stories from local people in Southmead', community is not mentioned once? There are poems about animals, plants, hunger, homelessness and a huge variety of other subjects, but among over 200 pieces, only a couple even mention Southmead. Silences, however, are not only within Southmead; there are silences about it that are part of what Foucault calls masking processes, part of the mechanism of power: 'power is only tolerable on condition that it masks a substantial part of itself. Its success is proportional to its ability to hide its own mechanisms'.[88] Despite all that is written and said, awareness is still needed about the unwritten and unspoken.

Second, what about cultural expressions in which words are of minor importance? Two of the most popular forms of expression in Southmead are music, with numbers of bands who both regularly

---

[85] Bristol Community Safety Partnership, 1999a
[86] Bristol City Council, 1996a
[87] Foucault, 1979: 27
[88] Foucault, 1979: 86

---

play live and record their own music[89], and sport. I have been told, in no uncertain terms, at a meeting held in the Southmead Rugby Club bar, which is adorned with display cases of the international strips collected by a local hero who has played for Scotland, that art is middle-class, and sport is what working-class people from Southmead want[90]. Henri Lefebvre points out that to underestimate non-verbal sets of signs, symbols and activities 'amounts to the overestimation of texts, written matter, and writing systems, along with the readable and visible, to the point of assigning these a monopoly on intelligibility'.[91] There is a further advantage gained by realising the significance of the non-verbal. It helps with the process of putting verbal discourse into quotation marks, thus recognising different languages and their import. Below are two very different examples of written languages collected for this book. First, some academic writing about place. Ed Soja in *Postmodern geographies* writes that localities can be defined as:

> ... particular types of enduring locales stabilizing socially and spatially through the clustered settlement of primary activity sites and the establishment of propinquitous territorial community. Like every locale, they are spatio-temporal structurations arising from the combination of human agency and the conditioning impact of spatio-temporal condition.[92]

This use of language provides us, just possibly, with an academic way of describing the phenomenon of Southmead. As an object, I can pick up that piece of language and not be overwhelmed by it.

A second genre of language in common use is that of professionals. The Southmead Family Project defines its aim as:

> To coordinate a strategic multi agency approach to work with a small number of families, offering positive programmes which seek to divert young people from causing major problems in the community.[93]

---

[89] See − or listen to − the CDs Fire It Up and kfs.
[90] At a meeting with Voice of Southmead, March 1997.
[91] Lefebvre, 1991: 62
[92] Soja, 1989: 151
[93] SCRiPT, 1996

The language of this piece consists of stringing together the highest number of the buzzwords of the moment as possible into one sentence. Part of the politics of protest in Southmead consists of challenging professional language such as that. At meetings of Voice of Southmead, there were continual demands from the floor for the public service managers there to make themselves understood: "We haven't had your education. What do you mean? We don't know these words."[94] As I read difficult texts, I keep hearing a memorable Southmead phrase used to challenge those who speak in long words: 'Stop bumming your chat'.[95]

While discourse analysis helps in the 'reading' of these different types of evidence, the quoted examples show how languages that are perfectly acceptable within their own language communities can really only be understood when, as Habermas says, 'we know the conditions under which [they] can be accepted as valid'.[96] Any reading is therefore a complex process, which is not just about extracting meaning, but is also about understanding, using Bakhtin's idea, the dialogic contrast of *languages*, which 'delineates the boundaries of language, creates a feeling for these boundaries, compels one to sense physically the plastic form of different languages'.[97]

While the method of putting everything into quotation marks can possibly accommodate this contrast, and through Foucault's understanding of silences and Lefebvre's emphasis on non-verbal significations, the evidence outside the merely verbal and the textual is recognised, there is still an issue with what this evidence then becomes. Discourse analysis treats discourses as objects: 'Discourse is about objects, and discourse analysis is about *discourses* as objects'.[98] Parker's approach acknowledges how the original material becomes objectified as it is placed in the text. This has the dangers of all other types of objectification: it can reduce what is dynamic to a form of stasis, and it tends to try to flatten wildly varying discourses into objects that look comparable. Discourse analysis can become a double objectification, an ironic result when trying to avoid an objectifying representation of social processes.

As we look at the data in the next chapters, we will see how different discourses do have effects, and how Southmead is constructed through

---

[94] Notes of March 1997 meeting.

[95] From Jill Truman's research notes for the book Alive and kicking! (Truman and Brent, 1995).

[96] Habermas, 1987: 313

[97] Bakhtin, 1981: 364

[98] Parker, 1992: 9 (emphasis in original)

---

them. However, during this process, it is important to avoid thinking that Southmead is merely a representation, that it appears in writings but has no material presence, that its people just talk but do not act, that all that is required for change is different thinking rather than different action, and that the way out is to form a 'correct' representation. The process does, however, indicate that an effective way of comprehending Southmead is through analysing the discourses that surround it.

Re-presentation

Throughout this book, examples of the data are re-presented to the reader, either as direct quotations, pictures or second-hand accounts. Atkinson writes of the ethnographer's use of exemplary materials like this in the text: 'They provide the reader with concrete − sometimes vivid − if fragmentary vicarious experiences of the social world in question'.[99] By this use of material: 'The ethnography ... can be a complex text with various levels and voices'.[100] The text consists not just of the voices of the author, but also of the elements found by the *bricoleur*. However, this approach to the reproduction of the evidence ignores what happens to it as it is being *re*-presented. There is a change, at least of tone if not of meaning, as these different 'voices' are replayed to the reader in their quotation marks.

There are young people in Southmead who have seen for themselves the effect that context has on the meaning of their own representation of the area. In 1995, a group of a dozen of them took a series of photographs to express what they felt about the place in which they lived. They themselves selected those they wanted to be displayed, and the photographs were put on show in a gallery as the Southmead Photo Album. As part of the media coverage, a group of them went to the exhibition venue to be interviewed by the local radio station. When they saw the display panels (which they had already seen and approved in Southmead) in this new setting, they became very uneasy and defensive in their interviews, as the photographs now looked different. They said of them, "They might think it's a rough area, but it's not really when you come up. It might not look like it, but it's good atmosphere and good fun", and, "They shouldn't look at the pictures and judge Southmead straight away".[101] Context changes meaning.

---

[99] Atkinson, 1990: 82

[100] Atkinson, 1990: 95

[101] BBC Radio Bristol, October 1995. There was greater discussion about the issue on the journey home, but I was driving and could not write down the comments.

When 'raw' material exists in the text, it becomes a different, treated form, and is unlike the original. The experience of the original through the reproduction of material can only be imagined, can only give a sensation of these other voices, not their full flavour, a possibly vivid but certainly not concrete experience.

The change from spoken to written language in this text loses a major marker of Southmead's difference – the accent in which people speak, an accent confined to the housing estates of Bristol. One of the most striking features of the film Rush is hearing the narrator speak. His accent on screen surprises viewers both from within and outside Southmead, because this accent is not usually heard in the public media. The accent is what makes Rush such a recognisably Southmead film, but one that I cannot re-present through writing.[102]

In the translation process, there can be an assumption that the language of the 'centre' is the default language, into which the languages of the margins need translating – what Bakhtin calls 'the incorporation of barbarians and lower social strata into a unitary language of culture and truth'[103] – but this imposition of such a unity is opposed to what he calls the 'realities of heteroglossia'.[104] In re-presenting the material gathered to the reader, that heteroglossia can get lost. What Benjamin said about translating Baudelaire from the French operates as much within national languages; the 'relationship between content and language is quite different in the original and the translation'.[105]

It might seem that I am overly concerned by this translation process, but one of my tasks as a participant in the area is as a translator. Translation must not be written off – I have, after all, just quoted a German writer (in translation) about translation, and a Russian about different languages. As a participant, I regularly translate from the words of official documents into the vernacular, and from vernacular accounts into official documents. Through the summer of 1997, after the various Voice of Southmead meetings that demanded better sporting facilities at the youth centre, there was a series of meetings to work out how this could happen in practice. This involved putting demands into certain formats: application forms for money, a job description for a youth sports worker. This translation did not seem oppressive, nor did it seem as if meaning were being lost. If anything, meaning was gained as a group

---

[102] I am aware that other writers do try to transcribe accent, but the result feels patronising (for example, Willis, 1980).
[103] Bakhtin, 1981: 271
[104] Bakhtin, 1981: 270
[105] Benjamin, 1969: 75

of people from different interests and positions bargained together to create a sports initiative of which all were proud.[106] However, that translation can be a bitter experience as well as a positive one. It is one that happens everyday, outside of this book, as ideas are re-presented across language and social differences.

Writing

It is by writing about it that the material collected through accumulation, reading and re-presentation is analysed. Writing is an interpretative process, and as such transforms that material.[107] In my commentary on representations of poverty, and their transformations, there were two questions that kept on recurring and underlaid much of my criticism: the questions of the position of the writers, and the psychic dimensions of the writing. In my own writing about Southmead, I can avoid neither of these questions. I too write from some kind of position, and from some form of desire that transforms the material.

The question of the position of the author has often been put as being one of whose side they are on. Walter Benjamin, in his often-quoted address 'The author as producer' given in 1934, said, with a certainty that now feels very dated, that the progressive writer 'places himself on the side of the proletariat'.[108] Writing, he said, exists within the relationships of production of the time, and the author was a producer, in the same relationship to the means of production as other workers. Any other relationship by the 'man of mind' to the proletariat, such as well-wisher or ideological patron, is impossible.[109] It is the criticism of the mere well-wisher, as Hal Foster has commented, that make these lines scathe as they question the basis of the relationship of writer to subject.[110]

However, this idea of 'being on a side' is highly problematic. First, claiming a side, as Foster points out, usually results in confirming the distance between people: 'Identification with the worker alienates the worker, confirms rather than closes the gap between the two through

---

[106] An example of that translation is the Southmead Youth Sports Development Initiative: Business Plan 1999. The pride is evident in the video Southmead Slamming (1999).

[107] Denzin, 1994: 504

[108] Benjamin, 1973: 85. See also Sennett and Cobb, 1977: 5 for a discussion of a similar position held by Sartre.

[109] Benjamin, 1973: 93

[110] Foster, 1996: 171

a reductive, idealistic, or otherwise misbegotten representation'.[111] Any attempt by me to 'pass' as a Southmeader, or as a young person, would be met either with deep suspicion or hoots of derision, as being so obviously sham. Second, though, even if I could 'pass', does the side exist? I have already shown the problem of there being simple 'sides' in my account of the bicycle theft and its aftermath.[112] If, on that occasion, I said I was 'on the side of Southmead', this assertion would immediately have to be followed by the question, 'Which version of Southmead?'. Both the thieves and the police could claim that they were on the side of Southmead – one set because they live there, the other because they were acting as its legal protectors. Taking sides was a difficult and ambiguous matter, both for myself and for those who eventually, ambivalently, supported me. However, in that incident there was also no possibility of being *outside* the situation, no neutral non-side.

Any assertion that I side with Southmead would only be with *my* preferred version of Southmead, one that I imagine: 'Siding with people becomes constructing people that exist only in the writer's imaginary'.[113] This point, made by Pile and Thrift, can not be overemphasised – in youth work, there is much bland assertion by workers that they are on the side of young people and in community work, there are similar assertions of being on the side of whatever 'community' the person happens to be working with at the time. In that version, our role is simple: it is to empower them to achieve what they want, which assumes that *who* they are, and *what* they want is unproblematic, rather than being the very questions that need to be asked.[114]

So there is no simple side to be on within the topic, and no simple viewing position outside of it from which to write. This lack of certainty of position creates an anxious desire to understand what can otherwise seem to be an overwhelming flux. Denying this desire, or even trying to compensate for its effects, would be counter-productive. As Slavoj Zizek points out, desire is itself necessary to see what we are looking at:

---

[111] Foster, 1996: 174

[112] See Chapter One

[113] Pile and Thrift, 1995: 16

[114] Abu-Lughod, 1994: 198. Compare Hammersley and Atkinson on the position of ethnographer who wants to advocate: 'There is often genuine uncertainty about what is and what is not in the interests of the group and of members of it' (1995: 253).

> If we look at a thing straight on, i.e. matter of factly,
> disinterestedly, objectively, we see nothing but a formless
> spot; the object assumes clear and distinctive features only
> if we look at it 'at an angle,' i.e., with an 'interested' view,
> supported, permeated, and 'distorted' by *desire*.[115]

To have *some* knowledge of one's own desire (it need hardly be said
that total self-knowledge in this area is inconceivable), to know the
angle(s) from which one is looking, possibly clarifies how one can
then represent this otherwise 'formless spot'. Without going into a
long process of self-psychoanalysis, although possibly undergoing the
'ethno-self-analysis' necessary prior to the ethnography of others[116], I
would say that my desire to write about Southmead comes from the
anxiety my relationship to it engenders. I am made anxious by the
relationship. I would like, through writing, to find some kind of answer
to the question as put by Edward Said:

> Perhaps the most important fact of all would be ... to
> ask how one can study other cultures and peoples from
> a libertarian, or a nonrepressive and nonmanipulative
> perspective.[117]

His word 'study' could equally well be replaced with the words
'represent' or 'act with'. It is an anxious question.

As soon as this desire is stated, the reasons for the impossibility of
its fulfilment start to flood in. The desire is a version of the ideal of
mutual recognition proposed by writers such as Jessica Benjamin and
Charles Taylor, of Habermas's ideal of communicative reason. But from
Derrida comes that reminder about the constant play of difference; the
word 'other' in Said's sentence cannot be deleted or ignored. And from
Foucault comes the further reminder that any exercise in knowledge
is also an exercise of power – an almost inevitable asymmetry in the
relationship, whether that power be creative, oppressive or a form of
resistance. However, it is because of the awareness of difference and
of power as constitutive of the forces without which Southmead
would not be a phenomenon to write about that leads to the desire
to write. The challenge is to write a representation of Southmead that

---

[115] Zizek 1991a: 11 (emphasis added)
[116] Augé, 1995: 39. This is similar to the idea of reflexivity discussed in Chapter Five
in greater depth.
[117] Said, 1978: 24

investigates these issues of power and difference rather than one that is yet another questionable survey of poor people.

Throughout the description of my research method, the words 'I' and 'my' keep on recurring. This is to openly acknowledge my relationship to the subject, in confirmation of Bahktin's point that: 'The observer has no position *outside* the observed world, and his observation enters as a constituent part into the observed object'.[118] Without the research descending into being totally self-referential, there has to be an understanding of this relationship. In writing, the process is even more difficult:

> The author's relation to what he depicts always enters into the image. The author's relationship is a constitutive aspect of the image. The relationship is extremely complex.[119]

My role within the image is made more explicit in Chapter Five.

Angela McRobbie worries whether researching prioritises intellectual work over action.[120] The tension between the two is articulated by the following diary entry[121]:

> *At the time of the most interesting events I am so involved in what is going on, uncertain of it and myself, and tired — difficult then to write it all down.*
>
> *Also difficult to make it an academic exercise for analysis. Maybe it should be though. At present I feel sceptical about academic knowledge.*
>
> *There is a kind of optimism about ideas, a playfulness, a feeling of power as they are understood and manipulated.*
>
> *There is a pessimism and depression when confronted by angry and violent young people — a feeling of powerlessness, of being unable to cope, of not being able to take on all the implications.*
>
> *Ideas can give you the run of the world — action is limited.*
>
> *People can (I can!) pronounce, pontificate, criticise. It is so different when face to face with problems that actually threaten oneself — physically and emotionally — test the sense one has of oneself, move one away from what one wants to be (for example,*

---

[118] Bakhtin, 1986: 126
[119] Bakhtin, 1986: 115
[120] McRobbie, 1991: 70
[121] Diary entry, May 1994

—

> *picking up young people and throwing them bodily out of the*
> *youth centre).*

In my defence, I have to say that this was written at a tempestuous time. The boy thrown out 'bodily' had already assaulted two other people before attacking me. Words completely failed on that occasion – not being particularly strong, I was left breathless and speechless by the effort, much to the amusement of the onlookers.

This research is about reflecting on such incidents in the hope of gaining insight and discovery. Accumulating, reading and re-presenting the material of the *bricoleur* are no guarantees of this; as Hobsbawm[122] pointed out, nothing arises naturally from that material. So how do we come to any findings? That process of discovery comes, says Richardson, through writing: 'I write because I want to find something out. I write in order to learn something I didn't know before I wrote it'.[123] The writing of this book, incidentally, is only possible because of my short-term withdrawal from being a participant, in the hope that the words come back for writing, and in recognition that writing is, for me, a different form of engagement with the area, but one, that by the end of this book, will have shown its uses.

Bakhtin likened the intention of a word, as it is directed towards an object, as taking 'the form of a ray of light'. The play of colour and light is not within the object, but within the word: 'The social atmosphere of the word, the atmosphere that surrounds the object, makes the facets of the image sparkle'.[124] Bakhtin, among all writers the one most aware of the numbers of very different voices that make up language, understands that 'for the prose writer, the object is a focal point for heteroglot voices among which his own voice must also sound'.[125] Denzin, a more recent writer on the research process, writes that: 'The story that is finally told becomes the researcher's accomplishment, his or her self-fashioned narration of the subject's history'.[126]

Accomplishing that narration, making the voice sound and the image sparkle, is a difficult process. Derek Walcott, in a poem from his book *Midsummer*, expresses the exasperation with language in keeping up with the shifts of place far better than I can:

---

[122] Hobsbawm, 1998
[123] Richardson, 1994: 510
[124] Bakhtin, 1981: 277
[125] Bakhtin, 1981: 278
[126] Denzin, 1994: 507

The lines that jerk

into step do not fit any mold. More than time

keeps shifting. Language never fits geography

except when earth and summer lightning rhyme.

...

     Too rapid the lightning's shorthand,

...

too slow the stones crawling towards language every

night.[127]

---

[127] Walcott, 1984: 19

THREE

The intelligent outsider? Official and media representations of Southmead

Introduction

A major theme, an orthodoxy even, is that in the battle of representation that is fought over Southmead there exist very different 'outsider' and 'insider' knowledges and representations of the area, emanating from standpoints that make this a two-sided battle. The difference between these two standpoints and their representations is used as one of the definitional markers of what Southmead itself is; the idea of 'out' and 'in' sets up Southmead as a bounded entity.

Throughout the book, the simple but powerful differentiation between inside and outside is questioned, but this cannot be done without first acknowledging how pervasive it is in representations of the area. In this chapter, I will look at official reports, surveys and media coverage of the area; these portrayals are considered as outsider representations of Southmead, both by those who produce them and by those about whom they are produced. The next chapter will look at representations that come from what is seen as inside. This approach to different knowledges of the area is very similar to that of standpoint epistemology developed by feminist and afrocentric thinkers, in which different standpoints of master and subjugated groups, in this case embodied as 'inside' and 'outside', lead to different, more or less distorted, knowledges.[1] In showing these two 'sides', however, I question whether these representations merely *reflect* two structurally different standpoints, or whether they themselves are intrinsic processes in the *construction* of those standpoints, which in turn create the object of Southmead. The idea of inside and outside as itself being part of the discursive formation of Southmead will continue to be investigated throughout the two chapters that follow this one. These issues are not unique to Southmead, nor are the types of representation. Looking at

[1] Compare Harding, 1986; Collins, 1990

how one area becomes an object in representation does not make that area any the more special than the hundreds of other areas subjected to the same process, but does enable us to look at the process in detail.

The Bristol Social Project

By far the largest and most thorough study of Southmead is the action research of the Bristol Social Project, carried out between 1953 and 1958. In some ways, it is comparable to this research of mine; it was concerned with Southmead, with active involvement, with young people and with the idea of community. It was, however, established on a very different footing:

> In 1952 a committee of Bristol's leading citizens drawn from a wide range of public life in the city submitted certain proposals for an action–research project in the following terms:

> To investigate and take part in the life of a developing community in Bristol in an attempt to establish practical means of tackling those stresses and strains which arise in such a community in the form of delinquency and other disturbances. The main emphasis of the Project will be encouraging local initiative and on getting residents to take a greater degree of responsibility for their community life.[2]

This main committee consisted of over 40 members of the political, religious and academic hierarchies of Bristol. The membership list reflected official anxiety about juvenile delinquency[3], and its composition gave the research great authority, as overtly backed by the political power of the 'master's position'. Collins describes this as a process through which 'elite white men and their representatives control structures of knowledge validation'.[4] This was not research that hid its authorship to attain credibility – it blazoned it in a public display of power, perfectly illustrating Bakhtin's argument that 'authoritative discourse permits no play with the context framing it…. It is indissolubly fused with its authority – with political power, an institution, a person – and it stands and falls together with that

---

[2] Spencer et al, 1964: 3
[3] Spencer et al, 1964: 4
[4] Collins, 1990: 201

authority'.[5] Representation and power are shown as closely interlinked. The 11-strong research team consisted both of academics and staff providing the action of action research: adventure playground worker, social workers, three field workers and a group worker.[6] A full-length book and a paper were published: *Stress and release in an urban estate: A study in action research* (Spencer et al, 1964) and *Difficult housing estates* (Wilson, 1963).[7] The research was to cover three areas of Bristol, but virtually all of the material in the published reports relate to Southmead, under its pseudonym of Upfield.

The writings of the project were suffused by the medical metaphor of providing a cure for the ills of the area.[8] Spencer wrote that: 'In action research the client [that is, Southmead] is the patient'[9], and Wilson extended this medical analogy with the statement that there was:

> ... hope of accurate early diagnosis and consequent remedial action where debilitating deviant unconformity may otherwise be expected.[10]

This sets up a relationship between Southmead as a patient suffering social ills, and researchers as knowing diagnosticians. This is a powerful approach that meshes together a medical model of diagnosis and remedy with a discourse of social and moral normalisation, transforming social 'deviance' into a diagnosable, objective disease, a 'scenario', writes Melucci, 'that promotes the transformation of social relation into "problems" or "pathologies"'.[11] Despite the assertion of a clinical, purely functional approach, the language is intensely rhetorical, containing forceful alliteration and rhythmic stress (de*bili*tating *devi*ant uncon*form*ity) displaying connotations of strong emotion.

The project started with general surveys 'of certain overt symptoms of social disorganization'[12], but most of the research was carried out through action: the provision of an adventure playground (one of the very first in Britain[13]) and meeting rooms, both in existence 45 years

---

[5] Bakhtin, 1981: 343

[6] Spencer et al, 1964: 330–1

[7] A further volume by Spencer, Life on the outskirts, was promised, but I cannot trace a copy, and suspect that it was never published.

[8] Spencer et al, 1964: 25

[9] Spencer et al, 1964: 319

[10] Wilson, 1963: 4

[11] Melucci, 1989: 133

[12] Spencer et al, 1964: 10

[13] Benjamin, 1974: 32

later; work with a series of groups – mothers, toddlers, teachers, social workers and adolescents; and a neighbourhood study. The Bristol Social Project was a major piece of work. In order not to be distracted from the main purposes of this book, I am using only its published material, although its unpublished history would be a fruitful subject of further research. There are strong hints that the project was the subject of controversy, not merely in Southmead, where there was 'a general dislike of being stigmatised by the presence of a project'[14], but among its committees and sponsors. There are repeated suggestions that it is the decision makers at the top that need to change in their attitudes to estates, and criticism of the way policy was made *in camera* by the party caucus of the local authority, which even led to the research programme having to be changed.[15]

The major difference between this project and later surveys was its emphasis on the *newness* of the area. It was a place that people had moved to from elsewhere, some due to slum clearance, and some for the more 'respectable' reason of housing shortage, a distinction of origin important enough to be noticeable.[16] The move was not always desired:

> I didn't ask to be moved from my so-called slum – it was nice there. The people were nice, always in and out. The rats didn't particularly bother us, either. Now what do I want with a garden and a box hedge and all this respectability? Can you blame me for not caring. I want my comfortable slum, so I let the garden go.[17]

Haunting the project is the idea that this new estate (in common with thousands of other such developments) was supposed to be the answer to the social problems of the slums:

> Putting people to live on a new housing estate is to provide them with facilities for a full life that their predecessors did not have – notably space, air, the chance to exercise housecraft ... the chance for children to have healthy conditions of growth, and freedom for all from so close a

---

[14] Spencer et al, 1964: 34
[15] Spencer et al, 1964: 314. This controversy might explain the lack of a second volume.
[16] Spencer et al, 1964: 335
[17] Wilson, 1963: 12

—

press of humanity that it is possible to have a life of one's own.[18]

However the rates of crime, 'mental deficiency', truancy and mental illness in the area, compared with the rest of Bristol, indicated that the 'answer' was not working.[19] Poverty was not considered the major issue, as it was seen as a condition that was over: 'In modern urban conditions ... there is ... enough money for more than basic necessities'.[20] Instead, people's ability to cope with the changes caused by the growth of consumption was a concern:

> Mrs. D, whose background and tradition have been things of but slow changes ... finds she is pushed into a maelstrom of new ideas and big possibilities, surrounded by changing faces that she does not know and that are likely to judge her more by what she *has*, she thinks, than by what she *is*.[21]

Southmead was understood as part of a much wider world of moving social and economic processes, so much so that the idea of community, or neighbourhood, as cures for its problems was strongly rejected. There was detailed criticism of neighbourhood being a useful idea.[22] It was considered doubtful whether Southmead could be labelled a 'community'; it was not self-contained, had too much diversity within, and too much connection to and influence from the wider world.[23] There was a rejection of the idea of place-specific sub-cultures:

> The stereotyped idea of a 'problem sub-culture' ... in which the whole area subscribes to a set of values different from those held in the wider society does not apply to Upfield, nor, we consider, to estates of similar social structures elsewhere.[24]

However, this conclusion is undermined by some of the problems in the research, as illustrated by this account of a paper on 'the Fence',

---

[18] Wilson, 1963: 22
[19] Spencer et al, 1964: 338
[20] Wilson, 1963: 4
[21] Wilson, 1963: 11
[22] Wilson, 1963: 4–5
[23] Spencer et al, 1964: 19, 30
[24] Spencer et al, 1964: 287 (emphasis in original)

given by a member of the research team, and its reception by the committee:

> The Fence was a shopkeeper ... who carried out his ordinary business and at the same time received stolen property from local residents, advanced money on Family Allowance Books, and bought up household goods on which the hire purchase instalments had not been paid. These two rather different functions were known to different types of customers....

> The Committee was irritated by this paper, because the members were uncertain what they were expected to do about it. The Chairman suggested that its importance lay in the fact that alongside the attitudes of people like teachers, councillors, and clergy went the attitudes of people such as the Fence who to many residents on the estate seemed to be performing a far more useful practical purpose in the business of daily living than those conventionally thought of as leaders.[25]

The committee was unable to decide whether to tell the police, and some felt the chairman and director naïve in presenting such a paper to them. The account shows both that there were informal social relations on the estate, and that these were outside of, and very different to, the value system of official provision.

The youth worker's notes, written well before recent work on the interaction between local and global youth culture[26], has startlingly similar conclusions as to the relationship between global culture and local particularities, with in this case the way the language of film affected young people:

> *Gladys:* "You come down our street! A fine street it is! There's the man with the bald patch – he has been accused of murder but they didn't have enough evidence. Two gone mad. Oh, a fine street! You just come down our street!" Her voice was bitter and shrill, like the Teds portrayed in a film.[27]

---

[25] Spencer et al, 1964: 42
[26] For example, Massey, 1998
[27] Spencer et al, 1964: 197

The youth worker noted that the young people went to the cinema up to five times a week, and their main reason for attending the youth club was to rock-and-roll. The Espressos, a group of teenagers the project worked with, were seen as being more part of Ted culture and wider problems of adolescence than as a Southmead phenomenon, although they saw themselves 'as coming from despised families and a despised district'.[28]

This group, and the problems they caused, was at the heart of the project:

> They called themselves the Espressos, and in this collective capacity they exhibited intolerably bad behaviour, frightening, indeed, in its aggression, destruction and irresponsibility.[29]

There are graphic descriptions from field notes of the problems they caused, and the difficulties of the relationship between them and the youth worker, not least of which was the fact that the local hostility to them was extended to her for working with them. Her records detail swearing, violence, house breaking, vandalism and crude and promiscuous sexual relationships. Contrary to assumption, most of the Espressos were girls.[30] They mostly worked in laundries and the sack factory. The boys were unskilled labourers, coal delivery drivers' mates and fish porters – low-status jobs of the period that they drifted in and out of.[31] Here was that 'delinquency' that the original committee hoped that community life could overcome, which brought its own questions, framed in that medicalised language used by the project.

> To what extent were they the product of the society which rejected them? Should we describe them in the neutral terminology of the psychiatrist as disordered personalities, or in the more popular language of the community as young hooligans?[32]

The project felt that local people were not strong enough to take on these problems. The original desire of the committee to encourage

---

[28] Spencer et al, 1964: 197
[29] Wilson, 1963: 32
[30] Wilson, 1963: 34
[31] Spencer et al, 1964: 167-215
[32] Spencer et al, 1964: 63

community was deemed to be unrealistic. Instead, 'a high degree of special skill is required and that must come professionally from outside'.[33] For the Espressos in particular, 'time is needed, money is needed, patience quite out of the ordinary is needed, and a long professional training is needed'.[34] The whole tenor of the findings of the project is that problems such as the Espressos and unconfident young mothers were not soluble through existing social services, but that there was a need for a new sort of preventative and curative professional involvement that would substitute for the traditional support provided in 'the more isolated and self-contained communities of the past'.[35] Professionals, preferably with psychiatric skills, were to be the answer to the lack of community, with all its supportive networks, that is brought about by modernity. The project existed at an early moment in the process described a generation later by Nikolas Rose, in which community is 'transformed, no doubt for the best of motives, into an expert discourse and professional vocation'.[36]

Spencer did note a crucial problem: these healing professionals were not necessarily wanted by the people who lived in the area:

> It is a comparatively simple task to make an analysis of the symptoms; but to help the patient to understand the nature of the sickness itself and to take the appropriate medicine is entirely another matter. And so it proved to be. The patient wanted neither the doctor nor the medicine which was offered. He hadn't asked for it. Moreover, he was sceptical of the doctor's diagnosis.[37]

But the 'doctor' still claimed that he knew better than people themselves what was wrong, because of his superior and unquestioned rationality:

> It is impossible to overstress the importance of differentiating what people *feel* about situations and the situation as it looks to an intelligent outsider....The project report stresses again and again that to secure change it is necessary to penetrate to people's feelings, which is much more difficult than to

---

[33] Wilson, 1963: 40
[34] Spencer et al, 1964: 213
[35] Spencer et al, 1964: 288
[36] Rose, 1996: 332
[37] Rose, 1996: 25

talk cool sense to people on the assumption that they are in a rational state of mind.[38]

In this formulation, the scientist is superior to the subject.[39] However, this role of the cool professional claimed by the project was full of ambiguity, as they had to:

> ... on the one hand cooperate with others who have power and, on the other hand, to enter into the lives of the more difficult of the estate tenants.[40]

Two of the project team members were residents on the estate, and the field notes indicate a familiarity and affection with the 'clients'. The project saw itself as upholding humane values against those at the centre who would ignore the psychological needs of the people of Southmead, and against those 'respectables' within the estate who wanted purely punitive action taken against delinquent youths, thus claiming a place for itself separate from both its originating committee and its clients. The work of the project was, interestingly, contemporaneous to Raymond Williams' interpretations of community quoted in Chapter One. It was concerned with redefining what public service should do with (or to) Southmead, as opposed to being an expression of solidarity.

There are signs throughout the research of a variety of Southmead identities forming: the man who preferred rats to respectability, the defiance of the Espressos, survival through use of the Fence, and the people who denied they were from Southmead, but gave their addresses as if they lived in the neighbouring suburb.[41] There is also some understanding of the reaction to the presence of the professional. These strong elements in the development of a variety of collective identities in Southmead have persisted since, as will reappear through this book. Finally, the project stressed that:

---

[38] Wilson, 1963: 8 (emphasis in original). Rationality, of course, may not be to the advantage of the ruled: 'Under sharply asymmetrical power conditions, rationality of the ruled is, to say the least, a mixed blessing. It may work to their gain. But it may as well destroy them' (Bauman, 1989: 149, emphasis in original).

[39] 'Objectivity vs. subjectivity, the scientist as knowing subject vs. the object of his enquiry, reason vs. emotion, mind vs. body – in each case the former has been associated with masculinity and the latter with femininity' (Harding, 1986: 23). This insight may be applicable to any situation of unequal power, not just that of patriarchy.

[40] Wilson, 1963: 31

[41] Wilson, 1963: 13

> Difficult housing estates must be accepted as a potentially permanent feature of the social landscape ... it is only by recognizing the reality and seeking for an appropriate social policy that we can minimize the social and psychological damage that growing up and living in such areas can do.[42]

The major thread of the Bristol Social Project was its emphasis on Southmead as a problem. The people within it were pathologised, and the solution to their problems was seen to be intervention by professionals, represented as being the actors with the right credentials to take action.

The reports of the 1980s and 1990s

The variety of reports since 1980 that are either directly about Southmead or that feature it bears out that prediction that the area would continue to be seen to be 'difficult'. It has been the site of a wide range of professional interventions, and informing these is the major purpose of all of the reports. They come in three formats:

- Statistics and maps within surveys that cover either the city of Bristol, or the old county of Avon.
- Questionnaire-based surveys.
- Reports to or by committees of the local authority.

There are three reports generated locally that will be discussed in the next chapter.[43]

The production of the reports shows the importance of the local authority in the life of and knowledge creation about Southmead – Bristol City Council, and Avon County Council during its existence from 1974 to 1996. All but one were published or commissioned by the local authority, and the one that was not involved local authority staff.[44] None of this later research is on the scale of the Bristol Social Project, and its quality is variable. Rather surprisingly, none of the studies makes any reference to the earlier project, even though some of them take up the cause of the adventure playground that it set up. There is also very little continuity between the reports, a matter to

---

[42] Wilson, 1963: 41–2

[43] St Stephen, Southmead, 1988; Kimberlee, 1998; Newman, 1999

[44] Monaghan, 1993

which I will return. First, however, I want to look at their approach to a series of issues concerning the condition of life of the people who live in the area – housing and environment, poverty, crime, young people, image, community – before looking at their general effects.

Housing and environment

The Bristol Social Project praised the physical environment of the new estate for its spaciousness and health, but later in its history criticism emerged of the way the estate was built:

> The general environment has, for the most part, a bleak appearance consequent on a mixture of initial poor design and layout, compounded by failure to provide satisfactory landscaping for substantial open areas within the estate.[45]

This deficiency of the environment 'must at least subconsciously affect residents'[46], and has been seen as creating a difference that marks it out from other areas: 'Southmead estate has a monotonous consistency of building type and streetscape which emphasises its separation from surrounding areas'.[47] Photographs of the area taken by young people show 'typical' Southmead streets of pre-war houses, recognisably a British council estate. The inadequacy of the design, and its social and cultural connotations, were not considered in the earlier research, which saw the area as typifying improvement.

The houses themselves are praised for being well built[48], although there have been concerns at times with the number of 'void' properties that affect the feel of the area. On measures of quality such as ventilation, damp and condensation, housing in Southmead is far better than the Bristol average.[49] One of the supposed benefits of moving from slum conditions was the overcoming of overcrowding; years later, however, there was an above-average number of large households and crowded homes.[50] This is an important consideration in the public life of the area – for example, young people who do not have space at home have to socialise more on the streets and in clubs.

---

[45] Bristol City Council, 1985
[46] Bristol City Council, 1983: ii
[47] Safe Neighbourhoods Unit, 1991: 3
[48] Safe Neighbourhoods Unit, 1991: 3
[49] Bristol City Council, 1997a: 17
[50] Bristol City Council, 1991: 9, 37

Southmead was built primarily as housing rented from the local authority, but housing tenure has changed dramatically since the right-to-buy legislation of the 1980s. In 1981, 73% of houses were rented from the local authority. By 1991, the figure was down to 44.5%, although still double the Bristol average. The number of owner-occupiers increased from 23% to 48.6%, and privately rented houses from 1% to 3.1%.[51] It is difficult to gauge how these changes in tenure affect social relationships in the area. From talking to young people, I know that they are now able to rent privately in Southmead, instead of having to move to other areas when they leave home, and this creates different types of households.[52] Private purchase does not necessarily mean wealth; while there are no figures for mortgage repossessions in the area, the regular presence of 'For Sale by Public Auction' signs are an indication that they take place.

The difference noted by the Bristol Social Project between different types of tenants is a persistent feature of later reports:

> Certain streets or parts of streets have developed a reputation over the years because of so-called 'problem tenants' ... these problems seem to arise more on the pre-war estate.[53]

It was in the pre-war estate that slum-clearance houses were built[54], and it is that part of the estate that features most in surveys of poverty and crime.

Poverty

Geographical analysis of poverty started after the 1981 Census, with reports produced by Avon County Council and Bristol City Council looking at the geographical distribution of poverty within their boundaries.[55] I have already indicated some of the problems with these reports.[56] They are, however, methodologically painstaking, and act as a reminder that there are material and structural constraints on

---

[51] Bristol City Council, 1985: 16; Avon County Council, 1991: 46

[52] Diary notes, 1 and 10 December 1993

[53] Bristol City Council, 1983, section 2.1.8

[54] Spencer et al, 1964: 335

[55] Avon County Council, 1983, 1993 (the publication dates of these two reports are not given, but as they refer to the censuses of 1981 and 1991, they must have been a year or two later); Bristol City Council, 1985, 1988, 1994, 1996a

[56] See Chapter Two

relationships that a purely interpretative, interactionist ethnography can miss.[57] There is a geography of poverty that has important implications, including 'tough personal ones for people living in poorer locations'.[58] The resources available for community involvement, and the need for community support, are strongly affected by poverty, and public life and public spaces are very different in poor than rich neighbourhoods. This can be seen vividly in the film Rush, where the main character has to run to a bank in nearby Westbury-on-Trym; in Southmead there are no cash machines, only money lenders charging high rates of interest. Westbury has restaurants, wine sellers and patisseries, Southmead has cafes, off-licences and a very popular hot-dog stall; each area is its own '*socially ranked geographical space*', with its own style.[59] The relationship between the two areas is a regular feature of Southmead life:

> The nearest job centre is in Westbury-on-Trym village well away from the heart of the problems. Similarly the unemployment benefits office is also in Westbury, and whilst this might be a pleasant walk on occasion, regular attendance must be embittering.[60]

The *Poverty in Bristol in 1996* report shows high indicators of poverty in Southmead compared with the rest of the city, including the numbers of households on council tax benefits and of children receiving free school meals. These figures are for the whole ward. When split down into smaller areas, they become even starker. In the 'Trym'[61] area of Southmead, which is the main area of pre-war slum clearance housing, the rate of households on benefit in 1996 was 59.6%, more than a third above the ward average, and well over twice the Bristol average. Unemployment levels in the pre-war estate are also always higher.[62] The pre-war estate got poorer between 1981 and 1991[63], and the post-

---

[57] Jackson, 1989b: 173

[58] McCormick and Philo, 1995. 4

[59] Bourdieu, 1984: 124 (emphasis in original). 'Tastes (i.e. manifested preferences) are the practical affirmation of an inevitable difference.... Aversion to different life-styles is perhaps one of the strongest barriers between the classes' (Bourdieu, 1984: 56).

[60] Bristol City Council, 1983, section 3.4.9

[61] The name Trym for the old estate is not common usage, but exists mainly in census-based reports. Southmead is not called Southmead-on-Trym, though it lies as much on that river as Westbury does.

[62] Bristol City Council, 1994: 37

[63] Bristol City Council, 1994: 39

war estate entered the 'worst fifth' areas of poverty for the first time in 1996.[64] Poverty was not, as assumed by the Bristol Social Project, coming to an end.

Coupled with poverty is poor health, and Southmead has a significantly high mortality ratio for people under 65, and the highest rate of infant deaths in the city.[65] There are 'large numbers of children with coughs, above average number of babies with low birth weights, as well as high numbers of parents who smoke'.[66]

Poverty is a major part of the conditions of the lives of people who live in Southmead, and the description of poverty as a spatial phenomenon is a major element in the discourses constructing Southmead as a social idea.

Crime

The relationship between poverty and crime is perceived as an uncertain one. However, analysis of crime is also becoming spatialised, and a comparison of a map of Bristol's most deprived areas with a map of crime hotspots shows overlap, if not congruence, between the two.[67] Southmead features on both maps, and 'it is clear that residents and workers alike recognise the impact that lack of disposable income and other forms of deprivation can have in generating a range of social problems on Southmead estate'.[68]

Crime has long been associated with Southmead, as testified by the reasons for the establishment of the Bristol Social Project. It is an issue closely connected to ideas of what a community should be, and to the position of young people. In 1990, the Bristol Safer Cities Project, a Home Office initiative, chose Southmead as one of its priority areas, and sponsored the 1991 survey. This survey was of people's opinions on crime, and consisted of a random sample of dwellings in the area commonly described as the 'old' estate (thus immediately identifying the crime as a problem tied to place, and therefore the place as a problem) and interviews with young people.[69] The survey was carried out during a period of public unrest in the area, when the police view was that 'the most troublesome incidents are those of public disorder

---

[64] Bristol City Council, 1996a: 53

[65] Bristol City Council, 1997a: 24

[66] Bristol Community Safety Partnership, 1999a: 32

[67] Bristol Community Safety Partnership, 1999a: 7, 30

[68] Safe Neighbourhoods Unit, 1991: 63

[69] Safe Neighbourhoods Unit, 1991: 1

or threatening behaviour'.[70] The report starts, however, by showing how, at that time, recorded crime in Southmead was relatively low[71], but that crime was seen by residents as being as big a problem as unemployment.[72] The poor reputation of the estate was equated to crime.[73] The survey certainly showed that crime was a major issue in the area, but on a close reading of the results there is a question as to how valid they are, or how much people pandered to the questionnaire. For example, 93% of residents thought that young people under 25 were responsible for crime.[74] There must surely have been a number of hypocritical answers among the 383 respondents, blaming the easiest visible target to deflect attention from themselves.

What were not included in the survey were racial crimes. Bristol City Council reported that, for both 1993 and 1994, incidents of racial harassment suffered by council tenants were at the highest level in the city: 13 cases in 1993, 20 in 1994.[75] In the 1991 Census, the number of residents from minority ethnic groups in Southmead was lower than the Bristol average at 400 throughout the ward, a figure that included those who were not council tenants.[76] The number of cases cited above was related to households, not individuals, so we can extrapolate that a significant proportion of black and Asian tenants suffered harassment over that period.

The most detailed geographical analysis of crime in Bristol is the *Audit of crime and disorder in Bristol* (1999), drawn up in response to the 1998 Crime and Disorder Act. In this audit, Southmead is shown as a major area of crime, a top 'hot spot'.[77] It was a priority area for domestic and commercial burglary, theft and handling of stolen goods, assault, criminal damage, domestic violence, home assault and drug seizures. High levels of truancy were reported.[78] In 1994/95, 39% of families reported problems with disturbance by youths.[79] The report

---

[70] Safe Neighbourhoods Unit, 1991: 9

[71] Safe Neighbourhoods Unit, 1991: 7

[72] Safe Neighbourhoods Unit, 1991: 33

[73] Safe Neighbourhoods Unit, 1991: 33

[74] Safe Neighbourhoods Unit, 1991: 46

[75] Bristol City Council Housing Services, 1994

[76] Southmead is much whiter than most of the 'problem' estates considered in Power and Tunstall (1995).

[77] Bristol Community Safety Partnership, 1999a: 30. 'Hot spot' is a term that continues the use of emotive language in supposedly objective reports.

[78] Bristol Community Safety Partnership, 1999a: 32

[79] Bristol Community Safety Partnership, 1999a: 27

listed 20 community safety initiatives in the area[80]; action against crime is a major local activity.

The connection between the discourse of poverty and the discourse of crime emphasises the point made in Chapter Two, that it is the *behaviour* of the poor that is considered to be of social concern, not the poverty itself, and it is this that brings professional interventions into the area. The method by which crime is represented as a spatial phenomenon itself labels areas and so creates them as socio-geographical entities.

Young people

In all the reports, young people are seen as a cause of crime, their behaviour a problem. The crime audit answers its own question about Southmead – 'Who are the offenders and why are they offending?' – thus:

> In keeping with the largest concentrations of young people in the city the area has high levels of truancy and youth unemployment. A minority of young people on the estate experiment with drugs and some have become addicted to hard drugs. Many burglaries and thefts are committed to fund drug habits. There is boredom and a lack of prospects amongst young people leading to crimes such as criminal damage.[81]

Throughout the reports on Southmead, young people are the *only* group that are identified as criminal, their large concentration seen as a problem. Even in discussion of domestic violence, men are not named as the major responsible group. Yet although the presence of young people is seen to be an indicator of crime in Southmead, another part of the audit states that '74% of crime is committed by people over 18 years of age', and young people are more likely than any other section of the population to be victims of crime.[82]

In the 1991 survey, there was a separate section in which under-18-year-olds were surveyed. They were asked if they had been victims of

---

[80] Bristol Community Safety Partnership, 1999b: 33-5

[81] Bristol Community Safety Partnership, 1999a: 33. The list of members of this partnership (on the inside front cover) is impressive, but not as impressive as that of the Bristol Social Project committee.

[82] Bristol Community Safety Partnership, 1999a: 25

crime (14% had been – not dissimilar to the adult rate[83]), but were also asked questions that the adults were not asked. Had they ever played truant? Had they been involved in crime? And, 'During the last year have you had an alcoholic drink or taken any drugs?'.[84] Asking them questions that were not asked of adults clearly demonstrates how surveys create a perception of young people as a problem and manufacture data that maintain this perception, showing how the questions asked in surveys are not themselves innocent. This process occurred again two years later in a survey of drugs misuse in Southmead that also concerned itself exclusively with young people – the only adults questioned were those who worked with young people, and adult drug use was not mentioned.[85] Of 150 young people questioned, 37 said they took drugs. From this small number were extrapolated a range of bar and pie charts that claimed to be a profile of drug use in Southmead. This survey makes one wonder why people have to endure such poor research, and shows how 'research' is used to maintain existing discourses of young people as problematic.

The Bristol Social Project also only talked about crime in relation to young people, except in an appendix where it gave rates of male criminal convictions for Bristol and Southmead. Overall, the crime rate in Southmead was over twice that for the rest of the city. The rate for 10- to 14-year-olds was about 40% above the Bristol average, and for 15- to 19-year-olds just under the average. For 25- to 34-year-olds, the rate was over three times the average, and higher than that for the adolescents. The rate for 50- to 54-year-olds was six-and-a-half times the average. Adult crime, however, was not identified as being a problem.

The 1991 survey had two answers for the problem of young people. One was to offer better facilities and support.[86] The other was, through housing allocation policy, to reduce the numbers of families with children moving into the area, and 'avoid concentrating households with children of the same age on the same street'[87], a cleansing of the area of this 'problem', an idea with chilling overtones.

This process of defining young people as a problem is not confined to Southmead. Sheila Brown, researching community safety in Middlesbrough, wrote:

---

[83] Safe Neighbourhoods Unit, 1991: 43, 57
[84] Safe Neighbourhoods Unit, 1991: 57
[85] Monaghan, 1993
[86] Safe Neighbourhoods Unit, 1991: 67-8
[87] Safe Neighbourhoods Unit, 1991: 65-6

> Young people in local – communities? – become successively defined as the 'criminal other', and these definitions find their way into policies and practices to the point where many policies bear little or no relationship to the everyday lives of young people or to crime.[88]

The discourses of crime and young people are joined together, and become important elements in the discourses of image and community.

Image

Various reports, from the Bristol Social Project onwards, are concerned with the image of Southmead. The 1991 survey stated that:

> The estate has had an image problem virtually since the first tenants moved in over 50 years ago. The area was used to rehouse many families from inner Bristol areas and quickly developed a poor reputation.[89]

It has been pointed out that poor areas have a 'geography of stigma' to contend with[90], which can help keep them poor:

> Employers – including Southmead employers! – often give strong indications of being prejudiced against even interviewing young people from the Southmead catchment because of its general reputation as an area with problems.[91]

Lash and Urry point out how the image of place can be crucial in 'the contemporary global economics of signs and space'.[92] Image has economic effects; having the wrong image can be a new element to blame the poor with.

It is interesting to contrast the images of Southmead and of Bristol used in official reports. There has been a change in the production and design of reports over 20 years, from pages and pages of duplicated

---

[88] Brown, 1995: 47
[89] Safe Neighbourhoods Unit, 1991: 3
[90] McCormick and Philo, 1995: 16
[91] Bristol City Council, 1983, section 3.4.4
[92] Lash and Urry, 1994: 326

lists of figures[93], to conscious and sophisticated design, made attractive with colour, maps and illustrations.[94] The designs of the reports exude competence on behalf of the authorities that produce them. There is a process of converting a wide variety of information, much of it concerned with social malfunction and distress, into colourful maps. It is through this process, by which problems are represented as images on a page, that these maps, in Phil Cohen's words, 'render the world as real and rational, by denying the existence of the Other as a locus of the unknown'.[95] All is known, therefore controllable – part of the image creation of Bristol as a competent city. This process is continued through the use of photographs. On the front cover of *Indicators of Quality of Life in Bristol*[96], which contains information about unacceptable levels of pollution and bad health in the city, there is a romantic photograph of sky, woods, the Clifton Suspension Bridge and the replica heritage sailing vessel, *The Matthew* – symbols of the good life. The cover of the *Southmead Survey 1991* is very different: a mother wheeling a pushchair across a broken pavement in front of a boarded-up church – symbols of the bad life. Both photographs act as myths; they have 'an imperative, buttonholing character'.[97] The reports themselves, to continue with Roland Barthes' useful idea of myth, hide nothing (all the facts are there), but in their presentation distort the full meaning. In that distortion, they compound the stigmatic image of Southmead that they decry.

Community

The same reports that are concerned with the image of Southmead are also concerned with the lack of community – even in the same sentence:

> The estate has acquired, from the past, a tough and unpopular image, and there is no strong tradition of community leadership.[98]

---

[93] Avon County Council, 1983

[94] Bristol City Council, 1997a; Bristol Community Safety Partnership, 1999a. The first two poverty reports had illustrations of despair; the more recent ones are unillustrated, perhaps indicative of an uncertainty as to what kind of images to use.

[95] Cohen, 1988: 56

[96] Bristol City Council, 1997a

[97] Barthes, 1973: 134

[98] Bristol City Council, 1985: 16

The existence of community is itself seen as an image of respectability. Due to its absence, it is the professionals, as with the Bristol Social Project, that have to fill the gap:

> With very few exceptions the major community groups or projects that exist are led by or involve either local Councillors or professional officers working in the area. There seems to be very little grass roots level activity.[99]

The obverse to that approach is that it could be the way that professional officers work that deter community initiative:

> Many of the Black residents consulted expressed the view that local agencies and organisations have a low opinion of Southmead residents. Their experience of Council officers was that they were 'talked down to'. Other residents do want to have greater opportunities for consultation and participation on the estate but suggested that Southmead people have insufficient opportunity for participation.[100]

All these reports expound a very municipal and orderly discourse of community. Community is seen as a rational system that can, or should, fix social problems, particularly crime. There is no recognition of the dynamic and aesthetic aspects of community to be discussed in later chapters, or of how reducing people to numerical ciphers and problems could reduce their capacity for action. The reports give no indication of any informal networks that might exist, or how people survive – none, for example, has discovered the modern equivalent of the Fence, which type of community activity lies outside of the understanding of these reports. They do, however, give plenty of indications of problems that are either obstacles to community or are the result of lack of community: crime, domestic violence, racial harassment, fear of walking the streets at night, divisions between rough and respectable, the othering of young people. When reading the reports, one wonders how people in Southmead survive at all, portrayed as they are as victims, not actors.

---

[99] Bristol City Council, 1983, section 3.1.4
[100] Safe Neighbourhoods Unit, 1991: 19

The general effect of official reports

Throughout discussion of designated 'problem areas' like Southmead, there is a pervasive, if unconscious, desire that they be reduced to knowable objects, usually as a prelude to attempts to manage and control them, despite all the historical evidence that they will keep on acting like subjects that keep on challenging or evading that control and 'cure'. The reports all possess an almost fetishistic belief in map and census material, which transposes Southmead into lists of figures or into a shape. There is an irony that it is the very aliveness of the Southmeads of the world, indeed of all social relationships, that leads to demands for a knowledge that attempts to reduce them to an inanimate objectivity that substitutes 'statistical ensembles for social actors'.[101] Mapping creates hopes that data about social chaos and conflict can be organised to lay bare an order that can be defined and mended. It posits a knowledge of an under-the-surface depth, despite being two-dimensional representations of surface.[102]

In all the reports, Southmead people are talked about, but, to use hooks' phrase, 'remain an absent presence without voices'.[103] In the questionnaire-based surveys, which claim to represent people's voices, all the recommendations are based on the interpretations by the researchers of the data collected – for example, nowhere in the 1991 survey questions or answers is there any mention of reducing the number of young people in Southmead. Of the 28 recommendations in that report, only five arise directly out of the answers given to the questionnaire questions, and 15 refer to issues that were not the subject of any of the questions.[104] None of the recommendations in the report on drug use relates to the questionnaire data.[105] So even when people are asked loaded questions, their answers are ignored. In the poverty reports, there is a strong argument that technical expertise is

---

[101] Touraine, 1988: 5

[102] For more on the practice and effects of mapping, see de Certeau, 1984; Duncan and Ley, 1993; Pile and Thrift, 1995, Harvey, 1996.

[103] hooks, 1991: 26. hooks is here referring to black people in the US. Again, as with the arguments I have taken from feminist writers, the same mechanisms of thought appear to operate across different situations of unequal power.

[104] Safe Neighbourhoods Unit, 1991: 63. To give just one example, I can not find any information in the survey to back the recommendation that 'in the longer term, consideration should be given to the consideration of new build sites on the estate for development by housing co-operatives, associations or self build schemes' (Safe Neighbourhoods Unit, 1991: 66).

[105] Monaghan, 1993: 19

required, but in the questionnaires the researchers take over the role of interpreting other people's views, which they then override with their own solutions. They purloin people's voices even while claiming to be attentive to them. The process by which the researchers reach their interpretations from the data is unclear; the data are presented, and are followed by a list of recommendations without a connecting argument, almost as if the data are put in first to justify recommendations that would have been made anyway.

The reports treat Southmead as an ahistorical entity, one subject to scarcely changing, ever-present problems; they freeze the area into an object static in both time and space. They are all synchronic snapshots, with no historical depth, in which the only movement for Southmead is the way it clambers up and down the rungs of the ladder of deprivation and criminality. The only change is in its ranking. The poverty reports contain no economic analysis at all – not the capitalist economics that would look at the effects of the business cycle on the area, and certainly not the radical economics that argues that '"poor places" are a structural problem of capitalism'.[106] Within this synchronic approach, the problems identified as important by the reports change. The reports have their own history, which reflects the concerns of social policy makers; the history of these reports as they veer between looking at crime and poverty is more about the history of social policy concerns than it is about the history of Southmead.

This lack of historical perspective is particularly acute when looking at the situation of young people. The huge changes that have affected young people and the idea of youth over the past 50 years are nowhere mentioned. Only by close reading can one see how the experience of young people has changed – from being porters and sack factory workers in the 1950s, to the YTS (Youth Training Scheme) and YOP (Youth Opportunities Programme) schemes of the 1980s.[107] The fact that these initials, and the approaches they stood for, were out of date by the end of the 1990s emphasises how quickly the experience of work and education has changed. In their work on young people in late modernity, Furlong and Cartmel write that 'young people today have to negotiate a set of risks which were largely unknown to their parents'.[108] But in all these reports all the multitude of changes in schools, colleges, benefit arrangements and work that affect young

---

[106] McCormick and Philo, 1995: 4
[107] Bristol City Council, 1983, section 3.4.2
[108] Furlong and Cartmel, 1997: 1

people are not mentioned, only their criminality and drug taking – their behaviour, not their condition.

This synchronic approach leads each report to its own series of short-term 'answers', with no reference to any previous answers, and leads to a situation in which projects that are supposed to provide answers are also short term. In 1957, after two years, the Bristol Social Project withdrew funding from the adventure playground.[109] The playground struggled on, but its history has been severely affected by a lack of long-term commitment, with fallow periods punctuated by bursts of finance provided after reports (1983, 1991). A common experience of working in poor areas is this periodic resurgence of interest leading to a cash injection, and those who have worked in the area for a long time, such as both the playground worker and myself, develop cynical strategies of taking the money while it is there, as insurance against the years of drought. All the answers proposed by these reports concern provision, or 'initiatives'[110], rather than changing the power relationships that affect the area. Their public service ethos creates more public service. Unfortunately, 'helping deprived places is not necessarily the same as helping deprived people ... those jobs that have been created in deprived areas have rarely gone to the urban poor who live there'.[111]

There is little consideration of how 'initiatives' might actually compound problems, for example, in policing. Labelling an area as criminal can lead to greater police presence, more arrests and a reinforcement of the labelling:

> The activities of the police are organised on the premise that criminality is a subcultural phenomenon and very much related to place. One of the consequences of patterns of police surveillance is that members of disadvantaged social groups are more likely to be charged with offences and, as a result, can face difficulties in the labour market, thus increasing the odds that criminal careers will continue.[112]

Finally, one of the strongest, and strangest, effects of these reports is the way they encourage an area identity. They may, in the words of Barry Wellman, be using the wrong boundaries, ones that assume locally based

---

[109] Benjamin, 1974: 35
[110] Bristol Community Safety Partnership, 1999a: 33
[111] Goodwin, 1995: 73
[112] Furlong and Cartmel, 1997: 94

social ties founded on 'extrinsic mappings of local area boundaries'[113], but in doing so actively create and reinforce boundaries that might otherwise not exist. The process starts with areas being used as 'arbitrary data collection points'.[114] These then become the administrative units of policy initiatives. Benedict Anderson, in raising the question of how colonies that were administrative units in the South American countries of the ex-Spanish empire became conceived of as 'fatherlands', says that 'one has to look at the way administrative organisations create meanings'.[115] As the reports use maps, so too are maps used locally to signify Southmead, as adverts for local events, or on local publications. The labelling of the area is a process that tends to:

> broaden the practice of *self-labelling*, through which the individual internalizes the external definition of his or her condition, thereby reinforcing the circle of dependence.[116]

Part of the creation of Southmead as a source of identity is not only in its differences in wealth and taste from surrounding areas, but also through the way it has been labelled, mapped and surveyed.

Media coverage of Southmead

There is a long tradition in Southmead that the press never covers anything that is good about the area, as voiced by this character in the community play:

> … 'cos the slightest bad thing that happen and all the press come swarming up here like flies looking for a story. And

---

[113] Wellman, 1979: 1202-3

[114] Agnew, 1989: 9. The arbitrariness can be illustrated in the fact that the 'Southmead' of all of the reports issued since 1981 has three different boundaries, each to suit the purposes of the report. The boundaries used are that of the ward (which also changes periodically) (Bristol City Council, 1991, 1996b, 1997a, 1997b 1999; Avon County Council, 1993; Bristol Community Safety Partnership, 1999a); workplace zones (Avon County Council, 1983; Bristol City Council, 1985); two of the sub-wards (Safe Neighbourhoods Unit, 1991; Bristol City Council, 1994); three sub-wards (Bristol City Council, 1996a). All very confusing, reinforcing the idea that Southmead is more an imaginary place than a real one.

[115] Anderson, 1991: 53

[116] Melucci, 1989: 134 (emphasis in original)

all you ever get is a negative story, they never tell about the good things that go on up here.[117]

The community play (discussed in the next chapter) was the subject of considerable media coverage – television, radio and all the local papers.[118] In that coverage, there was always a *but*, which supports the view that the 'bad' side is never forgotten:

> Southmead is often in the news for the wrong reasons, *but* now more than 150 people have come together to show there is still a strong positive spirit.[119]

The media does present 'good' stories about Southmead, but on *its* terms, which trivialise the lives of people who live in the area. The local media have a clutch of clichés they continually apply to the area.

The local press loves drama, but then so do its readers. On 3 June 1994, I could not buy a copy of the local paper in Southmead – all the shops had sold out to people wanting to read the main story, entitled 'Armed police smash their way into house. Drug fort'.[120] I had the same problem on 22 September: 'Wanted man in rooftop siege. Nowhere left to run' was spread over three pages, with colour photographs.[121] These major press dramas are always about crime.

Also in 1994 there was media coverage throughout the year of the build-up to the community play, and of Radio Southmead, that was positive and upbeat, if silly: 'Poptastic debut for radio kids'.[122] The two types of articles pander to two conflicting stereotypes: that Southmead is full of crooks, often young (as in a 'photo exclusive' of a teenager 'Caught in the act' of stealing a car[123]); and that children are innocent. These are separated by only a few days and maintained simultaneously: one is about a major drug dealer; the other is of gap-toothed infants laughing at a Punch and Judy show. There is no connection made between them, and anyone trying to form an understanding of

---

[117] Beddow, 1994: 66

[118] Diary entry, June 1994

[119] *Bristol Observer*, 24 November 1994 (emphasis added)

[120] *Bristol Evening Post*, 3 June 1994. This raid was extensively covered that evening on local television news, with the cameras following the police in as they smashed down doors.

[121] *Bristol Evening Post*, 22 September 1994

[122] *Bristol Observer*, 12 August 1994. Radio Southmead is described more in the next chapter.

[123] *Bristol Evening Post*, 21 February 1994

Southmead from these articles would be very confused. The media deal in fragments that assume a pre-existing knowledge of Southmead as an object within the popular imagination.

In more serious articles, the press recognises the difficulties of Southmead, but also takes the approach that they can be solved by 'initiatives'. Every time a scheme is launched, or there are reports of money being spent, the media reports treat these as if they will fix the problems of the area. For example:

> The final touches are being put to a plan that will breathe life into a run-down North West Bristol estate. Youngsters and ex-drug users will do up empty and derelict properties – providing them with valuable training at the same time as boosting the area's image.[124]

What is a good piece of work, like this plan, becomes seen as an almost magic solution. In 1997, there was coverage, each with several stories, of several new initiatives: a new supermarket, a drugs project, a proposed sports centre, a new counselling service, an arts show, an arts group, a young homelessness initiative, Voice of Southmead, an advice centre and a European Union-funded initiative to provide cheap food. Each was given the same magic ring. During the same year, there was also massive coverage of joyriding, drugs and sexual abuse – a rather dramatic, but ultimately static, staging of the area as consisting of an apolitical series of 'problems' and 'solutions'.

A common press solution, within this good–bad dichotomy, is 'community'. The community play was praised in an editorial for showing the 'Real spirit in the community'[125], and Voice of Southmead received considerable press support as an example of the community fighting back – considered such a 'good' that it received national coverage in a TV documentary.[126]

The image of Southmead is constantly filtered through the binaries of good/bad, problem/solution. Any confusion or subtlety gets removed, and local voices, even when asked to speak, get lost in the dominating media image of the area. I want to give two examples of that process in action. In November 1993, there was a campaign to promote National Youth Work Week in the local media, and I was asked to arrange for some articulate young people to talk to the media. Two unemployed

---

124 *Bristol Observer*, 22 August 1997
125 *Bristol Evening Post*, 1 December 1994
126 The Big Story, on ITV, December 1997

young men met with a reporter, and talked with her very seriously for some time on the issues she raised with them, those of unemployment and crime. They were both keen for their views to be heard. At the same time, a photographer took pictures of a young girl weightlifting, smiling into the camera. It was this photograph that featured in the subsequent 'good news' items, with a quote from a campaign spokesperson saying that young people 'don't get any attention when having to grapple with the hard reality of difficult circumstances'. Much to the puzzlement of the young men, their interview was not reported at all. They received none of this attention, although they were the ones doing the grappling. They were hurt, and they wondered what they had done wrong.[127]

In March 1995, I was approached by the makers of a weekly TV discussion programme to take part in a debate on policing. The local chief constable was being interviewed in the studio, and they wanted him to debate with people from Southmead, a criterion I met for the purposes of the programme. They arranged to film us not face-to-face with the chief constable in the studio, but in a local pub, thus staging an atmosphere of two 'sides'. I was initially asked to bring young people with me, but there was concern about the programme getting out of hand, so no young people were invited to join the debate. The panel was set up in a corner. None of us was a pub regular, as we were reminded by those who were ("Smelt the camera, eh?"). There was a local councillor, a neighbourhood watch representative and other local activists. Our right to represent Southmead was questioned by the pub regulars. The reporter did try to get them involved, but they refused. A local activist was the first to be interviewed, and she spoke, very hesitantly, in a strong Bristolian accent. She was nervous in front of the camera, and the reporter soon cut from her. He fixed on the more articulate of those present, and it was obvious how powerful fluency was in that situation. The reporter tried to stir disagreement on the issue of police effectiveness, and those of us on the panel felt that we were being pushed to be controversial, as if we were TV fodder for making a good programme.

Two men from the pub did finally come forward to speak. They offered the camera the seemingly authentic voice of the man in the bar, and complained about the deficiencies of the police. They gave the performance that was needed to make a good programme. This caused a lot of hilarity among the pub regulars, and I was told afterwards just what a couple of rogues these two were, how much they had been

---

[127] *Western Daily Press*, 22 November 1993; *Bristol Evening Post*, 22 November 1993; diary notes, November 1993

'taking the piss'. The sister of one told me that she would have hit him if she had been there, as he was being such a hypocrite (he dealt in stolen goods himself). The chief constable coped easily with their points.

The TV company set the whole tone of the debate. The programme traded on a stereotype of Southmead as a high-crime area with a pub culture. In doing so, while overtly giving a platform to local people, the local voice was actually silenced. People's real experiences with the police were too difficult to communicate on such a programme – it remained a subjugated knowledge that could not be spoken except by clowns. As with the questionnaire-based surveys, the opinions of 'the people' were used as a foil against which the experts could speak. Their subaltern position was reinforced.[128]

Conclusion

'Discourses', writes Parker, 'do not simply describe the social world, but categorise it, they bring phenomena into sight.'[129] Official reports and media representations create Southmead as a phenomenon, an object of social concern, always containing problems. Object is a crucial term here: there is a reliance in the official representations on statistical and cartographic techniques that reduce relationships to numbers and shapes. Being reduced to object, Southmead becomes a phenomenon to which things are done by others to solve its problems, by what Melucci typifies as a technological, 'resolutionary' approach. This approach, he says, 'renders listening impossible' [130], and I have shown that, far from listening to local people, the reports devalued their views as irrational, and ignored or silenced them even through processes that claimed representation of them. The reports all validate professional intervention, parallel to the magic solutions of the media, while ignoring both the power of their own representations and the actions of local people.

The major discursive process of creating Southmead as a problem object is to present it as an aberration and a pathology: poor, criminal, lacking both community and image. Lives, as Melucci points out, are marked by this process:

> Lives have turned into spaces for attention and manipulation
> by teams of experts circumscribing problems and

---

[128] This account is assembled from diary notes taken at the time.
[129] Parker, 1992: 4–5
[130] Melucci, 1996b: 2

manufacturing solutions. It is chiefly the policies pursued by the social and health services that are responsible for bringing this tendency to its current head. Preventive measures now operate according to a logic whereby preliminary classification is drawn up of groups within the population, based on social, geographical and epidemiological indicators decided in advance. Belonging to one of these groups and, hence, being directed through one of the preestablished channels for treatment of a problem (defined as either a pathology or the risk thereof) becomes the characteristic attached to every one of us, marking our individual life-histories thereafter.[131]

One could add collective life histories to this.

The representations studied in this chapter, while similar to the role of the 'master's' view in standpoint epistemology (discussed further in the next chapter), are more complex in operation than being merely distorted views of an existing reality. They do not possess the neutrality they claim to have, and have major effects on that reality, socially (the relationships between people), materially (money and housing) and culturally (being able to speak). They change, even create, what is 'inside'. The argument then is whether these outsider views can be challenged, and whether in creating an object of Southmead they create a standpoint for resistance from within.

---

[131] Melucci, 1996a: 83

FOUR

Knowledge from within: community art and local representations

Introduction

The 'insider' views of Southmead that are examined in this chapter set themselves up as different to official and media representations. The insider approach is that these outsider representations are generated from a position similar to the master's standpoint as described by Sandra Harding:

> The logic of the standpoint epistemologies depends on the understanding that the 'master's position' in any set of dominating social relations tends to produce distorted visions of the real regularities and underlying causal tendencies in social relations.[1]

In place of this outside knowledge, the knowledge of subordinate, inside groups is privileged in terms of understanding. It is claimed as clearer and less distorted than the knowledge, gained through secondary experience, of those who occupy dominating positions in social life. That people within a situation know most about it is a widespread, if contestable, argument, common within Southmead. One of the participants wrote of the community play, which was based on local experience:

> I have lived in Southmead all my life and I think this is an excellent chance to show people what Southmead is really made of.[2]

---

[1] Harding, 1986: 191
[2] Life Lines souvenir programme, 1994

'Insider' knowledge claims are based on a primary concrete experience of the situation, and it is this experience that provides their credibility.[3]

Vincent Berdoulay, a French language geographer, writes that 'our scientific understanding of it [place] cannot be artificially separated from people's account of their place'; in fact, 'a place becomes explicitly into being in the discourse of its inhabitants'.[4] This is a different argument from that in which Southmead is created as a social space through the discourse of social policy, and is an argument that sets out to challenge the supposedly neutral and rational knowledge that that discourse generates.

Looking at knowledge about Southmead that comes from Southmead involves a very different approach to that of certain strands of sociology that are summarised thus in a book on community: 'The analysis of any problem in sociology cannot make people's opinions of that problem its point of departure'.[5] Instead, it involves what Steve Pile and Nigel Thrift call a politics of location, 'a politics that makes no claims to second guessing others' experience, but still allows people to speak for themselves'.[6] Writing about this politics of location is not, however, a simple process. I have pointed out the transformation that occurs as representations made in one context are transformed as they appear in another context[7], and in selecting what to display from the large range of local material available, I am exercising a powerful mediating role.[8] By even handling this material, I could be sullying its truth. There is an undercurrent of belief, within arguments for subjugated knowledges, in what Stephen Crook calls 'the *purity* of the social'[9], and therefore the impurity of any form of mediation.

Over the past 40 years there has been a growth in accounts from 'below'. Foucault says that we might describe this 'as an insurrection of subjugated knowledges'.[10] Privileging the local is, ironically, a national,

---

[3] Collins, 1990: 209

[4] Berdoulay, 1989: 135, 136

[5] Bell and Newby, 1971: 193. This view bears a striking resemblance to those of the Bristol Social Project, quoted in Chapter Three.

[6] Pile and Thrift, 1995: 17

[7] See Chapter Two

[8] Roseanna Hertz, writing about reflexivity in social science, points out that: 'Authors decide whose stories (and quotes) to display, and whose to ignore' (Hertz, 1997: xii). This point can be made as strongly about the material selected to illustrate the previous chapter.

[9] Crook, 1998: 537 (emphasis in original)

[10] Foucault, 1980: 81

---

even international, phenomenon, a widespread trend related to the growth of forms of expression of subordinated experience within the feminist, gay and black movements, through working-class history, through history as seen through the eyes of 'ordinary' participants rather than the history of political leaders and victors, and through community histories.[11] There would surely not be so much local cultural production in Southmead if this wider phenomenon had not created it as a possibility, and if there were not new technologies that make new forms of expression and dissemination possible. For example, music has always been a popular cultural form in Southmead, but initially recording was expensive. Using new, affordable technology, the first CD made by a Southmead band was released in 1994.[12] Printing and video have also become more accessible, as reflected in the local materials listed in the References.

Foucault wrote that the 'local popular knowledges' formed by these disparate movements are seen as a sign of the elimination of 'the tyranny of globalising discourses with all their hierarchy and their privileges'.[13] The argument is that the growth of these knowledges is a power shift, which makes them important for this book not merely as 'knowledge', that is, what they tell us about Southmead, but also what they tell us about the possibility of local places having power in themselves. In Foucault's words, 'there is no ... knowledge that does not presuppose and constitute at the same time power relations'.[14] By producing their own knowledge, people in Southmead are also constituting their own power, and by studying that field of knowledge, we are also studying power relations.

As well as involving a different politics, looking at knowledge and expression from Southmead involves understanding a different epistemology in the 'alternative ways of producing and validating

---

[11] Prominent examples of this trend are the growth of women's publishing houses, such as Virago and the Women's Press, and influential works such as *The making of the English working class* by E.P. Thompson (1968) and *Blood of Spain* by Ronald Fraser (1979). The history of 'ordinary' people as witnesses is also a staple of television history, as in the BBC's major series and book, *People's century* (Hodgson, 1995). These examples are illustrative only, and scarcely do the subject justice. A full bibliography would be enormous. In one short essay, Joanna Bornat analysed over 50 works of community history from all over Britain, and her list is far from exhaustive (Bornat, 1993).

[12] Fire It Up, by Brabazon. The difficulty for this, and for the later CD kfs, was not its production, but its distribution. CD distribution is organised for mass commercial sales, not local small-scale productions.

[13] Foucault, 1980: 82, 83

[14] Foucault, 1977a: 27

knowledge' developed by subordinate groups.[15] Habermas writes that 'rival conceptions collide not only with each other but with conflicting standards of rationality as well'.[16] There can not be a straight comparison of reports and media from 'inside' with those from 'outside', as they come in very different forms, although there are locally produced surveys and sporadic examples of Southmead community newspapers. First, however, I want to look at three examples of productions that are from the genre that is loosely labelled community art: the community play Life Lines, a dramatic enactment of the history of the area; Radio Southmead, a short-term youth radio station; and Fresh Evidence, an art project and exhibition. I will also refer to other examples of Southmead's own insurrection of cultural production.

This chapter is not about uncritically accepting and presenting, or, in a word often used as a stock reaction to community cultures, 'celebrating' that local knowledge. Instead it will be questioning it. There is a deep tension in this approach, because of the claim of knowledge from below being rooted in a concrete experience that critics from 'outside' do not and cannot possess, and so are not equipped to criticise. Any critique could be seen as exemplifying that situation of unequal power between 'below' and 'above' that this knowledge production sets itself to challenge. The feeling of being investigated by experts is a received experience of, and orthodoxy in, Southmead, with defence of place being the antidote to being pathologised, as expressed by this poem:

The Committee

I honour you with a glimpse into my life

And betray you with the subject of my need

I strip you of the disadvantages we share

And leave clothed the appearance of your privileged past

I listen to constructed syllables of sound

And hear my own inadequate reply

I face in conflict the difference of our lives

---

[15] Collins, 1990: 202

[16] Habermas, 1992: 138. See also notes 38 and 39 in Chapter Three.

And in that conflict recognise defeat

I will in dignity defend my place

And cast the stone that ripples, outward and not in.

Kathleen Horseman[17]

An unresolved tension exists between accepting and applauding what is said in local cultural production because of its production by people whose voice is otherwise suppressed or derided, and a more critical and engaged, though not hostile, approach that creates ambivalence. This more critical approach runs counter to the strong tradition in 'community art' that 'a product of a particular project is presented in and of itself as an achievement, regardless of what it "means"'.[18] However, accepting uncritically the truth claims made by subjugated knowledge overlooks a danger contained within it, as identified by one of its champions, Collins. The danger is that it 'duplicates the positivist belief in one "true" interpretation of reality' and so, like positivist science, comes with its own set of problems.[19]

I am particularly sensitive to such arguments because 'telling it like it is', lauding the viewpoints of marginalised people, celebrating their lives and attempting to create a positive image to counter the problematisation of the area from 'outside', has also long been a major part of my own professional practice as youth worker in the area. I know how difficult it is to get local work taken seriously as art, and the delight that greets recognition, for example when the exhibition The Place We're In was covered in the arts section of the local newspaper instead of being relegated to being merely a 'good news' story about Southmead.[20]

I have been involved, to a varying extent, with all the examples I am investigating: marginally with the community play, the parish audit and community newspapers, but also as one of the organisers/coordinators of Radio Southmead, the Fresh Evidence exhibition and the young people's survey, and as a participant in local conversations. None of these events, as would happen in more structured action research, were set up

---

[17] From the second book of writings from Southmead, *A Southmead festival of words* (Bristol Broadsides, 1986).
[18] Rose, 1997: 193
[19] Collins, 1990: 235
[20] *Bristol Evening Post*, 25 April 1997

for the purposes of this research. In investigating them, I will be taking a critical look at professional practice as well as at local knowledge.

Life Lines: the Southmead community play

Life Lines was a play about Southmead that involved over 150 local people in performances in November and December 1994. There were recruitment leaflets, a souvenir programme, a poster, a T-shirt, the play script, a video, press coverage and a play-in-a-day by young people featured on the regional television news.[21] There were meetings, script sessions and rehearsals that started in January 1994. The community play was a year-long event.

The play was coordinated by the Avon Community Theatre Agency (ACTA), an organisation that 'gives people the opportunity to devise and produce their own theatre', and 'gives priority to areas with poor arts facilities'.[22] At an initial meeting, a worker from ACTA listed reasons for staging a community play in order to inspire local people: it brings people together with the same aim; it makes people look at their own area; it changes people's lives; it breaks down artificial barriers (age and disability were mentioned most); and gives a sense of pride and commitment. By finding community, people find themselves, and such a play, devised by working on people's own stories, was not something that would be imposed. The ACTA representative's speech was followed by someone from Southmead, who had seen a community play in another area. She said: "It was the spirit of community. You could see it. It was real". There was then a discussion about finding a 90-year-old woman (her age was emphasised several times) who 'knows all about Southmead', who was likened to being 'the spine of Southmead'.[23]

At the next meeting, of mostly older people, there was a lot of talk about Southmead in the 'old days', and concern that the play would only pick up on spectacular events, as outsiders do.

> "An ordinary lifestyle is more important than a spectacular one."

> "We don't want the play to be about joyriding. We've got enough of that in real life."

---

[21] Diary notes, 2 June 1994

[22] Statement in Life Lines souvenir programme

[23] Diary notes, 12 January 1994. The story of the old lady had the status of a 'founding narration' (de Certeau, 1984: 126).

"Other areas don't know the hardships we have suffered."

The difference between the two halves of the estate was discussed:

"We lived on the new estate. We had that distinction. We was posh."

Early Southmead was likened to paradise – there were stories of people arriving with their tin baths on their backs and finding that they had bathrooms:

"There was community spirit then."

"That is what we want to bring back."

"Everyone was poor then, going down to the pawnbroker together."

"Was there a pawnbroker in Southmead?"

"No, in town. You'd go down by bus. You could afford bus fares then."[24]

The theme of the play became a history of Southmead, proposed as a way of enabling younger people to find out about their inheritance. There was agreement among those involved that the past was good, and that the future should be good, but disagreement over whether the present was good.[25] That golden past era they were talking about was the era of the Bristol Social Project, which, as we saw, had argued that community was lacking. The rosy view of the past is a common one in community histories, called by Joanna Bornat, in her survey of the genre, constructions of community life through art and fable.[26] There was much anger at the negative image of Southmead in the media. The desire was to get away from 'Southmead again, big black cloud', and the message to outsiders was to 'Stop being negative about Southmead.

---

[24] Diary notes, 10 February 1994
[25] This is a common thread in thought about community, discussed further in Chapter Eight.
[26] Bornat, 1993: 30

Be positive'.[27] In her research on community art in Edinburgh, Gillian Rose shows how common it is for people involved in such projects to vent their resentment at press definitions of 'bad areas'.[28]

The play introduced itself with a show of defiance:

> They said it couldn't be done – This is our story, our lives
> we wanted to show you through Life Lines our community
> play – how we came to be here and how the community
> of Southmead is today.[29]

The local hall where the play was staged was turned into a Southmead street, with red-brick houses down each side. The play started with the song Southmead, Glorious Southmead, and was based around a contemporary 'fun day', with flashbacks to the past. In the 1930s, a family at a council office are offered a new house in Southmead as part of slum clearance, so long as they obey the rules, which the clerk shows them on a 'huge pile of paper'. They have to walk to their new home through fields from where the tramline ended. A rather curmudgeonly grandad, reminiscent of the character quoted in Chapter Three, complains about the inside toilets, but for the rest it is 'bloomin' paradise', albeit a paradise now lost:

> "My gran says that she used to be able to leave her doors
> and windows open when she went out. Can't do it now."

There is a scene of neighbours helping each other out when short of money, and one family having to pawn their wedding presents. This is followed by a conversation of how present-day young people are spoilt rotten, counterpoised to a scene showing just how mischievous children were in the 1940s. The wartime bombing of Bristol was followed by VE day street celebrations. There was a rock-and-roll night at the youth club in 1964. The argument about whether young people are dangerous, naughty or confused continues as a major theme of the play, with a teenager getting drunk, having a 'nightmare on Greystoke Avenue' (the main road through the area) and passing out. He is accused of stealing the money raised by the fun day for a kidney machine, even

---

[27] Diary notes, 7 April 1994. The theme of 'a deep sense of injustice for Southmead's reputation throughout Bristol' was highlighted again in the souvenir programme.
[28] Rose, 1997: 190
[29] Life Lines souvenir programme

though two other children had in fact taken it on themselves to deliver it directly to the hospital, so the play ends on a happy note.

The play upheld the view that Southmead has an unchanging nature, as expressed in the last main speech that compared the past to the present:

> "Different. I don't think so. Oh maybe the place looks different, but the people are the same underneath it all ... they don't change. Southmead people, they're special."

Continuity through history is the basis of the design of the poster for the play, with people from old and new photos placed together in a collage, giving the same atmosphere visually as the performance gave dramatically.

Life Lines ends with a song, A Sense of Belonging, with its chorus, 'Southmead is all about people'[30], a humanistic reaction to the objectification of outsider knowledge.

The play was full of themes with which we are already familiar – youth, crime, negative outsider images and the uncertainty of community – but this time recast into a quasi-nationalist format. All of these were seen through a Southmead perspective alone, as if these were only Southmead problems. There was no acknowledgement that, even close at hand in Bristol, there are other areas with similar histories. The history of Southmead becomes a rather static, closed heritage. Homi Bhabha, writing about nations, describes this process thus: 'The difference of space returns as the Sameness of Time, turning Territory into Tradition, turning the People into One'.[31] Although ostensibly about history, the play emphasised the difference of Southmead as a place while emphasising its similarity over time. The conflict in this place was not hidden, but transposed into what Benedict Anderson calls 'the reassurance of fratricide' that exists in nations and can only endure if there is an (imagined) fraternity.[32] The play built what Phil Cohen calls a 'nationalism of the neighbourhood'.[33]

There is a back-story to the play that is not as cosy. There were tremendous problems backstage, with fighting among cast members even as they were sweet and cooperative on stage.[34] There was some

---

[30] Quotes and story line all from the play script (Beddow, 1994)
[31] Bhabha, 1994: 300
[32] Anderson, 1991: 202
[33] Cohen, 1988: 33
[34] Diary notes, 1 December 1994

strong antagonism to the whole project, with a vociferous local faction resenting money being spent on a play when jobs and houses were more important, a much more materialist approach to local welfare. Some were physically threatened not to take part, and some members of the cast pulled out at the last minute.[35] The play aroused strong emotions, with some eagerly applauding it, and others refusing even to watch it. Those involved met after the play to plan a further production. There was a split, involving racial abuse and personal animosities, and a smaller group produced a much less ambitious, and much less successful, pantomime the following year, then collapsed completely.

The play was therefore not so much a representation of an already existing community, but a production that within itself created a performed community on stage. The 'selves' of the actors, which were supposed to be what grounded the play in reality, were produced by the performance, and only existed within it, as pointed out by a drama theorist: 'The self ... is produced by the performance it supposedly grounds'[36], inverting any claims to authenticity. The play created the presence of a community that was otherwise absent: the presence on stage, the absence behind the scenes. This 'acting' of community is not restricted to the community play – there have been actual fun days such as the one that sustained the structure of the play (one of these is mentioned in Chapter One), open air rock concerts featuring local bands (in the summers of 1993, 1996 and 1997) that raised money for good causes and matches played every Saturday and Sunday by Southmead sports teams, each of which could be seen as a performance of community.[37]

It is too easy to criticise what was a major piece of work that used up enormous amounts of energy, displayed the deep hurt that exists among people in Southmead and was a reassertion of themselves as people whose lives are worth something, who are reclaiming themselves, using Habermas's words, as 'communicatively acting subjects'[38] (bearing in mind the different meanings of the word 'act'). The arcadian and utopian messages of the play are important ingredients of popular accounts of the area, and the idea of community as performance in which people are actors hints at a possible way of describing the uncertain phenomenon of community.

---

[35] Diary notes, 28 November 1994
[36] Auslander, 1995: 60
[37] See my account of the 1993 concert in Brent, 1997: 74-5.
[38] Habermas, 1992: 141

Radio Southmead

Radio Southmead broadcast from Southmead Youth Centre on a Restricted Service Licence during August 1994.[39] There were five programmes, presented by local young people, using a magazine format, including jingles, quizzes, joke competitions, poems, interviews with local people, music from local bands and studio guests. An early decision was to generate all the content locally. Locality and self-production were emphasised in the station jingle:

> This station is
>
> A great big do
>
> It's run purely by
>
> And for you ...
>
> Southmead is
>
> The happening place
>
> Switch it on,
>
> It's purely ace.

Community radio is a movement wider than Southmead, with its own association and magazine. In the April 1994 issue of the magazine *Airflash*, there was an article entitled 'A broadcasting future for all – not just the powerful' – a phrase that could apply to the rationale of Radio Southmead.[40]

The station technique was very like that of *bricolage* – using what was there. And there was plenty of material in Southmead to broadcast. Local bands and the Women's Singing Group were featured, showing the strength of the (mostly male) music scene in the area. The music played was much more polished and articulate than the spoken word

---

[39] I was the station manager. This account is from my notes at the time, the final report on the project and material from the broadcasts themselves, all of which I have on tape.

[40] Mowlam, 1994: 12-13 (The article was by the then Shadow Secretary of State for National Heritage, the late Mo Mowlam.)

of the interviews conducted with local organisations, sports groups, churches and people on the street, which were full of hesitancies and people stumbling over their words. The station effectively showed that Southmead does have its own hinterland of activity, containing people who are not just objects or victims. This material was validated by being presented in 'real' radio format. One of the ingredients that made Radio Southmead a success was sponsorship by a local pizza company, and the free pizzas given out as prizes every day gave the station an air of legitimacy. Radio Southmead was popular. People listened and responded. The telephone line was busy, much to the excitement of the young people staffing it. There was a message from a retired dustman: "It's putting Southmead on the map ... I like it, it's real, not slick and professional". There was extensive media coverage, especially from the established local radio stations, but also on TV and in the press. It was noticeable at the beginning of the week of broadcasting how shy the young people were when they were interviewed, but how crisp and confident they were in handling the media when they came back just a few days later, after they had been doing the interviewing themselves. Radio Southmead was heard by people all over the Bristol area, many of whom phoned in with their congratulations.

Radio Southmead was one of the few occasions when young people have been seen as central to the process of community building rather than as a problem. Interviewees were delighted with them, and wanted to give of their best to the young interviewers.

As with the community play, Radio Southmead fetishised the place, with the regular repetition of the station jingle not letting anyone forget its provenance.

It was constructed around locality, which raised a series of issues:

- Narrowness. I met a group of teenagers on the street who were not involved in the radio and encouraged them to listen. They asked what sort of music was being played. I explained that it was all by local bands. "Ugh, just heavy metal then, we don't want that". They were into rave, and certainly did not like any of the locally produced music.[41]
- Exclusion. Attracted by the publicity, a number of young people who did not use the youth centre wanted to become involved. In the event, not a single one of these did take part. They were all pushed out by the regular users, not formally or violently, but they never showed up more than once. The swearing and rough way of

---

[41] The bands were not only heavy metal outfits, but also indie bands.

conducting relationships among the young people involved (albeit not on air) seemed more about forming a distinctive way of relating that was recognisably their own than stemming from any viciousness or hatred within the group. The exclusionary effect of this behaviour was very effective, creating a strong 'we' that outsiders could not join.

- Conventionality. There are claims, for instance by the black American writer bell hooks, that life on the margins can create a space of resistance that forms a new vision of social relationships.[42] Radio Southmead was more about affirming people as members of the existing society than challenging the premises of that society. Melucci points out that collective action need not be antagonistic or oppositional to 'the logic of the system', but is instead about claiming what is seen as one's rightful place within it, taking the form of:

> ... the expression of excluded social groups or categories pressing for representation.... There is no antagonistic dimension to this conflict; there is only pressure to join a system of benefits and rules from which one has been excluded.[43]

In both the community play and on Radio Southmead, people emphasised their ordinariness; on the radio a woman singer, and a woman who read her own poetry and told the interviewer that she had written a novel, both claimed their ordinariness as a virtue. The writer said, "I get my ideas from everyday life", and read a poem about cooking the Sunday dinner. This lack of challenge was recognised by the local media. A local commercial radio station lent equipment, knowing that Radio Southmead provided no threat to its own position. Radio Southmead was the acceptable face of alternative radio, different from the pirate stations, especially those run by minority ethnic groups, that challenge the hegemony of existing broadcasters.[44]

Fresh Evidence

While the community play and Radio Southmead were ambitious, but ultimately conventional, in their portrayals of Southmead, the paintings of the art exhibition Fresh Evidence were ambitious, unconventional

---

[42] hooks, 1991: 41
[43] Melucci, 1996b: 6-7
[44] Mowlam, 1994: 10-11

for a housing estate and made no attempt to portray Southmead.[45] The exhibition brochure explained the process thus:

> This exhibition is the result of a frantic three weeks at Southmead Youth Centre in the summer of 1996, when young people were given the opportunity to express themselves with paint, use their creative energy, and enjoy themselves.

Southmead is a large Bristol housing estate that, like many such areas, possesses a powerful mythology and notoriety, created partly from within, but largely by outsiders. Young people themselves are often demonised, bearing the brunt of the notoriety.

The exhibition consisted of a number of finished artworks, together with photographs of those involved, a display book showing the project in action, a video of the workshops and various objects from the project that all acted as a powerful testimony to the passion possessed by Southmead young people.

Forty young people took part in creating the paintings, with two artists. The project was not about expressing order or ordinariness; through its big canvases splattered with paint, it expressed disorder and excess.[46] Rose writes of community art that perhaps the subversive move is a desire for discursive excess that refuses to define, or be defined.[47] This excess challenges the 'objectivity' of the reports on Southmead, and has a very different view of community, more like the idea of community as extravagance envisaged by Corlett: 'an excess of possibility overflowing the boundaries of reasonable and orderly discourse'.[48] This was community art that, instead of creating a fixed identity for Southmead, challenged any tidy identity. It was a project that involved some of the roughest and most 'difficult' young people of the area, to whom asserting ordinariness and respectability was an alien concept.

A review in a local magazine summed up the difference of Fresh Evidence from most community art better than I can:

---

[45] My knowledge of Fresh Evidence comes from being one of its organisers.
[46] In the acknowledgements of help at the exhibition, special mention was made of the cleaners.
[47] Rose, 1997: 187
[48] Corlett, 1989: 159

The governing stereotypes of community-art work with
kids from a city council estate suggest a kind of dull
worthiness, best expressed, perhaps, in grainy black and
white photographs of old-folk carrying their shopping
home or graffiti art celebrations of gangsta-rap discourse.
This exhibition ... is the best corrective possible to such
a view. Instead of reinforcing negative images (and in
Southmead, there's plenty of inspiration) of urban alienation
or man's inhumanity to man, Fresh Evidence presents a
vibrant collection of large-scale paintings ... that could
look at home in the Saatchi Gallery's latest display of young
British artists. Damien Hirst or John Noakes-style spin
paintings ... share gallery space with luminous, hard-edged
abstracts, display-case installations celebrating the tools of
the trade and collectively-authored works in which bus-
shelter graffiti takes on the appearance of post-modern
script.

The kids in the project ... have produced work whose style
is both at the cutting-edge of contemporary painting and
yet also forms an eloquent testimony to the liveliness and
creativity of their own culture.

... Beautifully installed, brimming with energy and disclosing
a rare optimism of spirit, Fresh Evidence should win some
kind of award.[49]

The exhibition was in the smartest gallery in the Bristol City Museum
and Art Gallery, a space unusual for Southmead to occupy, which was
part of its surprise. It lost its impact when shown in the Greenway
Centre in Southmead, partly because that centre is not designed for
showing exhibitions, but mainly because there it did not possess such
a defiant intent. Strangely, its power was stronger away from its own
neighbourhood. What fascinated the young people much more than
that recognition by an institution to which they felt little relationship
was the contents of the exhibition's comment book, which became one
of the main artefacts of the exhibition, and was afterwards photocopied
and circulated in Southmead like some kind of *samizdat* publication.

---

[49] Article by Phil Johnson in *Venue*, 11 October 1996. This enthusiasm about the
exhibition from someone that none of those involved had ever met was a huge
boost.

They were impressed by the number of comments (nearly 200), but even more the contents and drama of what they said, from 'These paintings should be purchased for the nation' to 'Is this art? I don't think so' (and ruder).[50] The lively dialogue of the book, with its engaged praise and criticism, was far more interesting and far less patronising to those young people than being told that they had done well.

The exhibition was explicit about coming from Southmead. One of the images displayed was the Southmead 'S', a rather fascistic symbol found as a graffiti marker of ownership wherever Southmead young people go. There were gory photographs of an arm into which this symbol had been cut with a Stanley knife, and a large canvas with this 'S' painstakingly painted in acrylic – a strange transposition. The most popular single painting was 'Blue Car', another painstaking, but unfinished, painting of one of the cars most desired by young people at the time. Its very lack of completion suggests that desire most powerfully. Although based on Southmead, however, the exhibition was not stuck in its own nationalism, with local images being turned into abstractions giving wider resonances.

The very divided response to the paintings was replicated in Southmead. Many of them are on permanent display in community buildings. Blue Car remains in the youth centre, where young people have given it almost iconic status. There was also antipathy and cynicism. A local scrap dealer helped me take the paintings back to Southmead from the gallery. Flinging the paintings on to his truck, he said: "Is this art, eh? How much is it worth?".

Local surveys and community newspapers

Community profiling is a technique promoted both to discover the needs of local areas and to involve people in a community relationship while researching their own area.[51] It distinguishes between the needs identified by outside experts and professionals and 'felt needs by local people: these are the real needs felt or described by the people who actually live in the area'.[52] Community profiling considers itself an alternative to outsider surveys. They privilege the *reality* of the *local*, as if locality guarantees reality. Profiles are defined by Paul Burton as:

---

[50] These are from the comment book. Other comments are quoted in Chapter One.

[51] Burton, 1993

[52] Burton, 1993: 46

- a social, environmental and economic description
- of a given area
- which is used to inform local decision making. [53]

Community development in general, of which profiling is a part, is:

> helping people to learn about themselves, helping communities to express their identity and enabling communities to acquire the skills and power to clarify, create and take up opportunities for self-determination.[54]

The Anglican church in Southmead undertook an audit of the area in 1988, with the same aims as a community profile, but with an added religious purpose. The audit was structured:

> ... to make people more aware about their community and to enhance a willingness to co-operate with each other and God in answering the need highlighted.[55]

The audit pondered over census and poverty statistics, and tried to make sense of different boundaries by reproducing maps showing Southmead with four different boundaries. People were surveyed about their opinions of a range of local services, coming up with a list of likes, dislikes and conflicts in the area. These were not very clear; for example, one of the top 'likes' was 'community spirit', while one of the top 'dislikes' was 'split community and the insular attitude of people'.[56] The main recommendation was that the church should keep up its involvement. The audit was part of a process that led, three years later, to the establishment of a successful community work project by the church. This tells us more about the way in which church members engaged with the area, as part of a movement started by the Archbishop of Canterbury's *Faith in the City* report[57], than providing new information. Members of this and other churches in the area made up a significant number of the trustees elected to the new Southmead Development Trust in 1996, and in that May there was a church service

---

[53] Burton, 1993: 2

[54] Burton, 1993: 2

[55] St Stephen, Southmead, 1988: 1. Please note that this audit was carried out five years before the publication of Paul Burton's very practical handbook, which its authors would have found useful.

[56] St Stephen, Southmead, 1988: 21

[57] St Stephen, Southmead, 1988: 2

'to offer their support to the new Trust, to pray for God's blessing, and to make an Act of Commitment to work together for the common good of the community'[58], reminding us of the strong link between the idea of 'communion' and the sociality of 'community'.[59]

The *Young people's survey of Southmead 1998* was carried out to inform the development of projects under phase four of the government's Single Regeneration Budget programme, a phase called Youth Owning Urban Regeneration.[60] A university-based researcher worked with a small group of young people to develop and distribute a questionnaire, and analyse the responses. The research was met with a high degree of enthusiasm: 'Those asked expressed surprise that someone was actually interested in their opinion'.[61] The survey results showed that although overall young people had a positive view of Southmead, 'the police and the media are seen as having a very negative view of them as young people and the area of Southmead'.[62] Professionals who work in the area were seen as not listening to them. There was a real concern about bullying, a problem identified by one in five respondents in an answer to an open question about the worst problem they had faced. Young people were enthusiastic about the possibility of being involved in activities to improve the area. Two of them said that they enjoyed joyriding.

Because of this enthusiasm, and drawing on experience from previous surveys, a youth worker was appointed to take the survey results back to the young people to ask their opinions about how to respond.[63] Survey results are not the end of a process of finding out information, and themselves raise new questions; for example, more needed to be found out about the issue of bullying. Again, the young people involved were delighted to be taken seriously. From their responses, a project proposal was drawn up and tested on them. At the time of writing, this project working with young people on issues of bullying, youth involvement and public space in Southmead is under way.

---

[58] To my knowledge, four of the eight elected resident trustees were strong church-goers. One came from a group supported by the church community work project. Two were Labour Party members. I do not know the political or religious affiliations of the eighth member. The information on the service is from the invitation to attend.

[59] Communion features as a major ingredient of communitarian thought in Corlett, 1989. See also Amirou, 1989: 119; Maffesoli, 1996; Nancy, 1991: 10

[60] Kimberlee, 1998

[61] Kimberlee, 1998: 3

[62] Kimberlee, 1998

[63] Kimberlee and Cassidy, 1999. One of the benefits of participative research has been putting into practice the learning gained from reading other people's surveys.

This survey of young people does show how much people do want to be involved in decisions that affect them, how much better results are if people are treated seriously and how useful specific, focused surveys can be. It also gave a very different view of young people as participants in the area, rather than as the problems that they are categorised as in the majority of accounts of Southmead.

How much research should be about finding information, and how much it should be about providing a platform to voices that are not otherwise heard, are questions that pervaded a local research project on drug misuse.[64] The problem for that work was that, in its desire to validate the unheard voices of drug users, it was unable to use them in any systematic way. The quotes from its respondents are far more interesting than its recommendations, raising, but not answering, questions about the relationship between place and drug use:

> I lose count of the number of times I tried stopping and I couldn't.... I still had the same circle of friends and where I lived was still the same ...[65]

This repeating of voices alone provides no solution to problems, except as part of a process leading to action, a process to be looked at in later chapters.

One of the recommendations of the church audit was that there should be a magazine distributed throughout the community, and there have been a number of attempts to establish a Southmead community newspaper.[66] One of these stated that:

> Everyone we've spoken to thinks that a community newspaper would really help to establish better communications between local people and groups, and give a better image of Southmead, so that as one resident said, people would be proud and happy to live here.

However, it also listed the problems: 'lack of funding, training facilities, continuity, and community based commitment'.[67] Very few editions have ever been issued. The ones that have been all report on the various

---

[64] Newman, 1999
[65] Newman, 1999: 29
[66] *Say It! Southmead's Community Newspaper* (1991-93), *Southmead and Westbury-on-Trym Proclaimer/ The Proclaimer/ Southmead Community News* (1994-96)
[67] Southmead community newsletter, October 1995

organisations based in the area, and their concerns; they are rather formal, despite slogans such as 'Showing you the heart and soul of Southmead'.[68] They offer no alternative to the commercially run local press, and do not provide a regular or reliable local communication system.

The silences of community expression

In Chapter Three, I gave examples of how local knowledge and expression are silenced by the media. In this chapter, I have shown public expression of community being different from behind-the-scenes relationships. Public language is different, too; the young people involved with Radio Southmead spoke very differently on air to the way they talked among themselves. In the studio, there was a big notice saying, 'No swearing', but this was hardly necessary; the people involved knew what would be acceptable on air, and changed their language accordingly. Public personae are different from private ones.

There are more serious examples of stories that are silenced by, or cannot be spoken through, community expression.

At the same time as the start of the project creating the images of Southmead that would be shown at The Place We're In exhibition, there was a major court case in which a Southmead man, G, was sentenced to fourteen years imprisonment for 23 offences involving kidnap, blackmail, drugs supply and indecent assault.[69] Most of his victims were young boys in the area, and G was well known, and well feared, by young people. The case was being featured on regional television on a night that the two artists on this project were working with young people in the youth centre.[70] As they set up computers, there was a separate crowd intently watching the television, all of whom knew G. There was a palpable division between them and the 'outside' artists, who did not know him, and were not gripped by the programme.

The television had interviews with parents and victims, and scenes of Southmead. The main visual link was a constantly repeated shot of the legs of anonymous young men, 'victims', walking through streets that were recognisably in Southmead. Part of the art project consisted of giving young people cameras and asking them to photograph their neighbourhood. That evening they refused. They said that photographs

---

[68] *Southmead Community News*, May 1996

[69] *Bristol Evening Post,* 30 January 1997

[70] HTV Look West, 29 January 1997. This account is distilled from my notes at the time.

made Southmead look 'shit'. They were ashamed of Southmead, of those pictures of houses from which G operated that looked just like their own. Despite some of those present being victims, they seemed to feel that as they too were Southmeaders, they were all guilty. Self-expression, they felt, would not remove that stigmatic identity.

A youth worker tried to get young people to talk about the case on tape for the project. No-one would, openly stating fear of reprisal. Other attempts to discuss the topic were greeted with a fearful sexual flippancy and aspersions on the sexual motives of whoever raised it. However, the subject was talked about, on certain terms, to certain audiences. At unexpected moments, young men would disclose their experiences of G to me, but it was always them that started the conversation, and always on their terms. Driven by anger, numbers of them had talked to the police, despite fear of him, and fear that their own criminal records would make them be disbelieved. Anger led some of them to talk to the media.[71] What was important to them was that they chose their audiences.

The biggest silence of all was that of G himself. In September 1999, I had a conversation about him with one of his contemporaries. People around were saying "G, yuk", but he said, "G could say a lot about those children's homes he was in. He's got a lot of stories". But then, who would be his audience? As Ken Plummer writes:

> Stories can be told when they can be heard. There is usually no point in telling a tale without a receptive and appreciative listener.... To publicly tell a story to someone who will then mock you, disbelieve you, excommunicate you, sack you, hospitalise you, imprison you or bash you bleeding senseless to the ground may be brave but foolhardy.... It may well be better to be silent. [72]

The story of G was not mentioned at all in the exhibition The Place We're In, despite its local importance at the time. Situations like this remind us of the limits of community expression in articulating subjugated knowledges.

The nationalist slant of so much community expression silences other voices, those of minorities within the area. The year in which the community play was staged was also the year of high levels of racial

---

[71] Examples are in *Western Daily Press*, 30 January 1997; *Bristol Evening Post*, 24 March 1996.

[72] Plummer, 1995: 120

harassment in Southmead.[73] The chair of the play's steering committee, a well-respected local figure, was black, and she and a number of other black residents acted in the play. However, black people's different experience of Southmead was not featured, and the play made the area look like a multi-racial paradise, with no differentiation of experience between black and white residents. The play did not show that virtually none of the current residents had trudged from the tram terminal across fields to reach Southmead from their slums, but had been born there, or had come from, among other places, Ireland, Jamaica, Trinidad, Italy, Poland, Scotland and Wales. The oration by a representative of the Barbados Association at the funeral of a friend of mine, whom I knew only in his Southmead incarnation, concentrated on their boat trip to Britain from Barbados. Those making the trip didn't like the ship's food, so the captain asked if any of them could cook. My friend had said he could, and did so for the voyage. He was so good that he was offered a job on the ship for future trips, but turned it down so as to settle in Bristol.[74] Such migration stories of people who live in Southmead are not included in stories of Southmead. The attempt to create a public Southmead identity overrides these other identities.

One other great subject of silence in Southmead community expression is poverty. Workers on the play told me how shocked they were at the poverty they found in the area[75], but it only features in the cultural material produced locally as a condition of the past. Raising the subject as a contemporary issue leads to anger – chairing a meeting of the Southmead Arts Forum I had trouble keeping people in the same room together because one of the groups present had described Southmead as being deprived, and others were demanding that they withdrew that 'slur'.[76] Drawing attention to the poverty of Southmead is seen as insulting its people, and as an issue it is discussed far less than crime. Poverty, like criminal activity, is, it seems, a subject to be talked about only in the third person – others are criminal, others are poor.

Knowledge from below?

There is a title of an essay that sums up the dilemmas of knowledge from below. It asks, 'Can the subaltern speak?'.[77] Are the examples looked

---

[73] Bristol City Council Housing Services, 1994. See also Chapter Three.

[74] Diary notes, June 1997. The story was told with much greater eloquence, as befitted the occasion.

[75] Diary notes, 28 November 1994

[76] Diary notes, July 1997. A colleague told me of similar experiences in July 1994.

[77] Spivak, 1988

---

at in this chapter the voice of the subaltern people of Southmead, or have they actually not got a voice? I want to look at this issue, without getting bogged down in Spivak's complex and abstract arguments, by looking at the role of 'outside' influences on Southmead knowledge – the role of both the facilitators (for want of a better term) and the audience towards which the expression is directed.

In his book, *Telling sexual stories*, Plummer proposes a 'sociology of stories'.[78] Stories, he writes, are *'joint actions'* involving *'story tellers'*, *'coaxers, coachers and coercers'* and *'consumers, readers, audiences'*.[79] Stories do not exist in abstract, but are assembled around lives, events and happenings through a set of social relationships. Two of the most important aspects of the creation of stories are that they need to be *coaxed* and need an *audience* to hear them.

Plummer's description of coaxers is similar to the role of the various community artists and surveyors involved in the projects described above. They 'possess the power, at least momentarily, to provoke stories from people. Their line of activity is to seduce stories.... They probe, interview, interrogate'.[80] The person who took on this role for the community play, wrote:

> a period of research was embarked upon ... to find out about Southmead ... people's memories, impressions and opinions.[81]

These were then dramatised through workshops:

> My job at this stage was to take careful notes of the improvisation, conversations, characters, scenes and speeches ... making sure that all the material found its way into the final script....After a session where the second draft had been drastically changed I was told, "I hope you don't mind, but its important that we get it right, you see".[82]

One of the artists working on Fresh Evidence wrote of his relationship with the young people on a previous project, a dance film called FIRE. For him, the relationship was more dynamic than being a note taker:

---

[78] Plummer, 1995: 18

[79] Plummer, 1995: 20-21 (emphases in original).

[80] Plummer, 1995: 21. Questionnaire designers, too, are coaxers.

[81] Life Lines souvenir programme

[82] Life Lines souvenir programme

> The space between the artists and the kids was one of fundamental importance in being the place of interaction which then became the creative field. We as artists gave our skills and orchestrated the 'safe' place for them to precipitate some of their boisterous needs, they reciprocated by demonstrating their passion and between us we created 'FIRE'.[83]

The role of the 'artist' on community art has been the subject of much discussion. In 1984, Owen Kelly wrote that community art was 'ceasing to be a movement of activists, and beginning to become a profession'.[84] His concern was that community art could become a worthy part of the state, consisting of 'the kindly people who do good without ever causing trouble'.[85] The problem with this professionalisation is very clear to see. Nearly all of the writing on community art is about these artists and their concerns, and very little is written about the artworks themselves.[86] As Foster has written, the artist can come to stand for the community: 'Often artist and community are linked through an identitarian reduction of both, the apparent authenticity of one invoked to guarantee that of the other'.[87] He does go on to say that 'the relevant artists are aware of these complications, and sometimes they foreground them'.[88] However, even after a work has been completed, even if there has been good collaboration between artists and 'community', the 'work can be redirected to other ends' in the way it is used by galleries.[89] The work can become appropriated, with ownership passing from the producers to curators, with what Foster calls 'the inhabitants' having their work 'turned into anthropological exhibits'[90], a major problem for any community art.

However, without coaxers the stories would not exist. On a technical level, without the expertise of ACTA, the community play could not

---

[83] From an undated proposal for the painting project that became Fresh Evidence. The use of the word 'kids' can be seen as patronising, but that depends on who uses it. In my judgement, none of the 'young people' (my preferred, but longer-winded, term) felt at all patronised by this artist and his work with them.

[84] Kelly, 1984: 31

[85] Kelly, 1984: 1

[86] Braden, 1978; Kelly, 1984; Dickson, 1995; Felshin, 1995; Foster, 1996; Rose, 1997

[87] Foster, 1996: 198. At a packed public discussion of The Place We're In, on 22 April 1997, the speakers were the professional artists, myself, and the curators. None of the artists from Southmead was present.

[88] Foster, 1996: 198

[89] Foster, 1996: 198

[90] Foster, 1996: 196

have been produced. Without hiring radio transmitters from a different town, Radio Southmead could not have been broadcast. Without help from an experienced researcher, young people would not have been able to draw up a survey questionnaire and analyse its results. It is the relationship between these coaxers and the people with whom they are working that is crucial. It can go badly wrong. Coaxing can become coaching, which in turn can become coercing. There have been occasions in Southmead when people have felt exploited by the relationship. Each time that happens, the people involved become disillusioned with the very idea of expressing themselves.

An exciting moment in the production of local knowledge is when local people become coaxers themselves. They are the ones who go out and seek stories, and the relationship between outside professional and local person can become inverted. One of the young interviewers on Radio Southmead interviewed a professional community worker. He asked him what he liked least about the area. The reply was that what he disliked was not something just about Southmead, but about 'the world': "I wish people would do more together. People in Britain are not very community minded. If people work together they can solve some of their problems".[91] It is ironic that it is these 'outsiders' who are the great enthusiasts about community, and also, in the examples of the work, and the justifications they themselves give of it, are the most enthusiastic about community expression. The idea of community can be more important for them than for the people they work with, and is something whose worth these 'outsiders' are trying to convince 'insiders' of.

One of the major roles performed by coaxers is assembling the resources by which people can create their stories – money, equipment, exhibition space and so on. It is often possible to raise these resources because of the negative definition of the area that the resulting production is trying to challenge. For example, in the literature setting up the project that led to the exhibition The Place We're In, there is the following statement:

> [Southmead] is an area with a long and well documented history of poverty and social stress. Recently there has been considerable concern in the area about joy riding, vandalism, drug use and destructive behaviour by young people.[92]

---

[91] Radio Southmead, 9 August 1994
[92] From the project outline, 1996

Any community art or other form of knowledge creation starts in a relationship with those hegemonic definitions of the area, and this is common experience, as Rose found in Edinburgh.[93] Without that definition, the resources are not made available. Without support from an insurance company, the dramatic pictures in Fresh Evidence by the demonised young people of Southmead would never have been painted.

External perceptions of Southmead profoundly affect the work that is produced from 'within'. One can barely envisage a time when, in Southmead, '*the power to tell a story, or indeed not to tell a story, under the conditions of one's own choosing, is part of the political process*'.[94] Bakhtin wrote that 'every word is directed towards an *answer* and cannot escape the profound influence of the answering word it anticipates'.[95] The community play was particularly directed to trying to change perceptions, although in doing so did not then escape them. But without an answer of some sort, the expression itself is lost, and the powerlessness of the situation is emphasised. Charles Taylor, a communitarian philosopher, writes that 'denied recognition can be a form of oppression'[96], echoing Bakhtin's words that 'for the word (and, consequently, for a human being), there is nothing more terrible than a *lack of response*'.[97] The delight in response can be seen in Fresh Evidence. Knowledge from Southmead is not created from a neutral place and the perceptions of Southmead from outside affect expression by Southmeaders.

In this way, community expression is not a form of pure expression, but one that is affected by the relationships of production and of consumption that surround it. Crook, in writing of the myths surrounding 'everyday life', could also be writing about a simplistic notion of community art:

> Everyday life ... can represent an appealing image of wholeness and integration when compared to the diremptive and incommensurable complexities of modern culture. [There is an] idea that the communicative practices of everyday life retain the potential to heal the wounds of modernity and make it whole.[98]

[93] Rose, 1997: 191 (emphasis in original)
[94] Plummer, 1995: 26 (emphasis in original)
[95] Bakhtin, 1981: 280
[96] Taylor, 1991: 50
[97] Bakhtin, 1986: 127 (emphasis in original)
[98] Crook, 1998: 534–5

Community knowledge is no less complex than other forms of knowledge, and needs to throw off any ideas of being more 'real' than other forms of knowledge: 'Nostalgia for "real" experience feeds off a failure to recognise that human experience is always "mediated"'.[99] At its strongest, as with all social movements, it is 'a symbolic challenge to the dominant codes…. This confrontation signals the possibility of alternative experiences of time, space and interpersonal relationships, which in turn challenge the technological rationality of the system'.[100] At its weakest, it is a reinscription of those codes. What it cannot, does not, do is escape them. It may only be what one writer uses as a description of community in Kirkby, near Liverpool: 'vitality amidst fatalism'.[101] Most of the examples of local expression I have given so far have been publicly organised, in some way or another, but the strongest expression of vitality in Southmead occurs at Christmas, when, around the estate, there are houses ablaze with flashing lights, Santas on sleighs and gaudy crib scenes. This expression is certainly mediated by consumerism, but is no less vital for that. Above all, it is *public*; no tasteful Christmas tree kept just for the people inside the house, but a public display for all.[102]

Conclusion

While there have been exciting artistic productions that have come from Southmead, productions of an aesthetic quality not usually expected of a peripheral housing estate, there are problems with the claim of insider and subjugated knowledges as providing a less distorted view of the world. Participation within a relationship does not guarantee a purer understanding, nor does it necessarily lead to a challenge to the relationship. There can even be an acceptance of the framework of the relationship, with the aim being to invert this framework, not dismantle it. As Foster puts it:

> This work often assumes dominant definitions of the negative and/or deviant even as it moves to revalue them. So, too, it often allows rhetorical reversals of dominant definitions to stand for politics as such.[103]

---

[99] Crook, 1998: 538
[100] Melucci, 1989: 60
[101] Meegan, 1989: 228
[102] In my diary, I note the best sites, to visit again the following year. These are so kitsch as to be beautiful.
[103] Foster, 1996: 178

Thus the dominant definitions of Southmead as a crime-ridden area with problems of image and community permeate most of the insider productions. People who live within the area live within these discourses; discourses, as Parker points out, contain subjects who talk from within them, and who are interpellated by them.[104] They cannot escape them, even if they oppose them. Opposition takes the form of a kind of humanising nationalism. This asserts people not as merely one-dimensional victims, but with skills and creativity of their own, even if the possession of this humanity is only used to stress ordinariness against the pathologisation of the outsider views.

Ironically, this insurrection of Southmead knowledge, its assertion of its importance in the world, can subjugate and silence the diversity that is within the area in the very way it tries to create a *Southmead* voice. By the same process, it ignores the voices of other similar areas, making its woes singular to the one place, laying itself open to the criticism of the parochialism of community, an issue to be discussed further in Chapter Eight. Just as official discourses reify Southmead into being a problem area, so community expression is in danger of reifying it as a quasi-nation.

The major difference between insider and outsider knowledge, however, is the realisation that its producers are operating from within the relationships. These producers are comparable to the narrators of certain epics (my own favourite is the *Mahabharata*), who themselves appear within the text and whose storytelling is part of the action. The producers and performers of community expression exist within the frame of the story and are aware of being within the story, unlike the outsider representations that claim an objectifying distance. How stories and action are intertwined will be discussed further in Chapter Seven, when I will be looking at the importance of narration in community action.

In the examples given in this chapter, community is not being so much described as performed. This performance, though, is never whole and complete – the examples show a variety of voices, with no single, final view. They can be seen as being more about a search for community than its discovery. Raymond Williams describes this process:

> No community, no culture, can ever be fully conscious of itself, ever fully know itself.... A culture, while it is being lived, is always in part unknown, in part unrealized. The

---

[104] Parker, 1992: 9

making of a community is always an exploration, for consciousness cannot precede creation, and there is no formula for unknown experience.[105]

The concrete experience of living in the area provides a different approach to knowledge of the area, but no finished vision, no final word.

---

[105] Williams, 1958: 320

FIVE

The outsider within: crossing worlds

Introduction

Chapters Three and Four have investigated two points of view of Southmead: the view from without, the 'master's' position; and that from within, the 'subordinate' position. These standpoints impose a dualism on knowledge of the area. This chapter involves looking at Southmead from positions that cross between being within and without and question that dualism. The position of black women working as domestics in white households has been described by Collins as 'a curious outsider-within stance, a peculiar marginality'.[1] I have translated this idea to describe my own situation, the very different and more privileged position of public servant working in Southmead.

The idea of *stand*points as distinct and separate is difficult to sustain. The knowledges from outside have strong, almost solid themes, but their pathologisation of Southmead can be better described as a *force*, in the way they affect Southmead, than as an immobile *stand*. The relationship of those knowledges to Southmead is more complex than one of distortion, a relationship that would imply the existence of an undistorted, independent reality; these knowledges are in themselves a major part of the creation of the 'reality' of Southmead. The effect of power, as Foucault points out, is not to distort objects (such as Southmead), but to produce them, and the truths by which they are judged, a far more active relationship: 'Power produces; it produces reality; it produces domains of objects and rituals of truth'.[2]

The inside knowledges, in their complex, fragmentary and fluid way, are profoundly affected by their relationship with this created reality, a relationship they cannot escape. The two sets of knowledges are not autonomous *stands*, but exist in an interlinked relationship; any idea of Southmead as a bounded entity with an inside and an outside is constructed through powerful forces of social thought accepted by both

---

[1] Collins, 1990: 11
[2] Foucault, 1977a: 194

standpoints, even as they differ on the contents. Outside viewpoints create Southmead as object rather than subject; insider viewpoints assert humanity and existence as subjects. Ideas of Southmead as a unitary object are confounded by the disputes that these arouse. Anthony Cohen describes this process thus: 'The boundary as the community's public face is symbolically simple; but, as an object of internal discourse it is symbolically complex'.[3]

The ideas of inside/outside depend on the notion of a boundary, a skin, separating two sides: Southmead from the rest. This idea of boundary, central to Cohen as part of the 'symbolic construction of community'[4] makes Zygmunt Bauman cynical about the existence of community. There are, he says, no border guards, and 'the very idea of community borders ... becomes ever so difficult, nay impossible, to uphold'.[5] Community is, in his view, more a contentious *postulate* than a fact of life. Cohen's view, however, is that boundaries are not as solid and determined as borders, but are 'constituted by people in interaction'.[6]

In this chapter, I look at Southmead from a more fluid perspective, moving in and out and around, in order to investigate these ideas of boundary, entity and relationship. If there is an 'in' and an 'out', where and how do they meet? This involves looking at relationships that operate over space. To do this, I use *movement* rather than stationary position as a basis for knowledge. This approach still questions the possibility of the objectivity of knowledge, and holds that knowledge comes from movement through space and time, not from stationary location. This challenges the synchronic depictions of Southmead that become frozen into maps and tables, and the assertion of the unchanging nature of Southmead as a separate entity.

Various geographers use the idea of moving within place as an alternative to mapping. Pile and Thrift propose 'wayfinding', finding one's way around, as opposed to seeing the world as if from an aeroplane above.[7] De Certeau writes about 'walking in the city', rather than seeing it from the top of a skyscraper, which is, like a voyeur, 'to be lifted out of the city's grasp'.[8] By contrast, the walker in the city enunciates 'a *here* and a *there* ... establishing a conjunctive and disjunctive

---

[3] Cohen, 1985: 74
[4] The title of Cohen's (1985) book.
[5] Bauman, 1993: 44
[6] Cohen, 1985: 13
[7] Pile and Thrift, 1995: 1
[8] de Certeau, 1984: 92

articulation of places'.[9] But although while walking and wayfinding the observer moves among the observed, challenging what Habermas calls 'the objectivist fallacy according to which we could take up the extramundane standpoint of a subject removed from the world'[10], this does not absolve them from questions about their own gaze. There are problems with extolling movement in itself as an approach; it can become either the fashionable gesture of the leisurely *flâneur* strolling around Baudelaire's Paris, 'let the many attend to their daily lives; the man of leisure can indulge in the perambulations of the *flâneur*'[11], or lead to the exploitations of the explorer discussed in Chapter Two. Whether these dangers can be overcome through involvement and reflexivity will be discussed later in the chapter.

In a collection of short stories, the Italian writer, Italo Calvino, uses a quasi-mathematical approach to work out the moving relationship between observer and object. This emphasises the dynamic relationship between the viewing subject and viewed object. Calvino describes the slide from objectivity to subjectivity in describing a relationship:

> When I use the word 'objectively' it's a figure of speech, as it always is when you start out saying you're objective and then with one thing and another you end up being subjective, and so this business I want to tell you about is difficult because it keeps slipping into the subjective.[12]

An account of a day I had walking and cycling in and around Southmead is reproduced below, in which I consciously 'slip into the subjective'.[13] *Place* and *relationships* are the theme. The day in question was a particularly busy and stimulating one, which is why, at the time, I felt moved to write this account. Although it was a unique day, none of the events within it was unusual; they were exceptional only in their concentration into such a short period. The account throws up a number of questions that will then be discussed, about the nature of this thing called Southmead, and how people, not just myself, relate to 'it'. This is where I make my entry into the story, where my involvement and role will be made clearer.

---

[9] de Certeau, 1984: 99 (emphasis in original)

[10] Habermas, 1992: 139

[11] Benjamin, 1969: 172

[12] Calvino, 1993: 60-1

[13] I have given, in Chapters Two and Three, examples of when so-called objective accounts unconsciously slip into the subjective.

A day crossing between worlds[14]

8 April 1997 was sunny and hot, part of an early heatwave. The General Election campaign was under way, though scarcely noticeable until I watched television in the evening. During the day I criss-crossed to and from Southmead, moving between a number of different settings and different groups of people that felt, strangely for me as I travelled between them and had a part in each of them, as if they existed separately from each other, scarcely connected, despite the geographical distance between them being less than five miles, in the same city. Each setting had its own genre of language, behaviour and relationships, particularly noticeable to me as my purpose throughout the day was to try to make connections, to relate these settings and people to each other.

9 a.m. B

B was walking along the pavement as I cycled through Southmead, and greeted me, so I stopped to walk along with him. He is 15 or 16, and I have known him, as both wild and troublesome, generous and inventive, over the past four years. Some local residents see him as a total scourge and blight on their lives, but I have also experienced his enthusiasm when he has the opportunity to be creative, and his generosity to his friends. For some months he has been on bail, for a large number of offences going back over the last two years (car crime, burglary, assaulting police officers – about 25 charges), waiting for sentencing by the Crown Court because of the seriousness and number of the charges. His bail conditions include a curfew – 7 pm every weekday, 2 pm at weekends – and certain times when he has to sign in at the police station. Because of his curfew I don't see him often.

I asked him whether he didn't get really bored being on curfew (he said, non-committally, "S'alright"), and how much longer this was going to last. He reckoned on about another five months before he was sentenced. This period on curfew will not count against his sentence. Until he knows his sentence he can't really get on with life, there is nothing he can do to change the way he lives while he waits.

This short encounter with B left me with two feelings: of the frustration one gets when confronted by an injustice that one can do nothing about; and of the gaping difference between our lives.

9.15 a.m.-12.15 p.m. The youth centre

The youth centre office is my space. I work through correspondence, phone calls, petty cash records – nothing spectacular, just keeping the place going. I write a memo complaining about the lack of support given to me in running the place, particularly the length of time it takes to get building repairs done. The burnt-out car outside has not been moved, though it's been there over a week. Maybe

---

[14] This is a complete version of the account as I wrote it down over the week following the day in question. The only editing has been to disguise names.

this sets up my thinking about different worlds, as I have to work in a place that is not being cared for by those with the means, but who are at a distance. They do not experience at first-hand the growing dereliction, and the difficult and at times dangerous relationships this is caused by and causes.

The weekly group for children excluded from school is taking place. There are three of them present. The atmosphere is cheerful, despite the broken chairs and graffitied walls. They ask me if I want some of the burgers they are cooking for lunch, but I tell them I am having lunch at the BBC – I get teased for name dropping.

Just before I leave, a member of staff comes in, and seeing me about to go, says: "You be careful out there. It's like a rogues' gallery on the Green."

12.15 p.m. The Green

The Green runs between the main road and what shops there are - most of the first block is shuttered up, still waiting for the re-development that has been talked about and promised for the past five years.

On the surface, the scene is peaceful. Quite a number of people enjoying the beautiful sunshine. But scattered around are a number of men, from 20-year-olds to 40-year-olds, with the pinched and haunted faces of heroin users. For these all to be in the same place at the same time has a meaning. There is an air of concentrated expectancy. Supplies must be on their way, and nothing else is important to them – the presence of anything else is, as I am, an irrelevance.

12.20-12.50 p.m. The ride

The journey to the BBC is pleasant. I can cut through the woods by the stream, full of spring sunshine, and then I am into prosperous Bristol – I cycle past comfortable-looking houses, shops selling luxuries, banks, restaurants.

12.50-3.15 p.m. The BBC

The meeting I am attending is about involving young people in radio. First we meet in the canteen for lunch – clean, undamaged furniture, good, cheap food, relaxed atmosphere. We catch up on gossip. A world away from the tension of the Green. People look good, are well-dressed, polite. Speech is different in accent and form from that in Southmead – quieter, smoother, with less humour, irony, and anger.

We move to a meeting room, talk about the work of the youth radio producer, whose job is to create access to the radio for young people. The plan is to make a series of short radio plays written and performed by young people. The problem of money is discussed – we have to find money to work with the young people, but discover that we will also have to pay any costs of recording the plays, including engineers' time, even though we will be providing the BBC with broadcast material.

Young people can express themselves on radio so long as this is paid for. Access to have their voice heard, which is generally thought to be a 'good thing' depends on cash — in the case of this project, whether this cash can be raised from charities.

One world excludes the other. The more powerful one excludes with ease, at a committee meeting, politely, with no discernible violence done, with no contact between the opposing parties, nor even a realisation of opposition. No young people know of the meeting, no deliberate decision has been made to exclude them. It is just a fact of life.

3.30-5.15 p.m. The Watershed

Next stop was the Watershed, to see how the exhibition 'The Place We're In' is progressing. It is to open to the public in three days' time.

Most of the visual panels are up. Instead of bringing a different reality into the gallery, the reality that they are claiming to represent seems to me to become estranged in the gallery setting. That reality is other to the gallery itself, incompletely translatable into the genre of communication of the gallery. This is still a gallery, will never be a Southmead. The photos might upset or anger or excite people, but they themselves are inanimate, do not answer back or threaten. People who would not dream of visiting Southmead or envisage talking to the people in the photographs can stare at them uninterruptedly. They become aesthetic objects, full of the joy of colour and form, with their social context lost.

There was an urgent message for me to phone the University of the West of England about our material for the Bristol Digital City website. The representative there was concerned that it was controversial, and might have legal ramifications (was this last a smokescreen?), so might not be accepted at the editorial meeting later in the week. The website was intended, she explained, to give voice to the community, not to be controversial — as if these two functions are incompatible. I said that they would have to take all the material or none — we would not cut at their behest. I emphasised our credentials — that legal advice had been sought, that I work for the city council, that we had been extremely responsible. The argument about those without a voice having a right to have one seemed irrelevant, and the Internet lost its gloss of being a libertarian dream of free information. The site is controlled by Hewlett Packard, and it was up to that (large multinational) company to give approval for Southmead to have a place on the Internet!

I also gave an interview to the local paper. The journalist asked me if the exhibition was controversial. After my previous conversation, my reply was that it was 'thought provoking'. Again, I felt I had to be very careful to say what was acceptable in print, which was different to what may be acceptable as thought and language in Southmead.

Simon and Hannah, the artists, and I spend time listening to tapes of young people talking, to see how this material is best represented in the exhibition. The voices on the tapes seem distant, and insufficient in the gallery environment, curiously exposed and vulnerable, despite (or because of) their rough talk. What they are saying makes little sense when heard this way in this place, makes the logic of what they are saying, which is understood in Southmead, appear weak and untenable. We decide to split the interviews up into fragments, tasters of talk, to emphasise their incompleteness.

We then experiment with the security camera. I still have problems explaining to the others my intention, of making those looking at the photographs aware of themselves as surveying Southmead from a safe social and geographical distance, bringing out Southmead as subject, not mere object, which also looks back at them. However, some of the photos are strong enough to do that themselves, I hope.

Speech at the Watershed is similar to that at the BBC – no taking the piss, more wordy, a lot of use of the telephone. My speech too alters – and people notice if I talk in a way inappropriate to the particular place and moment. I hear myself talking differently than in my conversation with B.

6.15-7.15 p.m. The street, the club

That evening I return to Southmead. I am looking for young people who will talk to the local newspaper about the work at the Watershed when they ring up for an interview the next evening. I'm lucky – I meet the people I want out in the street. Other young people ask me for the postcard which goes with the exhibition, which is in great demand.

C is there – he comes into the club with me to look at the composite panel from the exhibition that is going to go into the library. Girl's Club is starting. Girls come in, L, the worker, wants to talk with some of them about their behaviour when they help with the Little Spacers Club for under-10s, and the abuse of the power that they accumulate through this help. The discussion is forthright, with real issues of power being aired, so good youth work, but C and I need to leave – we are the wrong gender. Power is an issue within place as well as imposed from outside.

7.15 p.m. The deal

Immediately outside the door of the building there is a group of some 10 or a dozen people, late teens/early twenties, some of whom I know, looking very agitated. I overhear the word 'police'. They are looking all ways, checking the roads on each side of the site.

They look unhealthy, anxious and are completely absorbed in their own activity.

We have walked into a heroin drop that has been disturbed by the sighting of a police car. No-one within the building is aware of it, though only separated by a door. That close.

C and I walk on and are soon back in the atmosphere of it being a lovely spring evening, on our way to the meeting of the Voice of Southmead. C tells me how he is losing his friends to heroin.

7.30-8.30 p.m. The meeting

The meeting is in the Southmead Rugby Club clubhouse. It is only meant to be a small meeting, to arrange a mass leafleting of houses over the next fortnight, but still there are 25 people there. There is some talk with the plainclothes policemen who now attend. The Voice of Southmead is a group determined to get drug dealers out of Southmead.

The meeting is informal – the bar is open, people get drinks, many are smoking. P however is a businesslike chair/leader, and has his proposals for action ready. No minutes or ceremony, plenty of swearing, but decisions and results. The room is covered with its own cultural artefacts – rugby cups, strips, club honours board, shield and so on.

The leafleting, to publicise the public meeting planned for 2 May, is to be carried out in large groups, to show strength. Sixty will start in a street where they know there are dealers, and then they will split up into groups of 15. One woman offers to do her street, but is told: "No disrespect to you, but we want all us blokes to be seen, to show them our strength".

There is talk about the street deals that are going on. P thinks it is because dealers are no longer able to deal from houses, so instead heroin is brought in by car. This is much more public, and should be easier for the police to stop. It is strange sitting in this meeting, only some 300 yards and 10 minutes away from the deal, still in Southmead, in such a different atmosphere.

There is discussion as to the difference between users and dealers. One man thinks that "they are all pricks", but the line of the group is clear – it is the dealers they are after. The users are victims. There is also talk about other things they can do in Southmead, after the public meeting, such as talk about helping the Southmead Project (which provides a drug education and counselling service) and the youth centre.

The group is described as a 'community action group' by the police, in a statement handed round. That is a shorthand description of a complicated process.

All white – like the BBC, Watershed. More male though than those places, with an emphasis on using this masculine strength to get results.

There are questions directed at me as to why I have brought C – his brother is a dealer. I tell them of the work C does with young people at the youth centre as a volunteer. I'm not sure if I convince them, and even I carry a faint question mark in my head about him. I tell C about their concern – but he knows all their past records too.

As in all the places I have been today, I am myself accepted without formality. I am not a stranger even if I am a slight outsider. Maybe it is rare to be in a group in which one is a full insider. My name here, as throughout Southmead, is either Jer or Jerry, as if I am a different person from the Jeremy of the BBC and Watershed.

8.45-9.45 p.m. The club

Two members of staff have left early, upset by the behaviour of the girls, so L is on her own. The girls are being rough, abusive.

A group of girls, most of whom I think are taking heroin, are plotting to get J, "that nasty little heroin dealer". Though he's only 16, his name had been mentioned at the earlier meeting. There is a lot of passion and energy around.

It's hot and sweaty. I'm glad when I can go.

10.30 p.m. Home, television

It's difficult to relax after such a day. I turn on Newsnight to see how the election is going. Tonight's programme is about inequality. Some bishops have just issued a report, and one of them is talking about it. There are clips of film of people talking about their poverty, and there is a selection of poor people in the studio: pensioner, single parent, unemployed. Also a millionaire, and three party spokespeople who have little to say about inequality, seem to want to hide what I have been seeing all day, seem to be in yet another world without nastiness.

An introduction to analysis

This account, like all accounts of Southmead, should be placed in the quotation marks of discourse analysis, hard for me as its author. To some extent, I leave it unanalysed, as a statement of context against which my analysis of other texts can be understood.

It is a very limited account, narrated from a particular viewpoint. The act of movement does not remove the prism of ideas through which this account has been written. There are familiar themes within it, concerning language, representation and power, which arise from my own interested view. Within the account it can be seen that there are people with other viewpoints, emphasising that this is a partial account. The questions it raises will recur in further chapters, as it contains within it questions central to the thesis: how to participate in and represent Southmead, and what sort of phenomenon is it that is being participated in and represented.

The themes I want to look at are: time, space and identity; places as multifaceted and divided; issues of outsider-within knowledge and reflexivity. I will start, however, with an update. The account itself is very precisely placed in a moment of time. This analysis is written two-and-a-half years later, so is looking back, as in all ethnographic accounts, 'from the "events" that occurred and were reported "then", to the reflection and reportage that occurs "now"'.[15]

---

[15] Atkinson, 1990: 83

An update

Three-and-a-half weeks later, the Labour Party won a landslide election victory. National political events affect local politics, and at the Voice of Southmead public meeting on 2 May there were expectations of the new government, with shouts at the newly elected Labour MP of "We elected you, what are you going to fucking do for us?".[16] Certain government policies, such as the New Deal and the minimum wage, affect individuals in Southmead. How, or whether this election, and the change in politics it signalled, affected the campaigning of Voice of Southmead, and the results it achieved, or other issues affecting Southmead, is hard to pinpoint. I suspect that it did, as the MP was present at a later meeting when deals between different agencies were being brokered.[17] Under a Conservative government, would the Voice have received the same response? Would the street heroin deals mentioned in the account still be occurring two years later, or, as has happened, be much reduced, so that public street life in Southmead has changed?

B went to court in the following August. He was given a non-custodial sentence, but has been in trouble with the law since. My own contact with him has reduced; the following year he drove a stolen car into P's sister's car, so has discreetly laid low.

The area around the Green was developed later in 1997, with the derelict building demolished and replaced by a supermarket, part of a German-owned chain.[18] The building work was carried out by a Welsh contractor, who had bilingual signs around the site, 'Danger. Perygl', a strange mixture of displaced locality and international business. The new supermarket has led to people coming *to* Southmead to shop, changing the flow of shopping traffic between Southmead and surrounding areas. The development has stopped the land in front of the youth centre being used as a dumping ground for stolen cars, and the youth centre itself was refurbished in 1998, the graffiti cleaned up, the broken chairs replaced, the atmosphere changed.

That was my last meeting at the BBC concerning youth radio. The website material was accepted in entirety. Judging by the exhibition comment book, the taped voices of young people we were agonising

---

[16] Diary notes

[17] Diary notes, 6 June 1997

[18] Please note, this is a different 'Green' from that mentioned in Chapter One, which by this date did not exist.

over as being insufficient were one of the most appreciated parts of the exhibition.

C became a fully trusted member of staff at the youth centre, and works closely alongside some of those who were at that time questioning his position. The political changes that Voice of Southmead was campaigning to bring about changed personal relationships between people within Southmead. One of the dimensions of collective action noted by Melucci is the relationship changes it brings about, with people 'making emotional investments which enable individuals to recognize themselves in each other'.[19] This is one example of that sort of shift; there were plenty of others.

The evening meeting was just one episode in the history of Voice of Southmead, a group aiming to change Southmead as a place by stopping the import of heroin. The account shows that there must have been a 'before', and that there was going to be an 'after'; the Voice was not a static phenomenon that could be encapsulated in that one meeting. By explicitly pinpointing time, that changes occur can be seen, if not the process of change itself. The account and its update show that there has been some alteration. Thinking that 'things never change' is a political fatalism from which poor areas suffer. It is the possibility of creating change that provides the optimism that fires collective action and community politics, as we shall see in Chapter Seven.

Moving through time, space, identity

One of the criticisms of creating taxonomies of place by which they can be compared (a problem that has long dogged community studies) has identified that places follow different trajectories through time.[20] History makes comparison difficult, one of the exasperations expressed by those looking for scientific objectivity in such studies. [21] Nor is the history of an area one simple strand. In the examples above, we can see examples of political history, personal history, economic history and collective history, all bearing some relationship to Southmead. It is difficult to know the significance of the events mentioned in terms of long-term economic, social, cultural or political changes. The presence of the German supermarket can be seen as tying Southmead into international capitalism, or enhancing the local standard of life by providing cheap food, or both. As Sharon Zukin argues, the more

---

[19] Melucci, 1989: 35
[20] Warde, 1985: 75
[21] Bell and Newby, 1971

places seek their own economic strength, the more they lose their autonomy to market forces. Using her descriptions, that small part of Southmead had changed from being a landscape of devastation to becoming a landscape of consumption, not due to local forces, but to the maelstrom of capitalism.[22] Capitalism changes place, place does not change capitalism: the new store came not only with its logo, but was built so as to be absolutely identical to all the other stores in the same chain.

I am not the only person who moves in and out of Southmead through time, both on a daily and a long-term basis. Movement is part of the relationship – whether it is visiting the dole[23], going to work or going shopping. Bauman's view of the lack of community borders applies to Southmead; it has no absolute border.

In an attempt to identify the borders and centre of Southmead, a few weeks before my written account I photographed my journey into the area, to its middle and out again. In those photographs, the 'border' can be seen only as a suburban crossroads, not as a frontier, the 'centre' as a featureless collection of shops, the Green a flat expanse without any drama, my meeting place with B a scruffy pavement. However, it is wrong to infer from that lack of physical boundary and distinguishing features that Southmead has no political or emotional boundaries; in my account, these could be seen in operation at the BBC and the Watershed, some miles away from the physical line that delineates Southmead on a map.

People, in their historical and spatial movement, relate strongly to the *meaning* of place: a *here* and *there*, a *now* and *then*. I have previously mentioned the immigration story of my friend from Barbados, and he is not the only person who has migrated to Southmead from another place. Migration is, of course, a major experience of the 20th century, not to be forgotten when looking at place. As well as those who have moved to Southmead, there are those who have moved from Southmead, through either willing or enforced migration. To add to my own account, here are two different accounts of the relationship between place, history, movement and identity that involve Southmead.

I had a visit from S. He was 31, and about to start his final year as a mature student at university. Here is a brief account of our conversation.

He said that up to the age of 20 Southmead was his identity – and that this was really strong. In fact, he did not know other people than those from

---

[22] Zukin, 1991

[23] See Chapter Three

Southmead. He laughed about his first meeting with people with Yorkshire accents. He met other people through smoking vast amounts of dope (though he added that he had stopped smoking anything 'five years ago last Sunday').

He said that for himself and his sister Southmead was like a skeleton in their past. He talks about it in his new life, telling stories about it. And he is not certain as to what he is now, except that he wants to be different from then.

He also told me that for about 18 months he had been heavily involved in crime, when he was around 16 – I had not known that at the time. He said how powerful it made him feel, just taking what he otherwise could not have, and how some people (he mentioned R) were like heroes.[24]

S's was a voluntary departure, to lead a life he could not live in Southmead. T, an Iranian, was driven out by racial harassment. He was still living in Southmead when we talked.

T has been living in Southmead about seven months. He told the story about coming home and wondering why there was a police car outside his house – he found that it had been rammed by a joyrider.

T said the problem was kids. They have been harassing him and his family. He is more worried about them than for himself, as he feels he can cope, as a man. His own children are OK at school, but it is different in the street. Kids shout 'Paki' at him – so he caught one and asked him what that meant. T told him he was not from Pakistan, but did not tell him where he was from, because that would give him a handle to abuse him.

We talked about him being sent on a high-status scholarship from Iran, then finding himself castigated as low on an English housing estate.[25]

A month later I was told by a local housing officer that he and his family had left. She said that this was the worst case of harassment that she had ever seen, involving 18- to 20-year-old assailants.[26] T and his family were victims of what Phil Cohen calls the 'rough and ready rituals' of territoriality articulated through racism.[27]

---

[24] Diary notes, September 1996. The following month I received a letter from another 'escapee' to university: "I finally made it" Incidentally, I had met R, who had remained in Southmead, the previous month. His greeting (friendly in tone, despite the words) was: "Hello you bastard. I bet you never fucking thought I would survive" (diary note).

[25] Diary notes, October 1994. Unfortunately, I did not take notes at the time. I had not expected this conversation, which took place in a pub. T told his story hesitantly, first testing me out when he knew I had a Southmead connection, but then talking more as I 'coaxed' and listened. As well as racial harassment, I have also witnessed harassment on grounds of sexuality (see Chapter Six).

[26] Diary notes, November 1994

[27] Cohen, 1988: 32

S was quite clear, despite his moving away, how much Southmead had affected his identity, and how moving away had changed him. Similarly, T's identity in Southmead was very different from his identity in Iran. In my own account, I show how my identity was different in different places, mostly through changes in language, which was the most noticeable contrast as I moved around, a demonstration of Bakhtin's idea of the almost physical boundaries that exist between languages, boundaries that are negotiated every day.[28] I talked differently in each of the different language communities that I took part in. I had a different name in different places. Change in place either permits or enforces change in identity.

Part of the received 'common sense' of those who work with young people is that they change if you take them out of their area. A social worker told a group of us planning to take young people on camp of his experience: "When you meet them on the street, they say 'fuck off'. But when they are away from Southmead, they are as good as gold." He told the rest of us about particular camps, when young people were dependent on the adults, rather than the other way around, as when they are in Southmead, and how this led to the formation of good relationships.[29] Underlying this was the stated belief that the 'real' person is discoverable when free from the bonds of place.

How much people change in different places was brought home to me when I met V Christmas shopping. In Southmead he is large, boisterous, charismatic, male: a nuisance, but alive. In the shopping centre:

V seemed really tense. "What are you doing here, Jerry?" "Buying Christmas presents." "So am I. It does my head in." All his bounce was gone – it was sad to see him so overwhelmed, out of place.[30]

His identity, so powerful in Southmead, was lost in this different place.

Pile and Thrift welcome, but question, the idea of identity being based on movement rather than place. The advantages are that:

> The ethnic absolutism of 'root' metaphors, fixed in place, is replaced by mobile 'route' metaphors which can lay down a challenge to the fixed identities of 'cultural insiderism'.[31]

---

[28] Bakhtin, 1981: 364, as quoted in Chapter Two

[29] Diary notes, July 1995

[30] Diary notes, December 1993

[31] Pile and Thrift, 1995: 10

However, redefining all identity as mobile 'by those for whom movement and mobility are unproblematic' ignores 'what is still a landscape of constraint for most people'.[32] T's movement across continents can feel threatening to those who are unsure of themselves when they go to the town centre because of the borders imposed on them.

People move in and out of Southmead. They can move out in order to change, as S did, or be chased out because of their unacceptability to a 'roots'-based identity, as with T. They can become more dependent on their social worker away from Southmead (a strange objective), or lose their strength, as with V. They move in and stay, finding a home that suits them. In all these examples, movement is not separate from place as an ingredient of identity, but is strongly related to it as departure point, destination or temporary stopping place. The experience of place may be liminal, people's lives may be lived in a zone that is 'betwixt and between'[33] and not fixed as landscapes themselves shift, but place itself still has a magnetism that, as with S, who has taken a route away, does not leave them alone, but fills them with stories. Without places, there are no reference points to be betwixt and between.

Place as multifaceted and divided

To see place as the starting, stopping off or finishing point of journeys gives the impression of it as a unity, a point. However, in my account there were very different, even incommensurable, activities taking place in close proximity, with only the thickness of a door between them. Southmead on that day was *both* a place of heroin deals *and* a centre of anti-heroin activity. It was the scene of gender conflict. It was full of controversy, not a cosy community with an easy message to put on a website. It did not even approximate to this definition given of community:

> Community *is an interlocking pattern of just human relationships in which people have at least a minimal sense of consensus within a definable territory. People within a community actively participate and cooperate with others to create their own self-worth, a sense of caring about others, and a feeling for the spirit of connectedness.*[34]

---

[32] Pile and Thrift, 1995: 24
[33] Zukin, 1991: 28
[34] Freie, 1998: 23 (emphasis in original)

In contrast to this uniting idea of community, de Certeau writes about all the 'micro-stories' of place that mean it is 'finally *polyvalent*'.[35] Rob Shields, in his exploration of the alternative geographies of modernity, is polygamous in his use of 'poly' words to describe place: place is polysemous, polyvocal.[36] It is the ability of place to have several different meanings and activities at once, while still maintaining a guise of being a unity, of being a *here*, that creates the difficult question of how it is to be understood. It eludes singular definition, which is part of its infuriation for those who wish to deal with defined objects.[37] One writer, recognising the multivocality of housing estates, distastefully called them 'a little explored morass of social worlds and processes that lend themselves to a great array of contrasting descriptions'.[38]

This is not, of course, an issue just for Southmead. Touraine writes that 'The most general problem of sociological analysis is to understand how a society can be both one and divided at the same time'.[39] Maffesoli, writing in his turn about the 'polyculturalism' of social life, enlists the idea of *unicity* in place of 'the dream of unity'[40]: 'While unity describes a closed condition, the medieval notion of *unicity* summons up a more open and heterogeneous situation'.[41] For Anthony Cohen, the 'multiplexity' of community is held together by symbols: a '*range* of meanings can be glossed over in a commonly accepted symbol'.[42] These symbols are malleable enough to encompass ambiguity, with each person able to give their own meaning to them.

So versatile are symbols they can often be bent into idiosyncratic shapes of meaning without such distortions becoming visible to other people who use the same symbol at the same time.[43]

Southmead itself is a place-symbol to which is attached a wealth of meanings, marking it off as different from other place-symbols. There is a cultural and symbolic delineation of places, with cultural differences – of looks, dress, speech and comportment – as the major markers of division between them: 'Culture is ... a powerful means of controlling cities ... it symbolizes "who belongs" in specific places'.[44] This

---

[35] de Certeau, 1984: 125

[36] Shields, 1991: 23, 25

[37] For example, Charsley, 1986; Duncan, 1989 (whose title is 'What is locality?').

[38] Rock, 1988: 108

[39] Touraine, 1988: 53

[40] Maffesoli, 1996: 105

[41] Maffesoli, 1991: 12

[42] Cohen, 1985: 15

[43] Cohen, 1985: 18

[44] Zukin, 1995: 1

delineation is created from outside as well as by collective self-definition from inside – as much ghettoisation as community consciousness.

Insider-outsider knowledge and reflexivity

Collins argues that 'an outsider within stance functions to create a new angle of vision on the process of suppression'.[45] In the course of one day, there is only so much active suppression taking place; in fact, most of what could be seen as oppressive, in regard to the BBC and the website, was passive, based on years of embedded practice. However, if I had not been there, I would not have known about it. I was the outsider within in those relationships, as well as in my relationship with Southmead. By being 'within', I was a witness: 'All ethnology presupposes the existence of a direct witness to a present actuality'.[46] This presumes a greater knowledge than that of being a casual observer of the *flâneur* variety: 'the casual observer will be quite unable to pierce the veil of ignorance'.[47] As casual observer, for example, I would not have known the signs of a heroin drop, nor cared about the website. Being part insider meant that I could converse with S and T, as we had enough common knowledge and trust for those conversations to take place.

Insider knowledge also means that there are places in Southmead I do *not* go, which I keep outside of, as shown by these notes about a detached youth work session I was working on with F.

F and I decided not to go into the pub where we would have found young people we should be in contact with. This despite F being born and brought up in the area. We ourselves would have felt uncomfortable, as well as the people in there. We would not have been going in for the simple and explainable purpose of having a drink, so the people inside would have tensed up and behaved differently. ... A naïve observer going into the pub would not be able to even tell the change in atmosphere, as this must be based on some kind of prior knowledge.[48]

It is knowledge that prevents me even attempting to enter certain 'insider' places, and makes me aware that not all boundaries are breachable.

The strain of being an outsider within is one of the daily issues of being a youth worker. This strain pulls in several directions. For example,

---

[45] Collins, 1990: 11-2
[46] Augé, 1995: 8
[47] Atkinson, 1990: 92
[48] Diary notes, 9 October 1996

in my dealings concerning the website, I was representing Southmead, and I expressed work at an outpost of a large organisation; within the organisation, my interests are equated with Southmead, while within Southmead I am a representative of the organisation.

A common answer to dealing with such problems is the necessity for reflexivity, being aware of one's situation, both as a researcher and a participant. By being reflexive, one is able to show where knowledge is coming from. Hertz describes reflexivity being accomplished through 'constant (and intensive) scrutiny of "what I know" and "how I know it"', and provides 'statements that provide insight on the workings of the social world *and* insight on how that knowledge came into existence'.[49] This small claim however, becomes a major claim as she argues that reflexive knowledge produces 'less distorted accounts of the social world'.[50] Being a reflexive outsider within, I suggest, merely provides a different set of distortions with its own set of perspectives.

Foster, in the sharp way that he has, punctures any self-congratulatory feelings one may have for being reflexive: 'The recent *self-critique* of anthropology renders it attractive, for it promises a reflexivity of the ethnographer at the center even as it preserves a romanticism of the other at the margins'.[51] I can *both* agonise about the ambiguities of my involvement *and* tell tales of encounters with the 'other'. The relationship can become one of co-dependency, in which the observer, or participant, becomes fixated and dependent on the relationship itself, and uses the subordinate position of Southmead to feed their own needs. Co-dependency is a term used to describe the friends or relatives of an addict, who end up needing that person's addiction as much as he or she needs the substance or activity to which they are addicted. The definition of a co-dependent person as someone who 'cannot feel self-confident without being devoted to the needs of others'[52] is a warning to those devoted to Southmead. There is often acknowledgement of this among people who work in Southmead. There is a continual 'emancipation/control dialectic' in welfare services.[53] These services would not exist without there being problems to solve. When the crime audit named Southmead as the worst crime hot spot in the city[54], there was as ironic cheer among my colleagues – our jobs were

---

[49] Hertz, 1997: vii–viii
[50] Hertz, 1997: vii–viii
[51] Foster, 1996: 182
[52] Giddens, 1992: 88
[53] Melucci, 1989: 131
[54] Bristol Community Safety Partnership, 1999a

safe! While showing us the relationships we are in, reflexivity does not free us from them.

The greatest enjoyment of being an outsider within several social worlds is the movement across them, the challenges of language and identity that they create, trying to find a place in each of them, the intersubjective challenge that leads us 'to redraft our map of the mind to include the territory of self and other, that space in which we know, discover, and create the world through our connections to it'.[55] The more the connections, the more exciting the territory.

Conclusion

In pursuing knowledge as an outsider within, I am, as part of my *bricolage*, using what is to hand – that is, my own experience, my own self. Valerie Walkerdine writes that:

> It is an impossible task to avoid the place of the subjective in research, and that, instead of making futile efforts to avoid something which cannot be avoided, we should think more carefully about how to utilise our subjectivity as a feature of the research process.[56]

By using myself in this subjectifying way, rather than in an objectifying way, I am laying my claims open to dispute by other subjects; the other too becomes subject. This, however, does not overcome otherness, and we must still, as Jessica Benjamin points out, 'tolerate the inevitable misrecognition that accompanies our efforts at recognition'.[57] By being reflexive, I am to a certain extent making myself a stranger, not quite part of all the situations I was in. This has been highlighted as one of the virtues of ethnographic research: 'Ethnographers ... must strenuously avoid feeling "at home". If and when all sense of being a stranger is lost, one may have allowed the escape of one's critical, analytic perspective'.[58] This otherness of the researcher can become a barrier between myself and those that do feel at home, and a barrier to my understanding of even what it is like to feel at home, that reassurance that is, for Corlett, one basis for community, 'a desire for foundations; a desire to escape

---

[55] Benjamin, 1990: 192-3
[56] Walkerdine, 1997: 59
[57] Benjamin, 1998: 25
[58] Hammersley and Atkinson, 1995: 115

the play of the world and stay at home for the night'[59], except that I was pleased to get home on the night of my account.

By travelling through and in and out of Southmead, I experience both fluidity and boundaries, a sense of Southmead being a *here*, and it being a set of very different *heres* to different people. The knowledge acquired through movement contains an acknowledgement of the formative power of the standpoint knowledges of Southmead, an acknowledgement of their discursive power. A moving epistemology travels around the objects built by power. That power is not directly visible: my photographs could not show its presence. Derrida writes that: "Force itself is never present; it is only a play of differences and quantities'.[60] (This 'play' can, of course, be brutal, as in the expulsion of T.) Instead of force as a total presence, there is a series of threads, each one of which is barely tangible, that weave together as a net, to use Foucault's metaphor: 'Power is employed and exercised through a net-like organisation'.[61] The threads are not just outside Southmead, but run through it, through its own internal relations of power. There is not a centre, a control point, but a web of a 'more-or-less organised, hierarchical, co-ordinated cluster of relations'.[62] In the different accounts we have seen relations of race, gender, education, the legal system, economics, language and so on; in Foucault's term, 'polymorphous techniques of power'.[63] These are elements of a system of relations in a 'thoroughly heterogeneous ensemble', that he calls a *dispositif*, or apparatus.[64] This net, to take the metaphor further, differentiates itself over space, creating knots, recognisable places like Southmead. This does not, as commentators of Foucault point out, remove the problem of analysis of 'what' the *dispositif* is, but is an initial attempt to describe it.[65] In so doing, this idea of *dispositif* nullifies any unitary views of place and community, while providing no easy alternative.

Tracing the threads can be a powerful position for the outsider within. Like a domestic servant knowing more about the cutlery than the master, I possibly know more about the threads and connections that bind Southmead than the residents do. When a documentary was being made about Southmead, I was concerned about how much I was the person providing information to the television crew. I was told by

---

[59] Corlett, 1989: 67

[60] Derrida, 1982: 17

[61] Foucault, 1980: 98

[62] Foucault, 1980: 198

[63] Foucault, 1979: 11

[64] Foucault, 1980: 194

[65] Dreyfus and Rabinow, 1983: 121

---

people from Voice of Southmead that this was fine, that I knew more about the history of the area than they did. In fact, one said that until recently he had not really considered it at all; he had got up and gone to work early in the morning, and returned late in the evening, and had not been concerned with what was going on in the area. However, though the crew used me for background information, they wanted 'authentic' voices with real experiences on screen. They found B (the one featured in my account), who was, they told me, 'the real thing', but could not cross the communication gap between his mumbling and their need for good footage. Not only was my reflexivity cut; so were the more reflective and complex statements by local people. They were expected to be 'real', not reflective; the final programme showed only the emotional and dramatic.[66] Use of movement and reflexivity does not stop depictions of Southmead that construct these powerful fictions of authenticity; they just witness the threads being spun.

In the description of Southmead in this chapter, it is seen as less solid than in the two standpoint representations. The boundaries that create the area are shown as multifarious and powerful, but also fluid and permeable. Time and historical change are shown as elements in the relationships that form the area. The position of the outsider being part of, even within, these relationships is far more explicit, a more problematic and ambiguous position than that of belonging to a distinct and separate standpoint. Standpoints are, however, still powerful; this account does not undermine them. The ability to move across boundaries may be an indication of power that is unfettered by place, but there is a different strength gained by having a place to speak or act from, of being able to take a stand.

---

[66] Diary notes, 1997. The programme was The Big Story, on ITV.

Young people and community: trouble and tribes

Introduction: young people and their relationship to community

We have seen in previous chapters that many of the concerns about poor areas are not about poverty or inequality, but about behaviour. The way people *behave* (or *act* – a word with different connotations) in these areas is bound up with ideas of community or its lack, with criminal behaviour and lack of community action identified as destructive of good community. I want to look more closely at this relationship between behaviour, action and community in Southmead; young people's 'behaviour' and adult's 'action' are the subjects of this and the following chapter.

The behaviour of young people features as a major issue in representations of Southmead. Outside surveys fasten on young people and their behaviour as a principal problem of the area, and the community play portrayed the vexations of young people's conduct as an endemic factor of Southmead life. This focus on young people and their behaviour as a problem to community is wider than Southmead. Saul Alinsky, an evangelist for community organisation from Chicago, first writing in 1946 but influential among community groups years later, wrote of the common example of problems of youth and delinquency as being 'one of the most frequent problems characteristic of the average community council'.[1] His view was that to treat these problems as separate from all the other problems that communities face was a fallacy, merely providing the trimmings of special programmes that do not tackle fundamental issues. He used the visible issues of young people and crime to lead into fundamental questions of community and power; for him, the two are inseparable. Sheila Brown, in her extensive survey of both adults and young people in Middlesbrough, which started out as a study of young people and

---

[1] Alinsky, 1969: 57. When I started work on the thesis behind this book, two community workers told me that I had to read his book, *Reveille for radicals*.

crime, but shifted its focus to the study of age as a social division, found the two issues of young people and community strongly intertwined in people's own accounts:

> Older adult attitudes towards crime and young people, then, may be fairly summarised as one which recognises the gravity of economic decline; which sees unemployment and poverty as contributing to moral decline; which regrets a perceived deterioration of order and community; but which in the end sees young people, not as victims, but rather as perpetrators and as both symptom and cause of the collapse of the moral universe.[2]

She continues by saying that community then becomes defined as containing only the 'middle aged and elderly residents of a locality', constructed as a defence against young people.[3]

That there is a problem of the behaviour of some young people in Southmead cannot be denied. F, a long-time youth worker with a strong commitment to young people in Southmead, told me:

Walking around the estate on Saturday I was so ashamed. The kids were being really horrible. I saw them attack X, and another old woman who used to work in the Post Office. They were throwing bricks at buses, and opening and closing the bus doors. Wherever I went on the estate there were kids behaving badly. They were collecting penny-for-the-guy. When people refused to give them any money, they followed them into the shops and pestered them. I feel that it is getting so bad that it can't get better. I was gutted and ashamed that I knew these kids. With this old lady they were jostling her in the street, and almost hit her.[4]

Describing incidents such as this (one of many[5]) initially raises an anger that mirrors that of the adults that Brown interviewed in Middlesbrough, whose 'punitiveness ... was virtually unrelenting'[6], and an understanding of why, in the United States, according to Myrna Margulies Breitbart, 'urban youth are increasingly defined as "undesirable" occupants of public space'.[7] In community safety discourse, teenagers hanging around is numbered as one of the 'incivilities' of

---

[2] Brown, 1995: 36
[3] Brown, 1995: 47
[4] Diary notes, 31 October 1994
[5] Including the bicycle incident described in Chapter One.
[6] Brown, 1995: 34
[7] Breitbart, 1998: 307

neighbourhoods in decline[8], although this view of young people may be a source of the problem. As Brown puts it: 'Given the negativity of adults' attitudes towards young people's use of the street, it is hardly strange that conflict escalates'.[9] Much of the conflict between adults and young people is about behaviour in public space. In public space, people are expected to behave with sociality, an ingredient within the idea of community.[10] Rob Shields explains sociality as people having 'to get along together'. Sociality is 'an affirmative power that restates the never-ending game of sociability, of solidarity and of reciprocity ... which anchors a sociology of everyday life'.[11] A noticeable facet of Southmead life is the number of young people using the public space of the streets, accounted for by the numbers of young people in the area, and the overcrowding of homes. Their use of the street is not, however, unusual, as is pointed out in a work on the geographies of youth culture: 'Studies on teenagers suggest that the space of the street is often the only autonomous space that young people are able to carve out for themselves'.[12] This attempt at autonomy brings them into conflict with other street users. In Brown's research, in place of a reciprocal sociality between young people and adults, there was a 'perpetual, never ending conflict over space which characterises much of the relationship between the generations in public'.[13]

In all these descriptions of conflict, young people are always mentioned in the plural. There is always more than one of them. The behaviour is collective. As Melucci writes, collective behaviour is 'never a purely irrational phenomenon. It is always to a degree meaningful to its participants, even when it appears to be anomic or marginal behaviour'.[14] I want to use his insight to examine this collective behaviour. The creation of collectivity is an important facet of the idea of community. Together with the idea of public space, it is closely linked to another idea often used as an ingredient of community: that of locality. The collective action and public spaces to be discussed are very localised. In looking at examples of young people's collective actions in Southmead, and their relation to public space and locality, wider issues of community are raised than just that of the behaviour of young people.

---

[8] Hope and Hough, 1988: 35
[9] Brown, 1995: 39
[10] On sociality and community, see Amirou, 1989
[11] Shields, 1992: 106
[12] Valentine et al, 1998: 7
[13] Brown, 1995: 40
[14] Melucci, 1989: 191

The idea people have of children, as distinct from youth, can bring them together in a more positive, if sentimental, manner. There are community events in Southmead, such as the bonfire night party at the adventure playground that ran, while regulations allowed, until 1997, and was attended annually by hundreds of people. At the 1996 party:

> In the crowd were adults and children of all sorts – the local criminals and drug dealers and those who act against or fear them. A community event that hid the divisions and problems, overlaid them with a warm sensation of togetherness for the night. Almost too comfortable. People there who had been going to the same event for years. People brought together by their children.[15]

The event was an example of sociality in practice – a 'community event' involving people otherwise in conflict with each other. Shields suggests that sociality is made possible by wilful suppression of individuality and the adoption of a sociable mask, or *persona*. On that occasion, it was the presence of children that gave the reason for those present 'to adopt a *persona* which allows convivial interaction at a given time and place'.[16] Getting together for the sake of children is a common form of community action, and informs some of the adult actions related in the next chapter.

Youth behaviour may be seen as destructive to community, but nostalgia for past youth is one aspect of community building. In Chapter One, I pointed out how people loved the shared history of a photographic display of themselves when young. In 1993, there had been a much more formal exhibition, called 40 Years of Youth Work in Southmead.[17] This was extremely popular, much more popular in the area than the exhibitions of contemporary work done by young people, and led to more people bringing in their even older photographs, and eventually the compilation of the book *Alive and kicking!*, full of memories of youth.[18] As Stuart Hall has put it, 'organic community

---

[15] Diary notes, November 1996. My emphasis at the time.

[16] Shields, 1992: 107

[17] This exhibition was extensively covered by the media. See, for example, *Bristol Observer*, 26 November 1993, with a photo of a man pointing himself out in a photo taken over 30 years before. These old photographs can be dangerous. When in 1996 cuts to the youth service were being discussed, some of the same pictures were used in the local newspaper to give the idea that youth work was old-fashioned, implying that cuts were modernising (*Bristol Evening Post*, 19 September 1996).

[18] Truman and Brent, 1995

was just always in the childhood you left behind'.[19] Shared memories of youth can be an important ingredient of adult community.

This chapter, however, is about the communal lives created by young people themselves. Before describing these, I want to look briefly at some of the particular problems of researching young people: first, at the relationship of the researcher to *their* voice; and second, at who this 'they' is. So far I have used 'young people' as a rather vague category, with no discussion as to what it means.

Writing with, or about, young people?

I have a strong feeling of writing *about* young people, not writing *with* them. I have fewer narrative accounts from them than from adults, although most of my working life has been with young people. This is part of the wider issue of audiences pointed out by Plummer: 'Youthful stories may not be heard easily in adult worlds'.[20]

In her research, Brown found that young people did not tell adults about the difficulties that they themselves have in public space, even though these were much worse than those experienced by adults.[21] They do not generally speak of these experiences because they feel that they will not be believed. Brown concludes that:

> It is hardly surprising that young people do not 'tell adults' or
> that they feel they 'will get into trouble' or 'not be believed':
> the conflict which exists between adults and young people
> impedes communication between them.[22]

The experience articulated by young people is that there is no sympathetic audience to whom to tell their stories. Responses in the *Young people's survey of Southmead* emphasise the point that young people feel that they are not listened to.[23] Without faith in an audience, stories are not told.

The coaxer is an important ingredient to the telling of stories. In terms of coaxing stories into the adult world, these are usually adults, and have the same barriers of communication to overcome; a coaxer has also to be a listener. This role is problematic; these interview

---

[19] Hall, 1991: 46

[20] Plummer, 1995: 22. See Chapter Four for a fuller discussion of his ideas.

[21] Brown, 1995: 37 has tables showing far higher levels of victimisation of 11- to 15-year-olds by adults than of victimisation of adults by 11- to 15-year-olds.

[22] Brown, 1995: 41

[23] Kimberlee, 1998: 5

transcripts show the coaxer's questions get longer and more desperate as the answers stay short:

> Tell me about yourself. What are you doing with yourself, are you still at school?
>
> *Yeh, I'm still at school.*
>
> What year are you in?
>
> *Eleven.*
>
> So you'll be leaving school this May then?
>
> *Yes.*
>
> And what are you going to do with yourself when you leave?
>
> *God knows.*
>
> You gotta have some really good ambition ... you can't just say 'God knows' – you gotta do something special with your life, what you gonna do?
>
> *Mechanic man.*[24]

This sort of interrogation brings inevitable silences, or lies:

> Tell me what do you think about the [surveillance] cameras out here?
>
> *Load a bollocks.*
>
> Tell me, is it a good thing or a bad thing that they've got out there?
>
> *Fucking stupid.*

---

[24] Transcript of interview recorded in February 1997 by a student youth worker, for The Place We're In exhibition.

Do you think the crime rate's gone down since they had it out there?

*No. *** was revving round Greystoke the other night, weren't you ***?*

In a Nova were you?

(Silence)

Ask me some more questions then.

What about yourself, have you ever been in any stolen cars for a joyride?

No. (Laughter)

You sure you haven't been in the cars joyriding?

No.[25]

The silences are necessary – speech may incriminate. This wariness of self-incrimination may not be because of crime (in fact, once people have been caught, they can be quite open about it, as we shall see in an interview later in the chapter), but because of uncertainty. The lives and events being experienced by young people may well not yet be clear enough to express. They are as yet unformed stories that are being lived, and are not ready to be told. The gusto of involvement that I will chronicle later in the chapter has not yet been reflected on, with engagement being the immediate dynamic, rather than recounting. While as a youth worker I enjoy many conversations with young people, these tend not to be in the form of narrated accounts.

Forming a relationship that leads to storytelling, what Plummer calls 'negotiated networks of collective activity'[26], is a difficult process. Young people are often in different networks from adults – their networks are the way by which they form themselves as *other* to that of adults. These are the networks I am interested in understanding, but by definition from outside, as in the following example. In January 1993, there was a minor epidemic of butane sniffing in Southmead. This is a particularly dangerous activity with a high fatality rate. The

---

[25] Transcript of interview recorded in February 1997 by a student youth worker, for The Place We're In exhibition.
[26] Plummer, 1995: 23

girls involved were sniffing in defiance of adults, leaving us in an impossible position – to actively disapprove would strengthen the groups' defiance, to condone the sniffing would be irresponsible. There was no outsider–within position available from which to work. Direct communication or negotiation on the practice was impossible, made so by the young people who wanted an activity in which adults did not take part, and stories about the high gained from the butane were not told to adults.[27]

Most of my encounters with young people are not so conflictual, but this example shows how any understanding of young people's collective behaviour comes through observation and interpretation, not through shared experience.

Who are young people?

'Youth' as a concept has a long history as a time of beauty and honourable rebellion, but from these noble ideas has been described as having deteriorated in late modernity into a rather negative period of life:

> Youth is ... a period of social semi-dependency which forms a bridge between the total dependency of childhood and the independence of adulthood. Consequently it is largely defined in the negative – by what it is not, rather than by what it is.[28]

Adolescence, a concept that is often elided with that of youth as being neither childhood nor adulthood, has obscure dividing lines, as David Sibley points out:

> The boundary separating child and adult is a decidedly fuzzy one. Adolescence is an ambiguous zone ... adolescents are denied access to the adult world, but they attempt to distance themselves from the world of the child.... Adolescents may be threatening to adults because they transgress the adult/ child boundary and appear discrepant in 'adult' spaces.[29]

This confusion about boundaries creates youth as a 'liminal' position that downgrades the period, suggesting that 'young people do not

---

[27] Diary notes, January 1993. Luckily, the epidemic passed without any deaths.
[28] Furlong and Cartmel, 1997: 41
[29] Sibley, 1995: 34–5

have any value in their own right ... rather they are valued only to the extent to which they are in the process of "becoming" an adult'.[30] In Chapter Five, I discussed the idea of community 'boundaries' and their indeterminacy – young people have another set of fluid boundaries and unclear definitions to negotiate. Not only are these boundaries unclear, they are changing rapidly, so that the experience that young people face is a growing period of dependency, with 'expectations of both the state and adults that the young should undertake certain obligational duties before they become full citizens'.[31]

Definitions of youth by age are vague. Brown uses 11-15. Kimberlee used 11-17, the age range for a particular government programme. The youth service uses 11-25, with 14-17 as the main target group. The adult minimum wage does not apply under 21 and full social security benefits are not available until the age of 25. Defining youth is a problem, including for legislators on issues such as the age of sexual consent. For Melucci, youth is no longer a characteristic of age:

> Youth has ceased to be a biological function and has become a symbolic definition. People are not young simply because of their particular age, but because they assume culturally the youthful characteristics of changeability and temporariness.[32]

Youth is therefore 'a social concept that lacks a physiological base', as Furlong and Cartmel put it.[33] Young people are those who take part in activities that are seen as being youthful, a rather circular definition. This can involve people as young as 10, as old as 25, but within this age range there is great variety of experience. For example, in Southmead there is a difference in the experience of bullying by under- and over-13- year-olds.[34] As a category, youth is often used to mean 'young men', who are blamed for their 'wildness'[35], but what then about young women? I will indicate in my examples the gender of those involved.

There are also important differences of race and class. By the late 1990s, young people in Southmead were predominantly white, although with a significant number of black and mixed-race young people. There were not enough of the latter to form a separate group,

---

[30] Valentine et al, 1998: 5-6
[31] France and Wiles, 1998: 66
[32] Melucci, 1989: 61
[33] Furlong and Cartmel, 1997: 42
[34] Kimberlee and Cassidy, 1999
[35] Coward, 1994

unlike in the early 1980s, when there was a large cohort of black young people living in Southmead with a strong local presence. One of the striking elements shown in the youth centre book *Alive and kicking!* is the racial changes in Southmead over time, from being 99% white in the 1950s, to having a strong black presence in the early 1980s, to becoming 'whiter' after about 1987. My field notes only relate to the 1990s, so although during the early 1980s my work was predominantly with black young people, I have not kept accounts of that period.[36] I have no doubt that if the incidents I describe later in this chapter had involved more black young people, the social and cultural meanings ascribed to them would have been very different. Finally, Southmead young people are representative of the class make-up of Southmead: few from professional or managerial households, most from households headed by manual workers or unemployed people.[37] Youth 'problems' is a term euphemistically used for lower-class youth behaviour.

There is one other distinction often made of young people – the 'good' and the 'bad', or 'disaffected'. These distinctions are far too neat and bear little close examination. Indeed, as Piper and Piper would argue, such distinctions are even 'wicked' in the way that they are used to pathologise.[38] Some of the young people that were involved in a 'good' project, like Radio Southmead, were, in other circumstances, categorised as 'bad'. Several of the boys involved in the bicycle theft described in Chapter One had painted wonderful pictures for Fresh Evidence, as had B from Chapter Five. The argument as to whether young people are *either* bad *or* good is finally a sterile approach to looking at the issues involved in young people living in a 'community', and puts all the onus of good behaviour on to them.

In the face of all the confusion created by attempts at neat categorisation, in the following sections of this chapter I will discuss certain incidents ascribed to young people, taking a 'common sense' definition. This is not because common sense is right, but because it is the perceptions of these incidents that lead to their categorisation. The examples I have chosen are dramatic, but not untypical.

---

[36] Truman and Brent, 1995. Despite the differences in counting, the census figures of 1981 and 1991 indicate a movement of black people away from 35 wards in Bristol into three inner-city wards – a growing racial division of Bristol along geographical lines.

[37] Bristol City Council, 1994: 53

[38] Piper and Piper, 1999

Young people, collective action and neo-tribes

The sight of large numbers of teenagers meeting together and enjoying themselves should be a cause for celebration for all those interested in the welfare of young people, especially when the young people feel 'empowered' enough to organise all their own activities – sitting around campfires, cooking food in the open, chatting, laughing, playing games, all with no adult supervision. However, the headline in one local newspaper was: 'Biker Grove! Beauty spot is ravaged by teen hoodlums'. The story went on:

> Police and park rangers are joining forces to clamp down on teenage motorcyclists who have turned a woodland beauty spot into an off-road race track.
>
> The move follows complaints from residents walking their dogs at Badocks Wood, in Southmead, about noise and dangerous driving....
>
> The area has been plagued by gangs of youths in recent months, who meet up on mopeds and use the wooded slopes and paths as an off-road adventure circuit.[39]

Despite its sensationalism, the newspaper coverage missed the full dramatic importance of the events in Badocks Wood for young people. The newspapers' perspective was only that of the outraged adults, and of the necessity for police action, and in no way reflected young people's perspective of pleasure as that area was taken over and used for a carnival of collective action and transgression (that this transgression was successful was confirmed by the tone of the article). The following description is compiled from my diary entries at the time.

Badocks Wood runs along the valley of the River Trym, here a stream. The plateau to one side of the valley is rough parkland, with long grass and young trees. It is on the borders of Southmead and the wealthier areas of Henleaze and Westbury; as well as being suitable terrain for the activities that took place, being border country maybe gave greater scope for breaking social rules. While during the day it is the province of dog walkers, at night through early spring 1996 large groups of young people congregated there. This area had become the place for them to be.

---

[39] *Bristol Observer*, 4 April 1996

Going around the area in the day (at night I would have been out of time and out of place[40]), I could get a sense of the excitement that the young people must have felt, as well as seeing the destruction caused. It was like a scene after a carnival. I could almost hear the shrieks of delight from the evening before. On a long stretch of grassland one could see the marks of wheels running up and over a dip. The ground in the woods was covered in skid marks from racing around among the trees and slopes. There were the remains of bonfires and food wrappers, and burnt-out wrecks of cars. Branches had been pulled off trees for firewood. There was the dramatic sight of a burnt out Metro on top of the old burial mound.[41] The fence around the mound and the post with its Ancient Monument information had gone, the wood used for fires.

Entry to the area was through a hole in the fence. The hole was small, so only small cars (hence the Metro) were being used. In the course of one week, there were eight wrecks in the area. The motorbikes were taken home at night.

The authorities cleared the area of this activity by a concerted operation; the aftermath of this was extreme anger among young people and antagonism towards the police and all other adults. It was a difficult time for staff at the youth centre, as angry young people moved there and vented their rage. The community police team felt the antagonism – they had a meeting with me to discuss the events, and struck me as being totally frustrated. They saw the issue as a matter of the law, as shown by this piece they put in the community newspaper:

> Once again, as spring approaches, the problem of off-road motorcyclists has re-surfaced in Badocks Wood.... Offences include dangerous riding and riding without due care and attention, for which fines of up to £1,000 can be levied.
>
> This has been an ongoing problem which causes great annoyance and danger to those living in the immediate area, and those who walk there. One youth was arrested recently for theft of a bike. We hope in the coming months to counter this danger to lawful users of the parks.[42]

---

[40] Compare the story in Chapter Five about not going into the pub.
[41] This strange sight was a reminder of the grotesqueness intrinsic in carnival, as pointed out by Bakhtin in *Rabelais and his world*, 1968.
[42] *Southmead Community News*, May 1996

All this illicit activity had resulted in one arrest. The events were virtually unpoliceable, with the collective activity of the young people leaving the police powerless until they used semi-military tactics.

At around the same time, there was a minor collective event that I witnessed directly. One evening young people started to pull up brick paving stones from the courtyard in front of the youth centre. Once one was loose, they could all be pulled up. This turned into a tremendous group effort, pulling up the bricks and loading them into trolleys taken from the local shops, wheeling them up to the side of the youth centre and building a wall from them – a proper wall, with the headers and stretchers of proper brickwork, if no mortar. I was struck by the immense enjoyment this collective activity brought, the creativity of the wall building, the great effort being put into a 'meaningless' activity, for the wall did virtually nothing; in fact, a gap was left at one end for people to walk through. K in particular was working hard and enjoying it – calling for people to help her push the loaded trolley. It did greatly annoy, perhaps because of its meaninglessness, and certainly because of its destructiveness of the yard. It frightened old people, who took another way to walk through. It unsettled the place, and made people unsure whether the path was blocked or not, safe or not.

Both these examples show a challenge to accepted modes of sociality, but also display an alternative, transgressive form of social behaviour. In Chapters Three and Four, I described municipal, orderly ideas of community as something that should fix problems such as crime, and showed how community expression can be the vehicle through which people assert their ordinariness. Neither of these approaches recognises transgression as a basis of community, 'the breaching of boundaries, the pushing of experience to the limits, the challenge to the law', seen by Jeffrey Weeks as a crucial moment in the establishment of community of radical sexual identity[43], and in my examples as a moment in the establishment of youth identity. This transgressive impulse leads groups of young people to embrace and celebrate (and even extend) the negative labelling of the area that respectable community activity is working hard to overturn.[44] This is not a rational, goal-oriented idea of community, but the experience of community described by Jean-Luc Nancy as 'the existence of being-in-common, which gives rise to the existence of being-self.'[45] Transgression and carnival bring people together in a different sort of community play in which there is self-

---

[43] Weeks, 1995: 108
[44] See Charsley, 1986 for a similar process among gangs in Glasgow.
[45] Nancy, 1991: xxxvii

discovery: 'Carnival does not know footlights, in the sense that it does not acknowledge any distinction between actors and spectators'.[46] Bakhtin calls this feeling of carnival 'the second life of the people, who for a time entered the utopian realm of community, freedom, equality and abundance'.[47]

Of course, it was entered only for a short time. These were not sustainable communities. Even without police action, their transgressive moment would have passed, even if reappearing in other guises at other times.[48] These short-lived communal gatherings are described by Maffesoli as 'the efflorescence and effervescence of neo-tribalism ... whose sole *raison d'être* is a preoccupation with the collective present'.[49] They are not stable: 'neo-tribalism is characterized by fluidity, by punctuated gathering and scattering', like a ballet, 'the arabesque of sociality'.[50] The basis of neo-tribalism (Maffesoli and others who use this term ignore any racial/racist connotations) is, for him, sensation, touch, performance, not causality or utilitarianism: 'The communal ethic has the simplest of foundations: warmth, companionship – physical contact with one another'.[51] This is not a description of community as being necessarily good – in fact, Maffesoli uses the phrase 'group egoism'[52] to describe such groups, a description that could fit the bicycle thieves described in Chapter One, whose communal activity was theft. He sees neo-tribes as being aesthetically, not ethically or politically based, although he argues that an ethics may develop from those aesthetics.[53]

The aesthetic aspect is portrayed by Beatrix Campbell, in prose that rises to the event, as she stresses the power of the performance of joyriding in Oxford, bringing together performers and a large audience in an immaculately staged dramatic event.[54] The following description by a joyrider from Southmead, being interviewed for The Place We're In, has a similar aesthetic quality.

---

[46] Bakhtin, 1968: 7

[47] Bakhtin, 1968: 9

[48] I pointed out in Chapter One how different spaces spring up as places where young people congregate. A few months after these events, a crossroads on another side of the estate (also on the boundary) became such an area, for a short while until that, too, was cleared.

[49] Maffesoli, 1996: 75

[50] Maffesoli, 1988: 148

[51] Maffesoli, 1996: 16

[52] Maffesoli, 1996: 92

[53] Maffesoli, 1991, 1996: 75

[54] Campbell, 1993: 254

How do you get into a car?

*You need a good screw driver ... right ... flat head ... make sure
the end bit's nice and thin bit ... fit in the door lock ... put in ...
put in the door lock ... turn in round whatever open the door ...
door open ... climb inside ... put your foot inside the steering wheel,
someone else grabs the other end ... turn it round ... snaps – steering
wheel snaps ... grab the casing from the back of the steering column
... rip it off ... get the ignition barrel head – file it down, put a
screw driver in the back of it, pop the black box off, put something
in the black box that'll fit in it – turn it, start it, drive off.*

What happens next?

*Drive round, drive it round, spin it round, kill it off – burn it
out.*

...

So last night, how many people would you say were on
the street?

Thirty, twenty, thirty.

Do you get a really big rush when you get it together?

*Yeh, sound funny ... watching the cars getting spun round, smoked
whatever.*

How do you manage to get the tyres to smoke?

*Foot down, handbrake up – put your foot down really fast, let the
clutch off fast and it smokes on the spot for ages, or sometimes you
put a brick on the accelerator ... leave it on its own ... just goes
round ... smokes on its own.*[55]

Accounts like these, with their disobedient, errant view of what is
'good', puncture the worthiness of much community rhetoric. They

---

[55] Notes of interview, February 1997. Later, the interviewee tells the interviewer
that he has been charged with about 30 offences. The identity of the interviewee is
anonymous; I do not know myself who he was.

remind us that 'human beings, rather than living for productive values such as balancing their accounts, live for unproductive values, such as the glory in deficit spending'.[56] This spending is forceful enough to depress whole forces of police officers. As Castells describes gang culture, it is 'a culture of the immediate end of life, not of its negation, but of its celebration. Thus, everything has to be tried, felt, experimented, accomplished, before it is too late, since there is no tomorrow'.[57] This collective drive for immediacy is a challenge to any established order.

These examples of collective behaviour have a romantic edge to them – in witnessing them and describing them, there is a sense of strong desire for shared, communal excitement.[58] John Freie says that 'lacking genuine community, yet longing for the meaning and sense of connectedness that it creates – the feeling of community – people become vulnerable to the merest suggestion of community'.[59] Maffesoli's view is that these small groups are created in interplay with the growing massification of society. A major theme of writings on community is that of loss of community as a 'natural' or 'organic' form, a loss that people strive to recover by inventing new community-type relationships within wider social relationships that are not communal at all, but are variously described as global, mass, bureaucratic, centralised, decentred and so on, a theme to be explored further in Chapter Eight.

The desire for connectedness can also be more vicious than this expansive, if destructive, longing. Forms of collective organisation are concerned with inclusion, exclusion and control, as in this account of control in a girl gang:

> *E came to club, asked for Y, told her about party. Y said she wasn't going. Later a group of girls came up, all done up, hair especially, carrying cans of lager and cider. E and E (12), L and R (15), J (16). Called Y out. Went around side of building, then J dragging Y by hair to front of building, where all could see – punching her, kicking her, banging her head against railing. I went over, stopped fight. Y kept asking for J to stop. Y went off, cut under left eye. Blokes*

---

[56] Corlett, 1989: 193. He is referring to the ideas of Georges Bataille.

[57] Castells, 1997: 64

[58] This despite the terror that joyriding causes. My diary entry for 20 April 1994 states how pleased I was to get out of the area that night, because of the presence of a performing car. The group of adults that was watching seemed beaten down by the activity, which was making their landscape even bleaker.

[59] Freie, 1998: 2

standing round took no part in it — not even to stop it when it became unfair. Consensus — J showing her power — do not leave my group, do what I want you to do — was the message. People predict that Y will toe the line.[60]

My very strong impression was of the establishment of an alternative power structure, maintaining itself very deliberately in public in the rawest possible way.

Here is an example of forceful public exclusion. In July 1996, the Hs, a family living down the road from the youth centre, were driven out by young people. On the evening it happened, there was a whole crowd in front of the house, hurling missiles and attacking the police even as they escorted the family away. I was told ferociously by young people to keep away, that 'this is the way we do things'. There was a strange sense of righteousness about this riot, despite its viciousness. Several were arrested.[61] A few weeks later, in a quieter conversation that took place while painting for the Fresh Evidence exhibition, I discovered their reasons for the attack from some of the girls involved:

The atmosphere was relaxed, and they started to talk about the Hs. They had a lot of stories to tell — to each other, to O (another girl), and by proxy to me, though they did not seem certain as to what I should know. They were amused at how they had welcomed the Hs, and taken R (girl of their age) under their wing, as she seemed so naive. In the light of what subsequently happened, "We were the naive ones!".

They obviously went round to the Hs' house a lot, and were there on the birthday of the father. There was drink, so they knew that they were doing forbidden things that their parents would not allow. The father then invited them to play strip poker, wanted them to sit on his lap, give him a birthday kiss, locked the door and wanted them to stay the night, helped in all of this by his sons. The daughter had gone to bed. The only way they got out was by pretending to be ill. They were laughing about all this as they talked about it, in the way one laughs about something that had been frightening at the time.[62]

Earlier in this chapter, I quoted Melucci to the effect that collective action always had its own meaning. E.P. Thompson writes of crowd actions having 'some legitimising notion', 'a moral economy of the poor' that justifies direct action.[63] In this case, there was a combination of a story that could not be told, which precluded adult involvement,

---

[60] Diary notes, 30 October 1993

[61] Diary notes, July 1996

[62] Edited from diary, September 1996, referring to conversation in August.

[63] Thompson, 1971: 78, 79

coupled with sexual propriety, solidarity and (in my view) enjoyment at having a moral 'cause' to justify the pleasures of battle.

In the story of the girl gang, Y was forcibly assimilated into the group, whose leader used what Bauman, from Lévi-Strauss, calls the 'inclusivist', *phagic* strategy of forcible absorption to maintain the gang. The Hs (and T, in Chapter Five), on the other hand, were expelled using an 'exclusivist', *emic* strategy of expulsion, or vomiting. Bauman argues that these strategies 'are applied in parallel, in each society and on every level of social organisation. They are both indispensable mechanisms of social spacing, but are effective precisely because of their co-presence, only as a pair'.[64] Together they are used to dominate social space; *phagic* and *emic* strategies are 'included in the toolbag of every domination'.[65] This is a harsher perspective on community to that of the desire for connectedness, which, in Bauman's words, hankers 'after identities which are neither phoney nor shallow', although even they, he continues, may be more 'like iron cages than cloaks lying lightly'.[66] The exclusion of adults from these events is an *emic* strategy, but adults too have *emic* strategies that exclude young people from their world. These are less visible and dramatic, and Sibley writes that:'It is the fact that exclusions take place routinely, without most people noticing, which is a particularly important aspect of the problem'.[67]

In all these examples, we can see processes at work that have been called, by Maffesoli, 'the secret and dense life of contemporary micro groups', that involve 'the ability of micro-groups to create themselves'.[68] These processes can be harsher in practice than the intrinsic romanticism of his approach. Although Maffesoli sees them as aesthetic rather than political groupings, they can be formed to political effect. In the autumn of 1996, there was a campaign against cuts to the youth service. K, whom we last met destroying a pavement to build a useless wall, became a leader of the campaign among young people in Southmead. The young people assembled a mass petition, made up of their handprints, each signed with a statement as to why they liked the youth centre. K met with councillors, and presented this document to Bristol City Council, being the first person under 18 to be allowed to address a full council meeting. The collective had been turned to

[64] Bauman, 1993: 163

[65] Bauman, 1993: 163

[66] Bauman, 1996: 81

[67] Sibley, 1995: xiv

[68] Maffesoli, 1996: 90, 96

a partially successful political purpose – the cuts in Southmead were fewer than originally proposed.[69]

Apart from this example of political campaigning, the various examples I have given of communal activity among young people are disruptive to a peaceful sociality of Southmead yet contain many of the elements associated with community – solidarity, collective action, boundary enforcement and control of space – and indicate a central component left out of more utilitarian descriptions of community – a strong aesthetic desire for connection. What they do not do is provide community as a solid and stable entity.

Young people and place

A major ingredient in the make-up of these moments of collective activity by young people has been that of place. I have quoted reports that criticised the bleakness of Southmead[70] – a landscape in which aesthetic resources are sparse. This is felt strongly by young people: 'Spaces send messages to young people about how an external world values or fails to value the quality of their lives'.[71] Young people in Southmead told the youth worker discussing the 1998 survey with them that 'Southmead is a shithole'.[72] Lefebvre argues that, in this architecture of the dominant system, it is only by way of revolt that adolescents 'have any prospect of recovering the world of difference – the natural, the sensory/sensual, sexuality and pleasure'.[73] In the events around Badocks Wood, this was a suitable space, in terms of size and potential, for such revolt. Using this border zone affronted the residents of the more respectable areas that surround it. The carnival disturbed more than just trees. Controlling place is also part of the collective activity of young people; the Hs, like T in Chapter Five, were physically expelled from Southmead, the place.

In some ways, the issue is simple. Place is important for young people who have not the qualifications or other resources to move away.[74] Locality therefore becomes recognised by young people as their 'community of destiny'.[75] Marylin Friedman has pointed out that, for

---

[69] Diary notes, November 1996

[70] In Chapter Three

[71] Breitbart, 1998: 308. See also Lash and Urry, 1994: 318, as quoted in Chapter One.

[72] She told me this in her report back, early 1999.

[73] Lefebvre, 1991: 50

[74] Callaghan 1992 documents this among young people in Sunderland.

[75] Maffesoli, 1996: 125

children, it is the community they are brought up in that has constituted them, using the American communitarian Michael Sandel's description of constitutive community as 'not a relationship they choose (as in a voluntary association) but an attachment they discover, not merely as an attribute but a constituent of their identity'.[76] This relationship is much stronger than that of communities of choice, which may, in Sandel's scheme, be either *instrumental* – 'individuals ... cooperate only for the sake of pursuing their private ends' – or *sentimental* – 'participants ... regard the scheme of co-operation as a good in itself'.[77] Being brought up in the social relationships of a place is constitutive, in one way or another, even if it is not as shaped as community in any of Sandel's senses. Place offers the possibility of face-to-face relationships that give an experience of social, potentially communal, relationships. It is a space in which young people can have effect, for the same reasons that adults are turning increasingly to local politics, as argued by Castells:

> The failure of proactive movements and politics ... to counter economic exploitation, cultural domination and political oppression had left people with no other choice than either to surrender or to react on the basis of the most immediate source of self-recognition and autonomous organisation: their locality.[78]

Local, known place has its own security. France and Wiles relate the creation of 'locations of trust – small bubbles of security in an insecure world'[79] as a reaction to the risks of late modernity. These locations are created by big business in, for example, secure guarded shopping malls that so often exclude young people. As spatiality is controlled against young people, creating them as a social category[80], it is no surprise that young people create counter-locations for themselves, their own bubbles where they, if no-one else, feel allowed. However, while for some young people this may create a security, for others it creates terror. Thirty per cent of young people surveyed in Southmead in 1998 said that they felt unsafe in Southmead, and the discussions after the survey highlighted the desire of many young people for safe places to go.[81] One of the groups run by youth workers in Southmead

---

[76] Friedman, 1989: 282; Sandel, 1982: 150
[77] Sandel, 1982: 148 (emphasis in original)
[78] Castells, 1997: 61
[79] France and Wiles 1998: 68-9
[80] See Massey, 1998: 127
[81] Kimberlee, 1998: 8; Kimberlee and Cassidy, 1999

is for those who feel too shy or intimidated to leave their homes to socialise. The rough and transgressive actions of some young people terrify others. The constitutive attachment to place is coupled with acts that are destructive of that very place, an everlasting conundrum: why are young people destroying their own? Piven and Cloward, in their work on poor people's movements, point out that people rebel at what is around them as they do not know what the outside forces are that are affecting their lives, nor how to reach them. Without strategic opportunities for defiance, people attack what is around them, act where they are located and with people that they know. The very powerlessness of their situation explains why their defiant behaviour can appear to be so inchoate. Piven and Cloward conclude that 'it is difficult to imagine them doing otherwise'.[82] The combined anger and zest of young people is often not *directed* towards a goal, but are emotions that are *expressed* where they live. Only when there are clear-cut issues, like cuts to the youth centre, or, in 1998, the closure of a local school, is anger directed at a political decision affecting their lives.[83]

Despite actions being local, the cultural symbols of youth are global. The youth culture of Southmead is not a closed culture. The local youth culture of Yucatec Maya investigated by Doreen Massey, where romantic preconception might lead one to expect a local 'authenticity', is also not 'a closed, local culture'.[84] She goes on:

> All youth cultures ... are hybrid cultures. All of them involve active importation, adoption and adaptation. This challenges the idea that 'local cultures' are understood as locally produced systems of social interaction and symbolic meaning.[85]

Young people in Southmead probably play the same electronic games she found in Mexico. I have related how one group of young people I met did not like the locally produced music of Radio Southmead, but wanted 'proper' music. As the action of young people is about giving a centrality to their own existence, so they will wear the designer clothes of the global market. Campbell observed in the early 1990s: 'All over peripheral estates across Britain teenagers were wearing designer

---

[82] Piven and Cloward, 1977: 18-22

[83] See *Bristol Evening Post*, 8 September 1998 and 25 November 1998 for examples of young people's campaigning views, that on this occasion were not successful.

[84] Massey, 1998: 122

[85] Massey, 1998: 122-3

casuals that signified their refusal to be peripheral, to be on the edge of everything'.[86] In a photograph in The Place We're In, the Nike swoosh is highly visible among those crowding around a stolen car. One of the titles considered for that exhibition was the Nike slogan, 'Just Do It', but there were concerns about using a copyrighted phrase. The phrase does, however, summon up an impulse of rebellion, even if from the safety of corporate headquarters thousands of miles away. There is a continual interplay between the global and the local elements of youth culture, with both having major effect. Locality is not autonomy, not separation from the rest of the world.

Conclusion: young people and questions of community

I started this chapter by recapping how much discussion of community in Southmead revolves around the issue of young people. What I have shown is how their collective activities, seen as being destructive of community, actually display facets of community, and question any easy idea of community as a space of peace and social understanding.

The neo-tribes, or micro-groups, formed and reformed by young people give a speeded-up version of the way a range of different ingredients are used in constructions of collective action, similar to that used in ideas of the construction of communities, albeit without the approbation that the term provides. As Raymond Williams has famously written, community as a term is one that 'seems never to be used unfavourably'; it is always 'warmly persuasive'.[87] To say that what young people are doing when joyriding is build community appears to be a contradiction in terms, but I would argue that this is what they are doing, and also what is being done with even more controversial activities, like heroin use, another collective activity that ties people into a group. Warner and Rountree have questioned whether strong community does lead to lower crime rates, as criminal activity can be part of an oppositional collective culture.[88] This means that community is not, of itself, an *answer* to these activities, although thinking about the needs and desires expressed through them might provide fruitful material for forming less destructive forms of collectivities (to use a less loaded term than community). These would have to take into account

---

[86] Campbell, 1993: 271
[87] Williams, 1983: 76
[88] Warner and Rountree, 1997

---

the issues of identity, activity, aesthetics, control and place, expanded on below, that these collectivities raise.

- **Identity.** The formation of young people's collectivities is connected to the formation of their identity as young people, as opposed to being children or adults. The joyrider who gave such an open interview said that, in five years' time, he would not be doing the same kind of stuff; he would probably be 'working an' shit'.[89] It is the uncertainty of the identity 'youth' that leads young people to form such dramatic tribal groupings. The lack of solidity in their lives leads to a search for it. As Bauman puts it, 'neo-tribes [are] conjured up with the intention of giving the choices that solidity which the choices sorely miss'.[90] This solidity is also what drug addiction promises, when choice is surrendered to an external force. Identity is craved for when it is least stable.
- **Activity.** This identity is achieved by activity and involvement, working together to be part of something, not being left on the sidelines as a mere spectator. All the examples given are active, even involving hard work, and in the case of joyriding, a lot of different skills (again, in that interview there was differentiation between those with the skills to steal cars and those with the skills to drive them). Lash and Urry point out that neo-tribes flourish in areas without resources[91]; the reasons for collective activities being mostly illicit may not only be about the joys of transgression, but may also reflect the paucity of licit skilled activity for young people to be involved with.
- **Aesthetics.** A major spur to the activities described in this chapter was to gain pleasure from otherwise barren physical and social landscapes. The activities were not utilitarian, and may even be shocking to a narrow idea of what is useful: cars were not stolen to sell for cash, but for the pleasure of driving and destroying them. Theatricality and performance are major factors in these activities, with the spectacle being the substance, a performance of community very different to that of the fun days and other community events described in Chapter Three.
- **Control.** Control can, of course, also be a pleasure, and all these activities involved some form of control, taking power over place (Badocks Wood), and people (Y, the Hs). These forms of control are

---

[89] Tape transcript, February 1997
[90] Bauman, 1996: 87
[91] Lash and Urry, 1994: 317

violent, the forms used by rebellious groups countering the ways that they feel controlled. Control both by and against these groups can be raw, but is itself part of the pleasure. 'Pleasure and power ... are linked together by complex mechanisms and devices of excitation and incitement'.[92]

- **Place.** The connection of community to place in these activities is both clear and obscure. There are strong reasons for emphasising the importance of place, both social and geographical, in all the events described. They always happen in place; each activity is very localised and could not be otherwise. However, they are not unique to specific places – such activities are replicated all over Britain and further afield. Specific locality does not create these activities, but it is the milieu in which they are created, and a milieu that they create. The activities themselves create the meaning of localities, using any cultural and physical means available.

How does this leave us with any idea of community? While I have identified these ingredients in young people's collective action, we will see, in Chapter Seven, how much they are also used in adult community action. There are several things that these actions are not: not necessarily utilitarian; not conformist; not lacking conflict; not permanent; and finally, not necessarily 'good', in the way that many arguments for community are about its necessity as a social good.[93] The desire for connectedness that appears to be so strong could be written off as chimerical – the communities formed are but dreams – or these dreams could be acknowledged as a major social force. However, these dreams are not necessarily unifying, but fragmentary, in themselves fragmenting places and people.

Community, or lack of it, is not the only factor involved in young people's behaviour. There are issues of power involved, issues that communitarians too often ignore.[94] All the activities described are gendered, even if they challenge traditional ideas of gendered behaviour. The behaviour is related to Southmead being a place of class and poverty. It involves the power position of young people, in terms of their rights, in terms of the resources available to them and in terms of the way power is exercised on them. The punitiveness identified among adults by Brown would like to achieve, in Foucault's words,

---

[92] Foucault, 1979: 48

[93] For example, Etzioni, 1988, 1995b, 1995c; Atkinson, 1994; Bellah, 1997

[94] Frazer and Lacey, 1993; Phillips, 1993

'docility and utility'.[95] However, it is this very negative use of power that strengthens transgressive resistance. The proponents of discipline as the major tool to be used with young people have not understood his dictum that 'if power were never anything but repressive, if it never did anything but to say no, do you really think anyone could be brought to obey it?'[96] Any community building in Southmead that wants to include young people needs to be creative and exciting, not disciplinary and forbidding.

---

[95] Foucault, 1977a: 218
[96] Foucault, 1980: 119

SEVEN

Four examples of community action in Southmead

Introduction

A recurring motif in the writing about Southmead from outside has been that of *lack* of community. In contrast, there have been assertions of community that come from within, as in the community play, but even in these instances community was seen as a thing of the past, currently lacking. Moving around Southmead, there is a sense of fluidity, of nothing as solid as something that could be called community. Instead, there is a strong sense of *place*, but place as *fractured*. The activities of young people described in Chapter Six display collectivities based on a yearning for *connectedness*, but a connectedness that is always temporary and shifting. However, despite all these signs that Southmead is not a community either *in* or *for* itself in any stable form, there are a number of vigorous organisations in the area that proclaim both Southmead and community as bases for social action, active users of the term community. This chapter looks at four of these organisations: the Southmead Project (SP), a drugs project; the Southmead Development Trust (SDT), a charity and limited company that runs a training and leisure centre; Southmead Parents' and Children's Environment (SPACE), a group of parents running activities for children; and Voice of Southmead, an anti-drug dealer campaigning group that lobbies for improvements and provides activities for young people.

This is by no means an exhaustive list of all the local organisations that exist. At a meeting of the Southmead Estate Working Party, a local umbrella group, in October 1994 (before three of the organisations mentioned above had been formed), there was a discussion as to whether it was good or bad that there were 28 different groups operating in the area: did this number show strength or division?[1] This question is considered crucial if unity is seen as important to community, what Bhabha calls the 'progressive metaphor of modern social cohesion – *the many as one* – shared by organic theories of the holism of culture

---

[1] Diary notes, October 1994

and community'.[2] I could not write about every one of these groups; even in writing about just four of them I will only be able to provide a limited discussion of each. I have had to choose which to write about, and have the following reasons for doing so:

- They are examples of organisations claiming community and locality as their *raison d'être* for action.
- They are contemporaneous. SP started in 1994, SDT was set up on an interim basis in 1995, with elections in 1996, SPACE started in mid-1996 and Voice of Southmead in early 1997. They were all still active in late 1999, the end of the period of analysis.
- They are different from each other. All occupy the same political terrain of wanting to improve Southmead through use of the idea of community. For three of them, drugs and young people are major issues, but each differs in its mode of operation, and in its approach to, and vision of, community. On occasion, they clash. One researcher has advised that 'focusing on community controversies as these erupt' is a fruitful method of research[3]; it is the differences between these groups that reveal much about community.
- I have a working knowledge of all of them, as an 'outsider within'. I was secretary to the SP committee for its first three years, have worked alongside the SDT, was first the butt of criticism from SPACE, but then organised some of the facilities they were demanding, and was initially criticised by the Voice, but have since worked closely with it. My work in Southmead has changed and benefited from all four organisations, although there has also been conflict caused by their different approaches to young people. My knowledge of them is simultaneously rich, partial and messy. Trying to understand them is part of my continued position of being both analyst and participant.

Although only part of the community activity in Southmead, these organisations were new and energetic, unlike, say, the Community Council, which, at over 40 years old, was unable to galvanise this generation of activists. They are also unlike the multi-agency groups that exist around Southmead, in which professional workers from a variety of different agencies (for example, social workers, police, health workers, planners) work together on issues of common concern in the area – a community formation of Southmead-based staff, what Lena Dominelli

---

[2] Bhabha, 1991: 294

[3] Abu-Lughod, 1994: 4

calls *community organisation*, 'a useful tool in the hands of management concerned with making the best use of resources'[4], although also used by locally based staff as a way of maintaining some autonomy from central control. These groups have been affected by the emergence of the four new organisations, and regrouped in their wake. To follow them would involve an organisational study of local and national state agencies, beyond the scope of this book. Multi-agency groups work effectively within the status quo – the 'community' organisations I am focusing on sought to change that status quo.

The majority of people in Southmead were not directly involved with these organisations, although, as Castells points out, all urban movements produce meaning 'not only for the movement's participants, but for the community at large'.[5] The wider effects of the organisations will be one of concerns of the concluding section of this chapter.

The Southmead Project (SP)

Founding stories are important in sustaining the sense of purpose and identity of community organisations. In the case of SP, it is a story often told, both to show how much the project was so initially grounded in local knowledge and experience, and to celebrate its triumphant, almost epic, growth.[6] In early 1994, a Southmead man with children, worried about the heroin use of a friend and the spread of heroin use among young people, approached M, a well-known local figure and trained drugs counsellor, to suggest that something needed to be done. Though M no longer lived in Southmead, he was closely involved with the area through the rugby club, of which he had been a founding member, and through the music scene – he had organised a big open-air concert featuring Southmead bands in July 1993. Five years after that first conversation, a local drugs agency had been established, employing counsellors and education staff, as well as a building company to employ former users and a counselling service for adults who have suffered sexual abuse: an impressive story.

Southmead Rugby Club features in the history of both SP and Voice of Southmead. Rugby in Bristol is not the upper-class sport that it is in other parts of England, but is, as in Wales, a popular working-men's

---

[4] Dominelli, 1990: 9

[5] Castells, 1997: 61

[6] It appears in the project's strategy documents, and in its annual reports from 1997 to 1999. I will not be giving all the ups and downs of the story, but points of relevance to this book.

sport. Southmead Rugby Club was set up in 1986 entirely on a self-help basis, and runs several teams, from an under-8s' team to adult teams, including one for women. It has a club-house and bar, built by members, who are proud of their achievement. Although set up for sport, it has a wider influence in the area; its members have gained organisational and committee experience, and there is a strong sense of camaraderie, developed, presumably, in the scrum. It provides a place to meet, and is a known image of male strength, invoked by both SP and the Voice against intimidation from drug dealers.[7]

When people have ideas and enthusiasm, they need some kind of structure to make them effective. Finding or creating such a structure is a problem for nascent groups, and as drug use among young people was increasingly dominating my work, so it was agreed that the charity Friends of Southmead Youth Centre would act as parent body for SP until it was strong enough to set up its own organisation three years later.[8] This provided a bank account, auditor, a committee that could sign a lease for premises and so on. A separate sub-committee was formed for SP. This involved a hybrid of people from the different constituencies, 'local' and 'professional', who made up the project. There was insistence that the project was *local*, distinct from bodies such as the Bristol Drugs Project:

> It is felt that the problem is best tackled locally, with people who know or are sympathetic to the area, who are trusted, and who understand and sympathise with the difficult situations people find themselves in. It is important for a service to be available locally, both for users and their families, and for there to be an effective education programme in the area.
>
> The strength of the Southmead Project is its energy, and its ability to mobilise local people with its community approach.[9]

This stress on locality was partly a euphemism for class, a reaction to middle-class outsiders who were seen as being unable to understand

---

[7] As well as picking up this knowledge just from being around, the club captain spoke of the history on Radio Southmead in August 1994. I have never been an insider of this club — I can't stand the game.

[8] M himself had also used the youth centre 30 years previously.

[9] The Southmead Project strategy for the period October 1995 to March 1997: 3

or communicate with users and their families. However, support from those very same professional outsiders was essential for the credibility of the project, in fund raising and attaining recognition from other drug agencies. Part of the process of creating credibility was a strategy document, in acceptable language agreed by these different social worlds, for which I was utilised as scribe. A lot of time was spent developing suitably worded aims and objectives in order to convince everyone from funders to local people to support the organisation. Finding the right language was crucial. Two main objectives were: 'To reduce substance related harm to individuals and their families and promote community safety within Southmead'; and 'To use local strengths to professional standards – a service from within, not imposed from without'.[10]

The bringing together of different worlds created a strain that SP experienced daily. It was difficult to be credible to local people, professionals and funding bodies, while at the same time implying that both worlds needed to change in order to reduce the harm that drug use was causing: professionals to accept the value of the life experiences of people from Southmead, and local people to accept the necessity for professional skills. Neither, in the SP's approach, could do without the other. To give an example of the stress involved, the police were an important and supportive presence on the committee, but when officers arrived at SP's office during the day, in full uniform while there were drug users present, there was consternation and anger from the local project workers, even though the police were delivering a cheque.

An inclusive approach (*phagic*, to use Bauman's term[11]) was central to the project, not only in this marrying of social worlds, but also in its approach to drug use. Drug users were not to be expelled from the community, but to be cared for, brought back in. To this end, a number of different ways of working were established, to tackle drug use at all its stages, an approach with holistic aspirations reinforcing that phagic, communitarian purpose. There was drug education for non-users, counselling for users, group support for their families and relapse prevention support for ex-users. To help with relapse prevention, a building company, Community Development Southmead (CDS), was set up, to offer work and training to recovering drug users with the idea of renovating the more run-down parts of the estate, thereby also

---

[10] The Southmead Project strategy for the period October 1995 to March 1997: 3. It is strange to 'quote' words that I wrote, although these words were changed and vetted by others, and became public property.

[11] See Chapter Six

tackling one of the perceived root causes of drug use. In association with the National Society for the Prevention of Cruelty to Children, a local Touchstone Project, providing counselling to adults who had experienced abuse as children, was set up to tackle another perceived cause of problem drug use, which was also the subject of a research project.[12]

Holding all this disparity together depended on forming common enemies; there was fury within the project when a major government grant that SP had applied for was won instead by the local social services department. This was felt to be a slap in the face for local aspirations and an external enemy was discovered that stood in the way of the project.[13] Voice of Southmead was first a friend, with M speaking at its big meeting in May 1997, but was then seen as an enemy, its tactics causing anger and its meetings boycotted.[14] Battling against the odds was a major theme of SP reports.

This activity needed to attract extensive external resources, from charities, statutory agencies, the National Lottery and businesses. This money from outside was raised by stressing the importance of a local, community approach, which tied in with the business–communitarian agenda of Business in the Community. Money raised within Southmead from fund-raising events was given huge symbolic importance in order to attract those external resources.

Legitimacy, credibility and political support were major concerns for SP. Although it worked through the provision of a series of services, support for these was garnered by evangelical zeal and lobbying. The local press was used skilfully to publicise the work and its crises.[15] There were events such as the opening of the premises by a local rugby hero and an open-air concert, both in 1996. In 1999, M was awarded the MBE, a useful lever of legitimacy. However, not all local people were supportive. There was such stiff resistance to its proposed headquarters from residents in one street that SP had to back down and find a more out-of-the-way building. The meeting where this was discussed was fiery, with the residents using their own claim of 'authenticity' of living in that street against the claims of a community-based approach to drug use that also claimed local legitimacy.[16] The Voice of Southmead view was that SP's counselling approach had not worked and that different

---

[12] Newman, 1999

[13] Diary notes, September and October 1996

[14] Diary notes, 2 May, 29 May, 4 June and 1 July 1997

[15] There were several stories each year in the local papers.

[16] Diary notes, 18 April 1995

measures needed to be taken.[17] These disagreements were difficult for local authority and other agencies that wanted community approaches in Southmead.[18] It put them in the position of having to choose which approach to support, or to try to bridge the divide, drawing them as active participants into community politics while being thought of as outsiders.

Southmead Development Trust (SDT)

Against this background, an aspiration of SDT was to speak for Southmead with one voice. In 1988, the Greenway Boys School had closed. The city council had the idea of developing its buildings and playing fields for the benefit of Southmead. This progressed under a new Greenway Trust, and created leisure facilities, offices, meeting rooms and a training centre.

In 1995, the trust was disbanded by the city council and replaced by the SDT. There were accusations that this was a move to give political advantage to the council and its ruling group[19], but its deeper politics lay in the formation of a new type of body, a development trust, elected locally, with a wider remit than merely running a centre. The growth of development trusts is a national movement, with its own Development Trust Association (DTA). The DTA assistant director told a local meeting that it was 'about the whole life and spirit of the community, not just bits of it', and listed certain 'core values': people before profit, community benefit before return of investment, community ownership and mutuality.[20] The formation of the SDT came during a period of much debate about, and changes in, forms of governance, a kind of restlessness about what the best forms are. Such changes affected school governing bodies and their responsibilities throughout the 1980s and 1990s. They also led to local authority reorganisation (affecting Bristol in 1996), and, on a larger scale, devolution in Scotland and Wales in 1999 and the introduction of elected mayors, with, as Nikolas Rose argues, 'the community' being seen as a unit and method of governance, a new '*imagined territory* upon which ... strategies should act','*government through community*'.[21] The rhetoric of all these changes is of people being able to control their own destinies at a level close to them.

---

[17] Diary notes, 22 May 1997
[18] The reports discussed in Chapter Three showed this official desire for community.
[19] *Bristol Observer*, 28 April 1995
[20] Diary notes, 12 September 1995
[21] Rose, 1996: 331-2

Development trusts are part of that rhetoric: 'Never before has there been such an opportunity for ordinary people to become involved in shaping the future of their own communities'.[22] Despite that rhetoric, SDT was not set up following demands from people in Southmead – it was created as a result of policy made elsewhere, a *dirigiste* form of community development.

The SDT describes itself as:

> ... a new kind of community organisation which is both a business and a charity which aims to stay independent by earning its own money wherever possible....

> Any surpluses or future profits are ploughed back into the Trust to increase its scope to improve the quality of life for people in Southmead, who the Trust is accountable to through its elected Trustees.[23]

The first elections for the trust were held in March 1996. Eight residents (out of 12 candidates), two local workers and two city councillors became the new board of trustees. Six hundred and sixty people voted, 8.8% of the electorate.[24]

This new trust took over running the Greenway Centre, which had its own Training and Enterprise Centre providing IT and business training, sports facilities, a summer play scheme, offices for local organisations and commercial lettings. A criticism made locally was that it ignored the wider estate, but the trustees explained that it would take time to branch out from running what was such a large undertaking. Lay members of the trust found their role very difficult, because of the complex legal and managerial decisions involved, and had to rely heavily on information and advice from paid staff, a continual problem of the power and function of management within a democracy.[25]

The trust won acclaim – it received a Times/NatWest Community Enterprise Award in 1999, for example – which it used to enhance its credibility, as SP did with the recognition it had gained.[26] However, despite its much-vaunted independence, its existence depended on

---

[22] The director of the Derry Inner City Trust quoted in the *Southmead Community News*, October 1995

[23] SDT information sheet for the trust elections of 6 May 1999

[24] Diary notes, March 1996; *Bristol Observer*, 8 March 1996, Southmead Community News, May 1996

[25] Diary notes, June 1996

[26] *Bristol Observer*, 23 April 1999

sources of public money and market forces over which it had little control. The trust had no tax-raising powers and when control was passed from the city council it had to raise its own income. It was highly dependent on grants from public sources, such as the European Union, the British government and National Lottery funds, but could only access that money if it met the criteria of the donor bodies. While it was well placed to attract such funds into Southmead, it was dependent on the policies of the donors. It raised income through charges, but this market operation tended to exclude the poorest, as they brought little income. Its prices were criticised by Voice of Southmead members, who said they wanted affordable provision, especially for young people.[27] Its greatest asset was its land, and over the years a number of attempts were made to sell some of this to raise capital. In 1999, a deal was reached to lease six acres to a private company to build a leisure club. The deal was publicly portrayed as a victory for Southmead, as it stood to gain up to £1.5 million for its own developments, and the company promised a 'community package' for local schools, 'excellent news for Southmead'.[28] This deal, however, made the trust dependent on trickle-down money from facilities provided for the wealthy – the very sort of facilities that marginalise poor people. It showed how much dreams of community are constrained by financial forces, making, as Zukin says, 'the local community submit more directly to markets enforced by financial controls'.[29] She continues: 'Local actors are far from autonomous.... Although they aim to preserve vernacular forms, they usually end up tying them to a landscape of power'.[30] The land deal was a clear example of that process.

There was a controversy in late 1996 that revealed very different ideas about how Southmead should be represented in this landscape of power. The Greenway Centre was used as the venue for a Business in the Community conference, which Prince Charles came to address as its patron. SP was to provide the catering, and its people came in T-shirts specially printed with drug messages. They were told by the trust manager that they could not wear these, and when Prince Charles came past the room they were working in the door was closed on them so they would not be seen. Angry debate followed as to whether the 'community' should be shown as it is or whether it should dress

---

[27] Diary notes, 13 May 1997, and meeting attended by local MP, 6 July 1997

[28] *Bristol Observer*, 27 September 99. The *Bristol Journal* reported the deal as 'Southmead boost', 3 September 1999.

[29] Zukin, 1991: 101

[30] Zukin, 1991: 275

up for the occasion in suits that people could not afford: maintain its autonomy or play the game.[31]

SDT provides a solid organisation within Southmead. It overlaps with the other three organisations – M was a trustee, as was a member of SPACE, and in the 1999 elections, a number of members of Voice of Southmead were elected to the board – but it has not itself been a campaigning organisation. It is instead a rather official body that has failed to provide unity.

Southmead Parents' and Children's Environment (SPACE)

SPACE is a very different group from the other three. It is a women's group, and although members of it are involved with SP, SDT and Voice, this group keeps a separate, female, identity. It is smaller than the other groups.

The youth centre was first approached by this group, whose members all used or worked in the local cafe, in April 1996, just after the ending of the young people's 'carnival' at Badocks Wood. They first contacted women staff members. They were angry about the behaviour of young people, especially their smoking, drinking and swearing, and blamed those of us working with them.[32] They wanted change – to Southmead, to the community. Their first meeting with me was aggressive, with bursts of generosity. I was the only man in the room with 15 women, and when they went on the attack they would ask every so often whether I was OK. This and subsequent meetings were riven with problems of power and communication. I was attacked and deferred to simultaneously – attacked as, in their eyes, a person with power who was not doing it right, and deferred to as a person with power, as if they questioned their own temerity in making this challenge to a 'professional'. The youth centre itself is staffed mainly by part-timers, most of whom live in the area themselves, and they, too, felt angry and threatened by the criticisms being made of their work by people using the umbrella of being 'community'. The atmosphere was full of conflict.

The women continued to meet at the youth centre, always arriving as a group. One of them had access to a computer and produced membership forms. At one meeting, they had a huge row about money

---

[31] Diary notes, 10 December 1996

[32] This is similar to the way the youth worker from the Bristol Social Project in the 1950s was blamed for young people's behaviour (see Chapter Three).

– no single person was trusted with looking after it. This formative period was a painful process. However, they decided that they wanted to work with the young people themselves. The problem was, that on the evenings that they came, young people stayed away. The young people did not like the authoritarian approach, and questioned me as to whom the youth centre was for, adults or them.

After this experience, the group decided to run a club for under-11s, and were pleased that this could be arranged. They called the club Little Spacers. Before doing this, they had to fill in forms about any past criminal convictions. Despite my concern that they might find this bureaucratic and official, these forms broke the ice. Instead of taking the forms home to be filled out in private, they were filled out publicly and communally. They were delighted to do it – it showed that they were being taken seriously. 'Is poll tax a crime, Jerry?', they asked (it was, but having a court order to pay was not), so they all wrote down 'no convictions'. Then TV licences were mentioned. Not paying is an offence that particularly affects women, and some had to cross out that 'no' for 'yes', and the same went for driving without insurance – all crimes of poverty that did not disqualify them from working with children. They were not the respectable church-going communitarians mentioned in Chapter Four.

Little Spacers became a successful club, with high attendance. SPACE organised coach trips and parties. The attitude of the women to the youth centre changed, and we became friends.[33]

It is easy to forget how powerless and ineffective people feel, and how it is only through group effort and anger that they break through the social barriers that keep them ineffective, even if that process only enables them to undertake a traditionally female activity – looking after children. SPACE became powerful only in a very small sphere. One of the criticisms levelled at community action is that it does not challenge power relations, but reinforces them by focusing on relatively trivial issues which disrupt broader-based struggle[34], a disappointment that it does not change the world.

Voice of Southmead

It was from one of the members of SPACE that I first heard about Voice of Southmead. 'The men', I was told, 'are meeting to do something

---

[33] This account is distilled from a number of diary entries over the period.
[34] Pratt, 1989: 98

about the drugs'.[35] The group was soon a major topic of conversation in the area, rumours flying everywhere. That it was men involved was stressed again and again; generally, community is seen as a women's sphere, maintained by women in spite of the activity of men.[36]

Voice of Southmead was the biggest mobilisation of people ever seen in Southmead. The spring and early summer of 1997 was a period of mass activity, with weekly meetings at the Rugby Club attracting 50 and more people, dramatic televised mass leafleting of the area and a large public meeting in May.[37] By September 1997, there was a visible reduction of heroin dealing in the area and one of the demands of the group had been met with the establishment of the Southmead Youth Sports Development Initiative. From then on the group became primarily involved in supporting this initiative, although the story of those early months was still used as a reminder of its power. Voice of Southmead became widely praised as a model of how community action could be taken against widespread drug use, with coverage on local and national media. On its first anniversary, the local newspaper ran a long article: 'Fighting back.... how the Voice of Southmead has helped turn the estate around'.[38] A year later there was further cause for pride – in July 1999, 200 members of the Voice attended the premiere of a video, Southmead Slamming[39], which told the story of the sports initiative and how it was raising money from national bodies as an example of good practice. The story of the Voice of Southmead from 1997 to 1999 falls into two periods that display different aspects of community, first mobilisation and then provision.

The spur to the formation of the Voice was the case of G[40]: 'It came to our attention through the media coverage of a Court Case where a Southmead man was found guilty of Drug and Sexual Abuse of young children as young as 10 years of age.... It was then it came apparent to us how the Heroin and Crack Cocaine Trade to young children has escalated'.[41] There was another major drug case before the courts at that time, too; the case of a man who had established a 'drugs fortress' in the area and was jailed for five-and–a-half years in June 1997. These

---

[35] Diary note, February 1997

[36] Dominelli, 1990; Bornat et al, 1993; Campbell 1993. This point is returned to later in the chapter.

[37] Described in Chapter Two

[38] *Bristol Evening Post*, 3 February 1998

[39] Commissioned by Bristol City Council, and directed by Dave Greenhalgh. A number of the audience cried during this première, overcome by emotion.

[40] See Chapter Four

[41] Voice of Southmead leaflet, June 1997

two cases became inextricably linked with the history of the Voice. Voice members soon learnt that when TV companies have dramatic footage in their archive, they will use it again and again.

I could not attend the first few meetings of the Voice - like others who work in the area, I was only invited later. Issues had to be resolved before attention was directed at the people and agencies that the Voice wanted to change. At these meetings, I was told later by people who had been there, three major issues emerged:

- Vigilantism. The group decided against the use of violence in driving out drug dealers. This continued to be a major issue. Certainly outside of the group, and in the local press, there was continual fear that violence would be used. It never was, although some drug dealers who were visited by large groups left the area very quickly, and the presence of a fear of a loss of control was significant. As Piven and Cloward say of other poor people's movements, 'Whatever the people won was a response to their turbulence and not to their organised numbers'.[42]
- Type of drugs targeted. Much debate led to the decision that the Voice was only against the use of Class A drugs – heroin and cocaine in this context – and not cannabis. This decision led to one of the main charges used against members of the Voice – that they were hypocrites who smoked cannabis.
- Grassing. The leading figures said that they were prepared to lose friends over the issue. They were going to split the community by breaking the local consensus of no grassing, although only about drug dealing. Later, the group met regularly with the police to pass on information about drug dealing.

When, in March 1997, I was asked to a meeting, it was like a summons – it would be against my interests not to go. There were about 70 people there. I was a spectator, unlike later meetings when I was put on the spot regarding my work with young people. I knew about a third of those present as ex-youth club users. Sixty per cent were men, but there had been a decision to bring wives to make the meeting less threatening and violent. Men led the meeting, but women spoke too. The room contained people with moving personal stories: ex-drug users, lifelong friends of dealers, parents of users, partners of users. Many had themselves been in trouble with the law. Like SPACE, these were

---

[42] Piven and Cloward, 1977: xiii. See also E.P Thompson (1971), who wrote of the effectiveness of the disposition to riot.

not respectable communitarians and they were aware of this – there was a modesty about themselves not being perfect, coupled with a determination that they had to take action. The meeting was full of rough humour. People restrained each other's anger, wanted to be serious and turned on one man when he arrived drunk, although they laughed when his Jack Russell terriers ran up and sniffed a policeman: "Watch out John, they're going to piss on your leg". The main guests were the police, and managers from the housing and social services departments. This is a précis of the principal exchanges:

> *Chair.* Our sole aim is to stop drug dealers dealing in Southmead. We are not vigilantes. We will work alongside police and the council.
>
> *Floor.* What do the police think of that?
>
> *Superintendent.* We are pleased to be here. The only way to defeat drugs is from within the community.
>
> *Floor.* (To police) You've not done enough. (To meeting) We can't hide behind no grassing.
>
> *Floor.* (Lots of anger about the housing rights of drug dealers.)
>
> *Social services/housing.* We need to work within the law.
>
> *Floor.* If 40 of us go round to dealers, with no violence, what do the police think?
>
> *Police.* You can challenge what people are doing.
>
> *Councillor.* What about a drug-free Bristol?
>
> *Floor.* We have got to start here. We are a small community.
>
> *Floor.* (To police) We are here because it's our estate, we've got the problems. You are here because it is your job.

Within the meeting, many of the major issues of community politics arose: relationship with the 'authorities', and who was most important, them or the 'community'; how the 'community' itself had to change; community demands versus the individual legal rights of drug dealers; and the remit of effectiveness. The message that the authorities were not doing enough, and that the Voice was demanding more, was loud and clear. After the main meeting, I was told the demand on my work: "We want more sport. This is a working-class community, it's keen on sport".[43]

The fear of the Voice continued. On 9 April there were rumours that the group was going to visit the youth centre. The atmosphere was very tense. People I knew to be drug users, but who did not use the centre, were outside armed with sticks and bars: "They are not telling us how to live". No-one came. Two days later, a group of young people asked me to invite the Voice to the centre so that they could put across their opinion, but when the visit did come, it was like an inspection.[44] This community action, like the collective actions of young people of the last chapter, was not warm and peaceful.[45]

During this period, P emerged as the leader of the Voice. He had no previous community or political experience, but was trusted and was good at dealing with the media. In the week of the drugs fortress court case, he appeared on local and national news bulletins and in live studio discussion.[46] He told me that he was put under a lot of pressure by his role, and had to remind those who wanted 'to do the business' on dealers that, as their public figurehead, his credibility was on the line. Another figure was a woman, one of whose sons was a heroin user, who was prepared to talk openly about her experience in public.[47] It would be overstating the case to say that their media-friendliness made them the voices of the Voice, but their skill with the media was a major factor in both their own credibility and the effectiveness of its campaign. There was a strong relationship between the political actions of the Voice and the media. Media appearances fed back into the campaign, with newspaper cuttings photocopied and circulated, to show, as with the SP, legitimacy and effectiveness. That it was called the Voice was no accident, as giving voice to experience was a major political tool; at one meeting P said to the various police and local authority managers there: "You don't understand drug problems, these people do".[48] This was representing Southmead backed by political

---

[43] The account of the meeting is from a diary entry for March 1997.
[44] Diary notes, 29 April 1997
[45] Diary notes, April 1997
[46] Diary notes, June 1997
[47] Diary notes, April 1997
[48] Diary notes, 6 June 1997

will and strength, and had a much greater effect in winning the respect of the media than the most skilful representations of community art. There were dissidents who questioned whether it was *the* Voice, and people from SP at one time suggested that a 'Real Voice of Southmead' should be formed.[49]

The big public meeting of the Voice the day after the general election firmly established it as a major force in the area.[50] The themes of the earlier meeting were aired again. Because of the attack on my work at the youth centre at that meeting, I went to the next regular meeting, when I was the focus of a three-quarter-of-an-hour onslaught, mostly of criticism of the artwork done with young people and of the separate Girls Club. The youth centre was important to their thinking; many present had used it when they were young. As I left, I was told, "You've got some bottle", and realised that I had been put through an initiation test, to see if I was worthy of inclusion.[51]

When the strength of the Voice was established, its approach to official agencies changed. Instead of criticism, I was asked what I did with young people, and was told that I had been working on my own for too long, and that they were prepared to help. There was a conscious shift of approach, with P stating that the Voice had begun by 'slagging off' the authorities, but now wanted to achieve change with them. There was a realisation that the local workers they met did not have much power over resources, and there was determination to reach the places where power lay, making it visible and accountable so that it could be negotiated with; Melucci identifies this process of making power visible as one of the fundamental roles of collective action.[52] The *emic* approach of excluding dealers became less pronounced, and became a more phagic approach of working with others to provide better facilities for young people. This process started with a meeting with the police superintendent, the MP and senior local authority and health authority managers, where these representatives of power were told: "We want to grab it now. This energy is special".[53] A series of working meetings followed, at which the Sports Initiative idea was fleshed out. By August I noted that: 'Oddly enough, I am *in* with the Voice.... Makes me realise how important and powerful that feeling of being *in* can be – and the power of exclusion and rejection'.[54]

---

[49] Diary notes, 1 July 1997
[50] See Chapter Two
[51] Diary notes, 6 May 1997
[52] Diary notes, 6 June 1997; Melucci, 1989: 77
[53] Diary notes, 6 June 1997
[54] Diary notes, 18 August 1997

To make the sports initiative work, resources were needed. The Voice was insistent that a paid worker was required – its members were at work all day, and were too tired to take on the responsibility. It was, however, prepared to help with additional money and volunteers. It ran the 1997 open-air concert, much to the fury of SP. The Voice had usurped its hegemonic role in the community and had the support of the local bands.[55] It kitted out local football teams with the money and provided volunteers to run them, but only after it was certain that the authorities too were providing money, and that its goodwill was not being abused. Several thousands of pounds were raised, including enough to set up a boxing club, an assertion of its type of sport. Money was provided through various local and national government funds to employ a youth sport development worker, and in November 1997 P joined the staff of the youth centre in that role.

The Southmead Youth Sports Development Initiative involved hundreds of young people in a variety of sports. Local volunteers ran the teams, the Voice raised money for equipment and it was supported by a committee of its members and the agencies who provided the salaries. Girls' sports were encouraged and given extra resources by the Voice ('Girls can do it too' was a message in Southmead Slamming). Matches provided a focal point for spectators, coaches had to be hired for the supporters for cup finals and large celebratory presentation evenings in 1998 and 1999, at the end of each season, involved hundreds of parents and young people. There were fun days in 1998 and 1999, with local specialities such as ferret racing, and several dances and discos each year.

The approach to young people became warmer as the project grew. P pointed out in the Southmead Slamming video that the amount of volunteer help 'shows that we are looking out for them'. All young people were welcomed, and there was a lot of patience shown towards the more 'difficult' ones – young people behaving in very similar ways to that of Voice members when they were younger. The agencies were delighted, and the police reported a large drop in the local crime rate (32% between 1997/98 and 1998/99).[56] The initiative was praised for the way different agencies worked together, made to do so by the community: the approach, said a government magazine, 'required the city council and other agencies to be flexible and allow the community

---

[55] Diary notes, 29 May 1997

[56] Report prepared by police 14/05/99, reproduced in the Southmead Youth Sports Development Initiative Business Plan

to set the agenda'.[57] In 1999, it was given a Community Safety Award and was chosen by Sport England as an Active Communities Showcase Project. My own role changed from defending inadequate youth provision to managing an ever-growing project.

Drug use did not stop in Southmead, but it was less public. There has been criticism in the drug treatment world of community approaches to reducing drug use in general, notably that it appears to be a radical but is in fact a 'form of utilitarian social engineering' that overlooks what is helpful in the long term for individual drug users, who lose out on services as the interests of the community are prioritised.[58] While drug use became a more private, underground activity, the concerns of the families of drug users moved into the public realm and were no longer treated as a private shame – public responsibility was taken for the wellbeing of young people. A major effect of Voice of Southmead was this shift in the boundaries of public and private behaviour, creating new communal, public responsibilities while turning Class A drug use into unacceptable public behaviour.

Themes running through community action

There is no single idea of community under which the histories of these organisations can all be subsumed, but I want to look at a number of themes running through their histories, some very similar to the themes identified running through the behaviour of young people in the last chapter:

- The activity of community
- Moments of community
- Unity/disunity
- Legitimacy
- Place and identity
- Narrative
- Public realm
- Movement of community
- Effects

---

[57] DETR, 1999
[58] Melville, 1994

The activity of community

All these organisations entailed a tremendous amount of effort and activity that both created a sense of involvement (as with the activity of young people discussed in Chapter Six) and demanded a strong commitment. Community action is not easy; it is hard work.

Moments of community

The formation of none of the four organisations could be taken for granted. Each happened at a certain community moment: an organisational moment for SDT and a time of conflict and crisis for the other three. At that moment of formation 'the energy is special', as was said about the Voice. As Melucci points out, 'since no actor is inherently conflictual, the nature of action assumes a necessarily temporary character'[59]; the moment passes. Sennett writes, less sympathetically, that community exists 'only by a continual hyping up of emotions', a hysteria.[60] This energy occurs at certain unpredictable times, almost as unpredictable as the sudden formations of young people. When I started the research for this book, there were no signs of these community movements.

Protest did not last long: the anger of SPACE lasted three months, and that of the Voice about four months. These early months are crucial, say Piven and Cloward: 'Organizers and leaders cannot prevent the ebbing of protest.... They can only try to win whatever can be won while it can be won'.[61] After that initial moment, institutional forms of maintaining the gains are needed, and this happened with all three organisations, with new forms of community provision in Southmead being sustained by organisational means (SP set up a charity, SPACE and the Voice used, but changed, the existing structure of the youth centre). SDT could be the institution that in future will be used to sustain the gains of any future actions, but institutions change too, as witnessed by the creation of SDT to replace the previous trust.

Coming together in community action is momentary, something that cannot be taken for granted. It resembles the short-lived passions of neo-tribes, but is no less powerful for that.

---

[59] Melucci, 1996b: 4
[60] Sennett, 1986: 309
[61] Piven and Cloward, 1977: 37

Unity/disunity

The 'we' of community is not only temporary, but fractious and fragmentary. 'Unity' is not part of the etymological make-up of the word community[62], although its phonetic presence produces the delusion that it should be. The word is based more on ideas of division than unity, a division of 'us' from 'them'. Elsewhere, I have argued that 'as community is based on division, it is not only an unattainable unity, but an internally and irretrievably split one'.[63] The holistic hopes of communitarians, summed up by Bhabha earlier in this chapter and labelled by Sennett 'the Myth of a Purified Community'[64] in which social division is solved, seem shattered by the division and difference between the four organisations under discussion. As they veer between emic and phagic modes, they cooperate with or anathematise each other. 'Collective action', explains Melucci, 'is not a unitary empirical phenomenon. Whatever unity exists should be considered the result and not the starting point, a fact to be explained rather than assumed.'[65]

However, this splitting, this disunity, is not necessarily as damaging as feared. It was the assertions of different approaches that created the energy of these community organisations. Lack of unity subverts the totalitarian danger of the united, apolitical communities in which there is no room for difference. The strength of community may well lie in its fractiousness; Robert Booth Fowler makes the point clearly:

> Community cannot be defined in theory or in practise as public consensus or the absence of disputes. If it is, then we may suspect that community has become a substitute for politics, and tyranny may indeed lie right around the corner.[66]

The four groups appealed to different views of Southmead and had different constituencies from within the area, emphasising the internal complexity of Southmead and its almost superabundance of community.

---

[62] Oxford English Dictionary, 1989
[63] Brent, 1997: 78
[64] Sennett, 1970: 32
[65] Melucci, 1989: 26
[66] Fowler, 1995: 93-4

Legitimacy

Phil Cohen writes that 'community has ... become a special kind of cultural capital'[67], and it is this capital that the four organisations all sought. Community is a legitimating symbol for action found as they 'rummage through society's cultural chest'.[68] Legitimacy was sought by all the organisations both from within Southmead and from outside in the form of media coverage and the recognition given by financial support, prizes and honours. However, community benefit was also claimed to justify the land deal with the private leisure centre. The way that community is used to justify very different relationships concerns Freie. He writes of the United States in the 1990s that 'virtually any claim of community will be taken seriously'.[69] In Southmead there are activities dressed up in such claims in order to deflect criticism.

This desire for legitimisation ties community into existing forms of power. Relations of power are apparent throughout the accounts, the strongest example being the dependence on male power of the Voice, used to combat the spread of heroin dealerships. Masculinity of itself does not preclude community, as is often argued. For example, Jessica Benjamin writes that 'male domination works through the cultural ideal, the ideal of individuality'[70] and Beatrix Campbell that: 'Crime and coercion are sustained by men. Solidarity and self-help are sustained by women. It is as stark as that'.[71] Men in both SP and the Voice acted with solidarity, albeit not reducing their own dominant strength. Through these groups men discovered community. There was one major difference between these two groups and SPACE: SP and the Voice each had an obvious leader, whereas SPACE did not.

By claiming community as a description of their activities, each group was claiming hegemony in the area. Fighting for 'their' community is a claim of owning that community, what Bauman calls 'the hard-won right to draw the charts of social space binding on others'.[72] When Voice members said, "It is our estate", the claim was not made just against the local authority, but over other groups in the area, as we saw young people make their claims. The different political visions

---

[67] Cohen, 1997: 38
[68] Melucci, 1989: 136. This rummaging is, for him, a characteristic of social movements.
[69] Freie, 1998: 32
[70] Benjamin, 1990: 173
[71] Campbell, 1993: 319
[72] Bauman, 1993: 162

of community struggling for hegemony and legitimacy were a major factor in the inherent disunity of community.

Place and identity

All four of the organisations named their identity as Southmead. What Southmead meant, though, was variable. SDT depended on the ward boundary. Its identity was as an institution and did not have the emotional force of the campaigning groups, whose identities gave them their expansive and energetic confidence to act. For these three organisations, group identity was based on a mixture of face-to-face relationships and an idea of Southmead, which were not necessarily the same. There were members of the Voice who did not live in the area and joined because of their face-to-face networks. M was not a resident. However, they considered themselves part of Southmead. Prior networks – the Rugby Club, the cafe, use of the youth centre 20 years earlier – were important in the formation of the groups. These prior networks were also the source of divisions: as well as a long-term building of trust, a major currency used for group cohesion, there were also long-term animosities and mistrust, similar to those in medieval villages as described by Phillips. He ridicules communitarians for holding these up as an example of community life: '[They] were riddled with petty conflicts, and hatred, fear, and violence were endemic'.[73] Long-term relationships do not inevitably lead to community, and communities based on them exclude those for whom movement between places is a major experience of life. Very few members of the minority ethnic groups from Southmead took part in any of these organisations, and the predominant whiteness was part of the 'we' that was created, not with racist intent, but with exclusionary effect.[74]

The chief claims to identity that made the groups different to the authorities that they were dealing with were their direct experience and class position (this last most explicit in the case of the Voice). Class was marked by income, language and culture (sport, rock music and ferrets), which gave people enough in common to work together.[75] Despite being based on experience, the moral stand against drugs was ambivalent, and a lot of work went into its construction in the first moments of the Voice. Identity was formed by the groups as they went

---

[73] Phillips, 1993: 107

[74] See Gilroy, 1987: 50 for a discussion of the racist effect of rooted English communities.

[75] See Sennett, 1970: 40 on people feeling '*the same*' (emphasis in original).

along, and did not exist prior to their actions. At the heart of their claim of community, there is what Nikolas Rose calls its Janus-faced logic[76] – community activists base their identity on a place or set of social relationships they are acting on to change. As Gillian Rose says: 'Community ... is about connections.... Connection itself changes what there is to be connected'.[77]

Community identity is often castigated as a retreat from greater forces in society, what Touraine calls '*social antimovements*'.[78] However, the various Southmead identities adopted by these groups were not used to retreat from the social, but to enter into it – what Touraine describes as an 'offensive identity'. That identity is 'no longer an appeal to a mode of being but the claim to a capacity for action and for change'.[79] This identity metamorphoses as action takes effect. One of the effects of these groups has been personal and relationship changes.[80] While an identity was necessary for their formation, their success means that this identity developed and changed.

Narrative

Plummer writes that:

> Communities themselves are ... built through storytelling. *Stories gather people around them*: they have to attract audiences, and these audiences may then have to start to build a common perception, a common language, a commonality.[81]

In the history of the campaigning groups, there were two sets of stories: the first was the story of the situation, the second the story of the campaign. The stories of drug use and personal and family pain that emerged into the public arena in Southmead from around 1994 drew people together. Both SP and the Voice relied heavily on these stories, to bring people together and as a spur to action: 'personal sufferings are (often) transformed into political ones through an emerging *political*

---

[76] Rose, 1996: 334

[77] Rose, 1997: 199

[78] Touraine, 1988: 99 (emphasis in original). This is also a theme throughout Sennett's work (1970, 1986, 1994).

[79] Touraine, 1988: 79, 81

[80] Noted in Chapter Five

[81] Plummer, 1995:174 (emphasis in original)

narrative and *rhetoric*.[82] Stories were used both therapeutically and politically.[83] These stories were continually referred to as the groups grew. The therapeutic nature of storytelling was developed by SP, where counselling was a major tool used to help people recover from addiction. The necessity of being heard was an important theme of the research sponsored by SP.[84]

These stories then led to the story of the struggle, stories of a community that cares, that takes risks, that fights dealers, that goes on TV[85], or of a project that grows from nothing and is now a major provider of help for drug users. People do not act without drama. These stories of heroism, struggle and drama were aesthetically sustaining. They were intimately connected to media representations of the struggle. In previous work I have described how, in an environmental conflict, the protesters rushed home after each incident to watch how it had been covered on TV[86], and the same occurred in Southmead. The way the media dealt with these groups became stories in their own right: how nervous the camera crew seemed when filming outside the drugs fortress, what it was like appearing on a live TV programme when the previous item was an interview with a senior politician.[87]

Inevitably, these stories were profoundly influenced by their audiences; the tellers wanted them to receive a different story from the usual representations of Southmead (similar to the motives of the community play). Which stories to tell to the public was one of the sources of intra-community conflict. I have mentioned a series in the local newspaper called 'The streets of shame'[88], and one of the arguments between SP and the Voice was whether it was right to give the press that image. The SP line was that it was true, and needed saying, whereas the Voice felt the shame. Changing the traditional media representations to Southmead was difficult. They did change from being problem estate to doughty community fighting back, but still in a trivial and melodramatic manner that left out the complexities of that new situation.

The strongest stories were those of SP and the Voice. SPACE's history was not as dramatic and SDT's not as heroic. Their stories did not have that aesthetic pull of narrative that is so mobilising, stories that

---

[82] Plummer, 1995: 110 (emphasis in original)

[83] As with the stories of the Scouts described in Chapter Two.

[84] Newman, 1999

[85] Diary notes, 6 June 1997

[86] Brent, 1992

[87] Diary notes, June 1997

[88] See Chapter Two

gave such pleasure that those involved wanted to keep on living in them and keep them going. Brian Fay, in answer to his own question, *'Do we live stories or just tell them?'*, writes that 'our lives are enstoried and our stories are enlived'.[89] The most energetic actions were those in which 'emplotment' (defined by Ricoeur as the process 'by which events are made *into* a story or ... a story is made *out* of events') was strongest.[90] These stories were a powerful part of 'the daily production of alternative frameworks of meaning' that nourish collective action[91]; the stronger the stories, the more prolific the action.

Public realm

The stories created a new public, and were part of what Phil Cohen calls the 'reassertion of the public realm'.[92] For the storytellers, public narration provided a relief from individual guilt, a sharing of stories of pain very different to the sharing of acceptable memories in the community play. Community politics is based on a public sharing of certain aspects of life, and the taking on of public responsibilities, in the case of these groups, variously, for drug users and young people. There is a retrieval of these responsibilities from official agencies: "it's our estate"; responsibility was neither private nor governmental, but public.

However, there are strains in this position, for example, around the legal rights of alleged drug dealers and their families and the individual needs of drug users, that were in danger of being swept away by calls for the public good. SDT is involved with the problem of providing public facilities in a private and marketised economy, seeking income from the second to provide the first. The public realm of community both combats the privatisation of life and extends the realm of public responsibilities against the tricky background of the protection of individual rights and the growth of individual consumption.

Movement of community

In the descriptions of the four groups one of the major features is not of community as a static form, but of movement and change, with community used as an idea for creating change. The groups come into

---

[89] Fay, 1996: 197
[90] Ricoeur, 1991: 3-4 (emphasis in original)
[91] Melucci, 1989: 70
[92] Cohen, 1997: 32-3

Castells' definition of urban movements, which focus on three main sets of goals:

> ... urban demands on living conditions and collective consumption; the affirmation of local cultural identity; and the conquest of local political autonomy and citizen participation.[93]

All the four organisations involved demands on collective consumption (facilities for drug users, the Greenway Centre, youth facilities); local identity (ideas of Southmead); and citizen participation. All emphasised their difference from political parties.[94]

However, there is a danger of lumping all collective action under a single heading of social movement. To avoid this, Melucci provides a taxonomy of eight different types of collective action.[95] The four organisations do not fit neatly into any one of these categories, but move across them. Melucci reserves the title *social movement* for collective action that is solidary, conflictual *and* breaches the systems limits, a description that could be applied to the opening moments of the campaigning organisations. There was change into what he terms *competition*, in which the conflict is within the system's limits, and is about shifting resources within the system. When these resources were shifted collective action became *cooperation* for the maintenance of the newly reorganised system. The four groups veered between these positions. A danger is that this cooperation becomes *reaction* if under threat. All these processes also involve *individual mobility*, as people entered new relationships (in some cases, new careers) and *collective rituals* (fun days, music and sports events) to maintain them. The four adult organisations considered in this chapter did not involve Melucci's last two categories, *individual resistance* and *deviance*, although these could be descriptions for some of the actions of young people described in the previous chapter.

Effects

One of the more cynical views of community action is that it changes virtually nothing, and that the basic asymmetries of power remain unaffected. Southmead remains a poor place. However, the actions

---

[93] Castells, 1997: 60
[94] Della Porta and Diani, 1999: 16
[95] Melucci, 1996b: 30

of just a few hundred people caused changes that should not be undervalued. The public devastation of drug use locally was reduced, even if the power of the international drug trade was scarcely dented. There was better provision for young people, provided in new ways. New representations of Southmead have arisen. Small havens have been built, even if heaven has not been achieved.[96] Local movements are not the wider social movements that aim at 'transforming human relationships at their most fundamental level, such as feminism and environmentalism'.[97] There are no major victories, but that can also be said of those wider movements. Melucci argues that: 'Conflicts no longer have winners, but they may produce innovation, modernization, and reform'.[98]

Between 1994 and 1999, new, innovatory (for Southmead) ways of approaching the local were established. There is an argument that, by taking action in such a small area, narrow solidarities are formed that blind people to a wider picture. This will be looked at in more detail in Chapter Eight, which looks at the question, 'What is community?'. Although community action uses the word with confidence, it provides no easy answer to the question.

---

[96] Castells, 1997: 61
[97] Castells, 1997: 2
[98] Melucci, 1989: 136

EIGHT

What is community anyway?

Introduction: the multiple confusions of a word

In order to tackle the major question of this book, 'What is community?', this chapter looks at different ways that community is theorised, in conjunction with examples and accounts of previous chapters. It takes the form of a series of complex arguments that lead to a conclusion that is open and discursive; community is not something easily encapsulated into a formula. This is the first of two concluding chapters, to be followed by a final chapter on the problems of engaging with such an open-ended concept.

A significant theme that has emerged is the many and varied uses of the word community within Southmead, uses that can either be in almost direct opposition to each other, or tackle different, if related, facets of collective life, for example, morality, territory, action, identity and control. The meaning and purpose of the word, and the actions associated with it, vary depending on who was using it, and the situation in which it is being used. To recapitulate from the start of the book, different uses of the term within just one incident were set out in the story of the bicycle theft. Different uses and contrasting estimations of community continue through the ways Southmead and its 'community' (or lack) are represented, in formal surveys and policy documents and through varieties of local expression. Moving in and around Southmead, while showing it as a site of powerful forces of difference, did not clearly delineate a bounded or centred entity of community in a way that would resolve the divergence between these uses and estimations. In contrast to ideas of community as a unitary harmonious social form, we have seen the conflict created by the collective behaviour of young people, and four contrasting examples of adult community action. Each of these claims to community existed in the same place and time, and while they share the same 'community repertoire', they use its 'terms and metaphors' 'selectively and flexibly'[1] and differ widely. No simple

---

[1] Potter and Reicher, 1987: 38

picture emerges of Southmead as a discrete community, nor is there a picture of what such a community would be like if it did exist.

The multiple uses of the term community have been widely noted; the confusion surrounding the term in Southmead is far from unique. Marjorie Mayo, discussing community and welfare, writes that:

> This word has been used to try to build credence for fundamentally different projects, projects which may be inherently controlling for oppressed groups, and projects which may be liberating, conjuring up images of mutuality, and mutual caring in human relationships.[2]

It is tempting, in the face of such confusing and contradictory uses of the word, to recommend the jettisoning of its use completely, and find more precise terms for the various social forms and movements that claim community. However, although community is what Goldberg would call a 'chameleonic' concept, one that is malleable and pliant (and therefore dangerous)[3], such a recommendation would have no effect other than as a self-denying ordinance. The use of the term is too widespread to be ended, and the use of language as social communication prevents any individual suppressing use of, or imposing their own meaning on, any word, although there are plenty who have wanted to do so by defining community in a particular way.[4]

What is striking about the term community is how widely it is used, despite (or because of) its ambiguity, the way it can change its guise to suit different circumstances and purposes. There may be no exact truth to the term, yet, as Wittgenstein points out, '["inexact"] does not mean "unusable"'.[5] It is not exactitude that gives words meaning, but their use; searching for an exact 'truth' of community blinds us to the use value of the word. More than that, its ambiguities may reflect the ambiguities of social life. It is this ambiguity, coupled with its ubiquity and politically charged use, that leads me to want to subject community to active interpretation, which, in Derrida's words, 'substitutes incessant deciphering for the unveiling of truth as the presentation of the thing itself in its presence'.[6]

---

[2] Mayo, 1994: 57
[3] Goldberg, 1993: 3
[4] For example, Phillips, 1993: 14 (quoted later in this chapter) and Freie, 1998: 23 (quoted in Chapter Four).
[5] Wittgenstein, 1976: 41
[6] Derrida, 1982: 18

This chapter draws together the incessant deciphering of the book by looking at a number of ideas connected with community: first (a widespread approach to community), that it is an illusion, that claims for its existence are mistaken or duplicitous and hide more important political and social issues; second, that it is an organic social form, in contrast to artificial organisational and economic structures; third, that there is the elision between place and community. The questions that these approaches raise are a prelude to a major problem: can community (or any social form) be defined anyway? I will contrast the temptation of definition with the lure of deconstruction. From these approaches, I want to develop a concept of community that takes into account the various levels on which it operates: material place, dreams, social relationships and actions. I will argue that any such concept must allow for incompletion, splitting, ambiguity and changeability. Finally, the use of community in language and action has material and political effects. These effects, and how they are created, give final clues as to how community is created.

Illusion or reality?

A major criticism of community, and communitarianism, is that as a concept of how society works it either ignores or denies wider forces and structures: the forces of globalism and capitalism that flow over the world, and the structures of race, gender and class that divide the world.[7] The idea of community, it is argued, replaces these flows and structures with illusions of an autonomy that withstands the flows, and of a wholeness that overcomes the divisions.

Marshall Berman gives this dramatic description of living in modern times:

> To be modern ... is to experience personal and social life as a maelstrom, to find one's world and oneself in perpetual disintegration and renewal, trouble and anguish, ambiguity and contradiction: to be part of a universe in which all that is solid melts into air.[8]

---

[7] Globalism, globalisation and the global are terms even more indefinite in their meaning than community. They are used here as other writers use them, as metaphors for big, impersonal economic and cultural forces that appear to move in unrestricted ways around the planet.

[8] Berman, 1983: 345

Life is in constant flux and solid social structures evaporate. By inference, any attempt to make a solid base in the face of this flux is doomed. Any solidity, autonomy or protection offered by community may survive for a time, but offers no protection against the maelstrom and will be dissolved in the turmoil. The maelstrom of the creative destruction of modern capitalism undercuts the power of place and replaces it with flows: 'from place to flow, from spaces to streams', as Lash and Urry describe the workings of what they call disorganised capitalism.[9] Castells sees as a major social trend 'the historical emergence of the space of flows, superseding the meaning of the space of places'.[10] I have already pointed out how uncertain are the lives of young people in particular, as the terms of their lives are subject to continual change.[11] Wider cultural influences in film, music and clothes, referred to in previous chapters, undermine the idea of local community as a simple repository of cultural difference, and within Southmead both large and small effects of the world of economic flows are visible, as shown by the following examples.

In the second half of the 1990s, there was a marked reduction in unemployment in Southmead, from 14.3% in April 1996 to 6.3% in January 1999. Despite Southmead becoming poorer relative to the rest of Bristol, the city as a whole was becoming wealthier.[12] This flow of economic activity cannot be traced to local factors or to the growth in community activity in Southmead in the late 1990s, but was part of a wider trend reflecting shifts of economic activity within Britain and its performance in the global economy. The upsurge of local community activity described in the last chapter came *after* the growth of employment. Although it would be difficult to argue how the income growth determined, caused or provided the motive for the passionate involvement in community activity, it could be argued that it made it possible by providing an increase in confidence and resources. Recognising relative prosperity as a contributory factor in community mobilisation is salutary, reminding us not to blame poor people if they do not have the resources to mobilise.[13] This flow to

---

[9] Lash and Urry, 1994: 323. The idea of the 'creative destruction' of capitalism is Joseph Schumpeter's, described in Zukin, 1991: 4.

[10] Castells, 1989: 348

[11] See Chapter Six

[12] Bristol City Council, 1996a, 1997a, 1999. The reports warn that these figures are approximate. They are also for the whole ward, so do not show how the poorest sub-ward was faring, but they are strong indications of a trend.

[13] Boswell (1990) argues, however, that community is not just an add-on to economic life, but that economic health and community renaissance are inseparable.

Southmead could ebb again, with the resulting depression and struggle for maintenance of individual existence having knock-on effects on community activity in the area.

Stock market discipline affects the community involvement of companies. After four years of financial support for projects in Southmead, take-over pressure on one firm led it, in 2000, to cut its community programme. The previous policy of the managing director (who lost his job in the changes), of employee and community value, was overtaken by the language of shareholder value. Resources for Southmead were thus affected by national and global changes in the world banking system, distant from local circumstance.[14] The transforming role of international capital in Southmead has been pointed out in the example of the building of the supermarket in 1997.[15] Each such example is a drip of change and together these drips form the flow of capital.

Such examples show how local place is buffeted by economic uncertainties. Rather than seeking refuge in an illusion of certainty, Berman advises that:

> To be a *modernist* is to make oneself somehow at home in the maelstrom, to make its rhythms one's own, to move within its currents in search of the forms of reality, of beauty, of freedom, of justice, that its fervid and perilous flow allows.[16]

A common theme among writing on community is that attempts to create community are merely reactions against the uncertainty that is social reality; they are understandable but doomed projects.[17] Corlett sympathises with the desire for reassurance, which he sees as one of the bases of community: 'a desire for foundations; a desire to escape the play of the world and stay at home for the night'.[18] More nihilistically, Maffesoli writes that the 'horror of emptiness drives one into indiscriminate association, making people gather together without

---

[14] Record of conversation with a company manager, 11 January 2000. Only six months before, the managing director had been extolling the business sense of community involvement in the video Southmead Slamming.

[15] See Chapter Five

[16] Berman, 1983: 345-6

[17] Harvey, 1990: 238-9

[18] Corlett, 1989: 67. Home for him is not in the rhythm of the maelstrom.

rhyme or reason'.[19] Sennett argues that the belief that community means resistance leads to retreat from the world:

> The emotional logic of community, beginning as a resistance to the evils of modern capitalism, winds up as a bizarre kind of depoliticized withdrawal; the system remains intact, but maybe we can get it to leave our piece of turf untouched.[20]

Such retreat is unsuccessful. A dramatic example of community failure emerges in Sennett's study of the Jewish ghetto in Venice in the 16th and 17th centuries. He shows the great efforts made to transform the ghetto into a community, so that 'an accursed space became a holy place'.[21] Despite the fact that a powerful and glittering social life was created out of this oppressed and segregated space, all this was erased in 1636, in one of the worst pogroms ever known in Europe.[22] Notwithstanding all the efforts of the Jews in the ghetto, they had not, through creating community, escaped oppression, but had even, possibly, strengthened it by accepting the reality of the ghetto even as they tried to invert its meaning:

> A group identity forged by oppression remains in the hand of the oppressor... It can be no reproach to say they [the Jews] had internalized the oppressor in making a community out of a space of oppression. But this communal life proved to be, at best, a shield rather than a sword.[23]

That this shield of community could not withstand attack, and gave only illusory protection, is a case that Sennett sees as more than an isolated historical tragedy. Phil Cohen, writing of working-class areas in late 20th-century Britain, agues that community is a 'make-believe that "*we* rule round here"'.[24] It is 'a magical device for creating something apparently solidary out of the thin air of modern times'.[25] Because the larger forces that drove the east end of London into poverty could not be resisted, this semblance of control was exercised through racial

---

[19] Maffesoli, 1991: 14
[20] Sennett, 1986: 296
[21] Sennett, 1986: 243
[22] Sennett, 1986: 248
[23] Sennett, 1986: 249
[24] Cohen, 1988: 34 (emphasis in original)
[25] Cohen, 1997: 39

exclusions. Phillips, using a wide historical sweep, says that: 'Racism, sexism, exclusion and even eradication ... are often involved in attempts to achieve community'.[26] The control gained by such community, does not, Bauman argues, provide liberation, but instead imposes group domination over individuals: 'communitarian "difference" stands for the group's power to limit individual freedom'.[27] Communities trying to take control of their destinies create new oppressions. Some of the examples in this book have shown this in practice.

There is a strong argument that by trying to create local solutions, based on an idea of the common good, community masks real issues, divisions and power relationships. Anthony Cohen shows how community is not drawn along the lines of major social divisions: 'Rather than being drawn at the point were differentiation occurs, the community boundary incorporates and encloses difference'.[28] The divisions of community identity cross and obscure structural divisions, as the geographers Peet and Thrift make more explicit:

> Movements tend to use a language of local community rather than a language of class or race or gender, so that they can neutralize certain issues (although these issues can return to haunt them).[29]

Formations such as community based on a spatial solidarity hide power relations, and need demystifying.[30] In fact, they do more than hide power relations − by their parochialism, they create what has been called a '*narrow* form of social consciousness' that leads to 'yet more sectionalism in the working class', so preventing capitalist power relations from being challenged.[31]

Barthes describes the workings of myth as being the way history, with all its political content, is transformed into nature.[32] Communities can be seen as such depoliticising myths, in their case turning social inequality into natural difference. Both the community play and Radio Southmead treated Southmead as a natural form to be celebrated (akin to the Jews of the Venice ghetto). The creativity of that community art

---

[26] Phillips, 1993: 176
[27] Bauman, 1996: 81
[28] Cohen, 1986b: 13
[29] Peet and Thrift, 1989b: 49
[30] Soja, 1989: 61
[31] Centre for Contemporary Cultural Studies, 1976: 17 (emphasis in original). This is typical of 'old left' criticisms of community.
[32] Barthes, 1973: 140

masked the social processes that created and maintained Southmead in the first place, mistakenly claiming this creation as the actions of local inhabitants. Sennett is, as ever, highly cynical about the masking effect of community; the masks that in performance theory enable people to act and in fact deceive: 'What is peculiar about modern community roles ... is that the masks, supposedly only the means to power, become ends in themselves'.[33] The identity given by these masks does not empower the wearers, but acts to naturalise their existence in the area. Southmead itself becomes masked as a place on the map, a natural feature. The creation of community in that place, lauded as the product of human agency, hides the forces under which people live.

Desire to escape these forces can lead to community being manufactured as a commodity, described by Harvey as 'packaged for sale by producers'.[34] John Freie calls these packages 'counterfeit communities'.[35] He writes of the 'common interest developments' (CIDs) that exist in the United States, counterfeit communities that give those who buy into them the illusion of avoiding social problems through the purchase of self-segregation and authoritarian rules.[36] These are simulacra, 'not just fantasies, but imitations of fantasies'.[37] While people do not buy into Southmead as a commodified community (in fact, the opposite is the case – it is the sort of place these CIDs are built to avoid), this criticism of fantasy community could be aimed at its own community activity.[38]

Within these ideas of community as an illusion, however, there is often a hint of the possibility of 'real' communities. Community may be an impossible illusion/delusion under present conditions, but the idea still has a utopian purchase on the imagination of many of those who criticise it. Similar to the views of those involved in the Southmead community play[39], there are those who believe that community existed in the past, in pre-modern times (as Phillips puts it, 'a concern with the disappearance of community ... has been a persistent theme in political and social thought throughout much of the nineteenth and twentieth

---

[33] Sennett, 1986: 304
[34] Harvey, 1990: 82
[35] Freie, 1998: 5
[36] Freie, 1998: 40
[37] Freie, 1998: 7
[38] See Bornat (1993) on community histories as fables
[39] See Chapter Four

centuries'[40]), and could be achieved again in the future. The validity of the future good of community in contrast to its present illusory existence is spelt out by Marx and Engels:

> In the previous substitutes for the community ... personal freedom has existed only for the individuals who developed within the relationships of the ruling class, and only insofar as they were individuals of this class. The illusory community, in which individuals have up till now combined ... [was] not only a completely illusory community, but a new fetter as well. In a real community the individuals obtain their freedom in and through their association.[41]

There is therefore a distinction between community as an illusory idea, never to be achieved, and as an illusory practice, not to be achieved under present circumstances.

These arguments as to whether or not community is an illusion in the modern, globalised world are based around three sets of ideas: first, the idea that illusion does not have a role in the tough world of social reality; second, the idea that community is too static to cope with the flows of the world; and third, that globalisation is a totalising force that precludes all other forms of social organisation.

In contrast to the first idea, Berger and Luckman argue that: '*All social reality is precarious*'.[42] Ernesto Laclau goes on to argue that myth is used in constructing that social reality: 'Myth is constitutive of any possible society'.[43] Even those, like Phillips, who are critical of the rhetoric of community, do not deny that this rhetoric has created social effects, even if these are harmful: 'The rhetoric of the common good has tended to benefit those with wealth, power, and privilege'.[44] Illusion and rhetoric are an important part of social discourse and action, which is not, as I have shown in Southmead (particularly in relation to young people), based merely on instrumentality, but has strong aesthetic and narrative components. Rather than rejecting community for being an illusion, the workings of community open the way for recognising how much illusion is part of social life. While illusions may be dangerous

---

[40] Phillips, 1993: 3. Nancy makes a similar point (1991: 1), as do Bell and Newby (1971) and many others, and saying that this is a persistent theme is a persistent theme in books on community.

[41] Marx and Engels, 1970: 83

[42] Berger and Luckman, 1967: 121 (emphasis in original)

[43] Laclau, 1990: 67

[44] Phillips, 1993: 168

(and there are plenty of examples of the dangers of community), they cannot be dismissed for being 'unreal'. They may appear to turn history into nature, but this transformation in itself transforms the social action that continues to make history.

The community activity in Southmead described in previous chapters is both conflictual and shifting. Community is not necessarily a form of social stasis. My accounts of community mobilisations in Southmead, and of the collective behaviour of young people, show community activity itself as a maelstrom, all about movement, with its young people even unleashing their own forces of creative destruction. I have argued that to typify it as static is defeatist, a tactic of social control. Community activities are messy and conflictual, the opposite of the stasis and pacification that would exist only if there were quiescent resignation to the forces around rather than mobilisations. These community activities were not defensive, but made offensive claims on the wider world. They were ways by which people entered the maelstrom rather than succumb to it. As bell hooks puts it, it is because of the risk involved in being radical, in making claims on the world, that 'one needs a community of resistance'.[45] The argument about the political worth of any particular community or community activity concerns the focus that it is built around, and the issues that it confronts. For many people, that focus is a matter over which there is not much choice, as an identity has been given them by virtue of exclusion or pathologisation, whether it be the Jews of 17th century Venice or, less violently, the working class of 20th- and 21st-century Southmead. While there may be disappointment with these communities that they do not radically change the social relationships that they are in, this should be directed at the asymmetries of power involved rather than at the people involved. The act of telling people that the understanding on which they base their activity is illusory perpetuates the relationship of the superior role of the social scientist to unknowing participants that we first encountered in the work of the Bristol Social Project.[46]

Finally, whether community and globalisation are antithetical is under question. Community growth and the globalisation of power are, Castells says, 'part of the same fundamental process of historical restructuring'. In the face of globalisation:

> People have affirmed their cultural identity, often in territorial terms, mobilizing to achieve their demands,

---

[45] hooks, 1991: 149

[46] See Chapter Three

organizing their communities, and staking out their places to preserve meaning, to restore whatever limited control they have over work and residence, to reinvent love and laughter in the midst of the abstraction of the new historical landscape. [47]

Communities and localities are therefore becoming more important, and the relationship between localisation and globalisation is not a case of either/or, but of both/and; as Stuart Hall puts it, 'the local' operating within the logic of 'the global'.[48] This logic raises questions both about community at a global level[49] and about how local communities operate within it. Janna Thompson argues that these local communities need to be far more complex than the simple definitions given by communitarians, in order for a global community to exist.

> Because their account of community does not fit relations in a modern state, communitarians tend to lapse into a reactionary position, expressed by a distaste for modern political complexities and uncertainties and a longing for a simpler political life.[50]

Complex local identities can, and must, be part of cosmopolitan theory, as a complex identity 'is conducive to the establishment of procedures for resolving conflicts between communities'.[51] Rather than rule out all ideas of community, it is only when ideas and formations of local community are simple that they are antithetical to global community, which aspires to be a humanising (if illusory) constraint on the flows and divisions that threaten people's control over their own lives. Neither local nor global community is sufficient without the other.

Community as an organic form

Castells suggests that community is a reclamation of life from abstraction. The idea of a reconnection of people and nature is expounded in a collection of essays edited by Rajan, using a strange mix of Buddhism, Gaia, Ghandi, Amerindian thought, ecology, post-modernism and

---

[47] Castells, 1989: 350

[48] Hall, 1993: 354. This theme occurs, in different forms, in Cohen, 1986a; Castells, 1989, 1997; Lash and Urry 1994; Maffesoli, 1996.

[49] Explored in the essays in Archibugi et al, 1998

[50] Thompson, 1998: 188

[51] Thompson, 1998: 187

feminism.[52] Community is a way of bringing the natural, organic world, back into politics, inverting the idea that community turns politics into nature into a positive attribute.

The strand of thought that there is a lifeworld, separate from, and possibly prior to, the systems of politics and economics, is not confined to the spiritual apostles in Rajan's collection. The idea of lifeworld is a major theme in Habermas' work. For him, 'Marx was the first to analyze this conflict between system imperatives and lifeworld imperatives'.[53] Money and power are the main examples of functional systems, that 'can neither buy nor compel solidarity and meaning'.[54] Our own alienation from ourselves is increasing as the spheres of economy and public administration expand, relationships become objectified and people become objects.[55] The idea is taken up by Melucci, who reaffirms that: 'The colonization of the lifeworld is certainly an observable trend in complex societies'.[56] Melucci distinguishes the lifeworld from economic activity, the political system and organizational systems, and describes it as 'that level of social relations through which the basic requirements of social life are maintained and reproduced through interaction and communication'.[57] While for him the lifeworld is but part of the social structure, incomplete without the other parts; for others it is separate, even superior. Maffesoli argues that we are witnessing a return to vitalism by which the *organic* and the life principle in social life is becoming more important than the *mechanical*; for him, the tendency is in the opposite direction to that charted by Habermas and Melucci, although he uses similar concepts, which he traces to the influence of Weber.[58] I have previously quoted Lefebvre's view on how young people act to recover the natural as a struggle against the dominant system.[59] The organic world, it is argued, is necessary; dystopia exists, in Augé's view, in places where there is no organic society: 'the non-place is the opposite of utopia: it exists, and does not contain any organic

---

[52] See Rajan, 1993: 5 and 15, and the various essays in this book, Rebuilding communities.

[53] Habermas, 1987: 349, 1992. 'Lifeworld' is a major part of the argument in both books.

[54] Habermas, 1987: 363

[55] Habermas, 1992: 141

[56] Melucci, 1989: 195

[57] Melucci, 1996b: 27

[58] Maffesoli, 1996: 3, 12. Bell and Newby point out that, in 19th-century sociology, 'The community ... was viewed as man's natural habitat'. This included not only Marx and Weber, but also Tönnies (Bell and Newby, 1971: 22).

[59] Lefebvre, 1991: 50, quoted in Chapter Six

society'. In his view, these non-places are multiplying; the non-organic is gaining ground.[60]

It is this idea of organic as opposed to artificial space that is often claimed for community. Freie writes that 'community is organic, not contractual or artificial'.[61] Alinsky's vision of community is as a natural formation, opposed to the unnaturalness of state power. In his writing, even the power holders in the community, the 'community leaders', are typified as being native and indigenous, without being tainted by the artificiality and oppressiveness of other forms of power.[62] Community, says Maffesoli, is how and where the '*puissance*' of the masses, a power of inherent energy and vital force, overcomes alienation from the institutional power, '*pouvoir*', of the economic-political order.[63]

This rather romantic belief in the role of the organic in social life has been criticised as tending to an idea of an ecology of social existence, an approach that Saunders berates the community studies of the Chicago School for holding.[64] In this approach, people adapt to their environment by creating community in whatever circumstance they find themselves, a highly conservative view that uses community as a natural salve for social conflict. Touraine is scathing about there being any such non-social definition of any social form, any 'metasocial guarantor of social order, such as the essence of humanity'.[65] We have seen the social policy approach that criticises Southmead for not having that salve, in effect blaming it as a unit for not naturally being able to contain the social pressures on it, with a hint of criticism of the humanity of the people who live there.

Southmead as a housing estate is certainly not a natural place, but was physically constructed due to the town and social planning policies of the mid-20th century, and socially constructed both from those policies, and the official and media discourses of poverty, crime and place.[66] In the various examples of community activity in Southmead, we see how it challenges those discourses, in a mode certainly distinct from other mechanisms of social organisation, although whether this is 'natural' is a moot point:

---

[60] Augé, 1995: 34, 111-12

[61] Freie, 1998: 21

[62] Alinsky, 1969: 64, 79. See also Potter and Halliday (1990), who point out that the category 'community' leader, unlike other power holders, has 'relative impermeability to criticism', even at the time of riots (p 919).

[63] Maffesoli, 1996: 1, 44

[64] Saunders, 1986: 52

[65] Touraine, 1988: 75

[66] See Chapter Three

- Apart from Southmead Development Trust, Southmead community action operates differently from state political power, and articulates its difference from the political parties that organise to control that power. These are not systems of governance of the area, but a challenge to those systems for not involving or representing local people, or providing for their needs. Much of the content of young people's collective action involves a transgressive challenge to, and resistance of, the agents of state power.

- These collective activities are not bureaucratic in their organisational forms, and are even militant in their endorsement of spontaneity as an antithesis to bureaucracy, as shown by the informality of meetings, and of unconstrained collective activity of young people. They are dependent on consensus more than organisation. The community art productions from the area were infused with a sense of humanity (the community play), or excess (Fresh Evidence) in antithesis to ideas of purely instrumental reason.

- The Southmead examples of community activity are not based on economic relations of production or exchange, nor are they based on remunity, a term used by Corlett to distinguish relationships of payment and repayment (not necessarily financial) from the mutual sharing of community[67], although neither do they offer an escape from these relations in other areas of life.

There is enjoyment in occupying this different mode of relationship, in its informality, spontaneity and insubordination, for example, the laughter as the dogs sniffed the policeman.[68] These forms themselves are, in Melucci's words, symbolic challenges to the dominant code.[69] However, while operating in a different mode, these community actions relate to the other systems, and are not so separate as to be completely different or autonomous. I have shown how the adult campaigns needed organisations to help fulfil their aspirations, and how all have used political lobbying and fund raising to good effect. I have also shown the importance of both coaxer and audience in community art, which makes clear that this is a constructed rather than natural form of expression. Only the most transgressive of the activities of young people were attempts to carve out carnivalesque space with no systemic involvement, and these inevitably succumbed to systemic control by the police.

---

[67] Corlett, 1989
[68] See Chapter Seven
[69] Melucci, 1989: 60

Visions of community as natural spaces are similar to Habermas' view of a world of communicative reason, where there is a 'mutual and constraint-free understanding among individuals in their dealings with one another'.[70] However, community in Southmead, as needs to be constantly reiterated, is not a form of harmonious natural equilibrium, but a conflictual and highly politicised space.

As well as the fact of existing in relation to institutionalised systems (including those that set up the construction of Southmead as an object) compromising any idea of the organic purity of community, the community actions described in previous chapters have also been riddled with their own relationships of power, gender, race and generation. Some have been the exercise of power against the isolated, the different and the weak. As Foucault reminds us, the most ethically based (even seemingly natural) forms of relationships between people include relationships of power and knowledge, sexuality being his major example.[71] These are not internally power-free zones engaging in battle against negative external powers, as in Alinsky's model, a model that cannot withstand Foucault's insight that 'Resistance is never in a position of exteriority in relation to power'.[72]

Claiming community as organic or natural is to assert the existence of a fundamental ground on which it rests, what Derrida calls 'a fundamental immobility and reassuring certitude'.[73] But, as he says, there are no structures of any sort that possess this certitude. No structure has an independent centre, either inside of itself (as a core), or outside (as a foundation), as what are seen as cores or foundations are themselves constructed as part of the structure itself. As Derrida points out, this lack of foundation is extremely difficult to conceive of; any structure without certainty at its centre 'represents the unthinkable itself'.[74] It is in the face of this unthinkability that the ideas of nature, organicity or *puissance* are used to explain community, to give community a thinkable foundation. Their use is as vivid *metaphors* to distinguish the difference between community and the more instrumental and formal lines of the state or the abstractions of the economic system. However,

---

[70] Habermas, 1992: 145
[71] Foucault, 1986: 387; 1979
[72] Foucault, 1979: 95
[73] Derrida, 1978: 279
[74] Derrida, 1978: 279

to claim these concepts as solid foundation for community can be problematic. There is no necessary congruence between natural and good; appeal to notions of nature can be used not only to explain a desire for connectedness (which itself can be used for a variety of ends), but also to justify vicious acts of domination. In Southmead, it was the collective activities of young people that relied most on spontaneity and aesthetic content (although driving cars at high speed is hardly a natural phenomenon) that were the least sustainable (and most destructive) of all the examples of communal activity given. Any good that is in community has to be argued for, and cannot rely on appeal to an idea of foundational natural good as explanation or legitimisation.

There are issues as to whether, albeit the formation of community is not organic, there is a thinkable (even if only through metaphor) life force that propels that formation, involving desire, spontaneity and aesthetics, a question to be asked of all social forms. A cursory look at advertising shows how desire and aesthetics are put to work as part of the economic system, how adverts play with connotations of lifeworld and excess, and how the exchange value of goods are based as much on their aesthetic value as their use value. The examples in this book show how social forms are not constructed purely by ideas of systematic instrumental reason. The study of community shows that, as well as illusion being an important part of social construction, so too are desires for spontaneity and aesthetic content.

Community and place

Throughout this book there has been little distinction made between Southmead as place, and Southmead as community, an unclear elision of meanings. 'Confusing place and community is widespread in the social sciences', writes John Agnew, and this reflects 'ambiguity in the language of community'.[75] However, in the accounts of community activity in Southmead, the place features as a vital ingredient in the concept of community. It was fetishised by the community play and Radio Southmead, and proclaimed in their names by all the organisations that assert community in Southmead. The place itself is both a meaningful part of identity, and the site of community activity, be it the illicit carnival in the woods, or the development of anti-drug initiatives.

In exploring this close relationship between space and community, one can see how separating the two out could make a different sense of the previous arguments; space the reality, community the illusion,

---

[75] Agnew, 1989: 10

or space the abstract notion that comes to life when filled by the organic presence of community. However, the relationship between the two is not so clear-cut. There have been constant attempts to define what space is, which parallel the attempts to define community, with as many different conceptualisations.[76] According to Lefebvre, space is not simply a geometric shape, or empty area: 'It seems to be well established that physical space has no 'reality' without the energy that is deployed within it'.[77] Furthermore, geographical space, says Bourdieu, 'is never socially neutral'.[78] Foucault points out that geographical terms and metaphors also always involve other ideas, which may be legal, economic, political, juridical or pictorial.[79] Community is, among other usages, a geographical metaphor that involves both spatial and other ideas. One of the important and recurring descriptions of Southmead as a *place* in official reports has been its lack of *community*; the two are closely, if confusedly, linked.[80]

Community is one idea of place. However, it does not exist inevitably in every place, and the differences between places are not necessarily based on the differences between them as communities. The major difference between Southmead and its neighbour, Westbury, is one of class.[81] Space is racially charged, with racial division reflected and reinforced by spatial separation.[82] The boundaries of place are not constructed as boundaries of community, or vice versa, and both are hard to find, as pointed out in my journeys to and from Southmead. One cannot separate out boundaries of space as being purely physical from boundaries of community as being social or symbolic. Place itself, as Berdoulay has pointed out, is also connected with narrative and meaning.[83] Attempts to have a more value-free conception of

---

[76] For example, Murgatroyd et al, 1985; Agnew and Duncan, 1989; Peet and Thrift, 1989b; Soja, 1989; Bagguley et al, 1990; Harloe et al, 1990; Shields, 1991; Duncan and Ley, 1993; Gregory and Urry, 1985; Pile and Thrift, 1995; Sibley, 1995. Important interventions are 'Questions of geography' in Foucault, 1980, and Lefebvre, 1991.
[77] Lefebvre, 1991: 13
[78] Bourdieu, 1984: 102
[79] Foucault, 1980: 68
[80] See Chapter Three
[81] Chapters Two and Three
[82] Goldberg, 1993: 187; Keith and Cross, 1993. Examples of the racial/spatial politics of Southmead are shown in Chapters Four, Five, Six and Seven.
[83] Berdoulay, 1989: 134-5. See also de Certeau, 1984.

the difference space makes, such as locality, have failed. Locality is as confusing a concept to define as community.[84]

For Freie, local space is essential to community, as it is only through face-to-face relationships that community can be built: 'A sense of place continues to be an important element of community: it provides a physical location and focus for human interaction ... the undermining of place has had devastating effects'. [85] In a communitarian pamphlet, the creation of urban villages is seen as part of a policy to strengthen community.[86] The authors of a study of Lancaster that tries to get to grips with the importance of space state that 'community forms of mutual support – which imply trust, a rough homogeneity of condition and lack of privacy – are unlikely to survive much geographical or social mobility'[87] The importance of trust was seen as important in the community mobilisations in Southmead, with that trust built up on long-term, face-to-face relationships made possible by people living in both geographical and social proximity with each other. Such a relationship, however, is extremely limited. Iris Marion Young points out that: 'Recognizing the specific value of ... face-to-face relationships ... is quite a different matter from proposing them as the organising principle of a whole society'.[88] We need also to remember that not all face-to-face relationships are necessarily communitarian in nature; they can include eyeball-to-eyeball hatred.

Most communities are not based on such close relationships. Except for the very smallest, they are, in Benedict Anderson's term, *imagined*: "All communities larger than primordial villages of face-to-face contact (and perhaps even these) are imagined'.[89] Face-to-face contact by itself certainly does not guarantee community, but in any case Southmead is itself too large for complete face-to-face knowledge and contact. This is an explanation for the profusion of community groups, in each of which there is face-to-face contact, although within these groups community is still imagined as being larger than just that group. Community exists as an imagination of relationships. But then Southmead, too, exists as an imagined place as much as a physical space.[90] The imaginings of place and community are linked.

---

84 Duncan, 1989: 247
85 Freie, 1998: 31
86 Atkinson, 1994: 37-8
87 Bagguley et al, 1990: 141
88 Young, 1990: 316
89 Anderson, 1991: 6
90 Argued in Chapter One

Not all social combinations that are conceived of as communities are place-based. Gusfield wrote that:

> Communal points of reference emerge in modern society without the kind of territorial and interpersonal experiences often seen as essential to the development and persistence of community.[91]

Jeffrey Weeks writes about the importance of sexual communities for affirming and sustaining identities[92]; there can be diaspora communities of race[93] and there is the contested idea that communities can be formed over the net.[94] All these realise that social relationships are wider than face-to-face, with communication systems operating over social space not limited by locality.

This book has not even started to look at residents of Southmead who see themselves as members of minority or transgressive sexual communities, although there is a local shop called Transformations, which promises 'Change from He to She in 15 minutes'.[95] There is the presence of a black diaspora, as shown by the Barbadan funeral in Southmead.[96]

> At the funeral there were many older Black people, but the younger people were Black, Asian, mixed. What was most visible was the smartness of the Black people there (communal pride?), but also the scruffiness and visible poverty of the white people. The Black people came from all around – London, different parts of Bristol. The white people all had a Southmead connection.[97]

On this occasion, the diaspora and place-based communities came together in joint mourning; as Mercer says, 'communities come to be united mostly in moments of tragedy and grief'.[98] On other occasions, diaspora communities are seen as such a threat to place communities

---

[91] Gusfield, 1975: 47

[92] Weeks, 1995: 106

[93] See Gilroy, 1987, 1993 for ideas on black diaspora and community.

[94] Doheny-Farina, 1996; Smith and Kollock, 1999

[95] Diary notes, 1997

[96] See Chapter Four

[97] Diary notes, June 1997

[98] Mercer, 1995: 15

that they are excluded or exterminated. In 1994, two of the Southmead pubs sported notices reading:

Sorry

No Travellers

or Gypsy's

Welcome Here.[99]

And, hanging over the 20th century, is the history of the non-national nation of Jews whose threat to the idea of fixed spatial boundaries led to their mass slaughter.[100] It is examples such as this, and the histories of former Yugoslavia and Rwanda (albeit these were about an 'enemy within' rather than a translocal enemy) that inform much of the criticism of the equation of place with community, as it leads to local chauvinism that is neither mutual within itself nor cooperative with those outside.[101]

> The ideal of a society consisting of decentralized face-to-face communities is undesirably utopian in several ways. It fails to see that alienation and violence are not only a function of the mediation of social relations but also can and do exist in face-to-face relations.... It fails to address the political question of the relations among face-to-face communities.[102]

In the case of community activity in Southmead, place is the communal point of reference, to the extent that it is fetishised and enlivened by that activity. Place and community activity exist in an interlocking metonymic relationship; Southmead is a part of community, and community is part of Southmead. Each is an attribute of the other, which makes it hard, when writing about them, to keep them separate. Each

---

[99] Brent, 1997: 75-6
[100] Bauman, 1989: 52
[101] For Rwanda and how the idea of internal enemy ended in genocide, see Gourevitch 1998.
[102] Young 1990:302

is imagined as much as actual, with the imaginings closely interlinked. The relationship between them can best be described metaphorically: space is a stage brought to life by performance; community is one of the shows performed.

Definition or deconstruction?

In the discussion so far, there has been a constant circling around what community *is*, a continual deferral of any descriptive or definitional formulation by which 'it' can be identified. Imprecise terms, such as illusion, myth and performance, have been used; there has been a reliance on figures of speech such as metaphor and metonymy, and an emphasis on relationships with other concepts (the global, system imperatives and place). There has been nothing more specific with which to identify community, although there have been various words associated with it throughout the book: connectedness, mutuality, utopia, resistance, politicised space, spontaneity, aesthetics, imagination, collective action, narrative.

In the face of this tangle of words, there is little wonder that there exists a desire for a definition, a desire not merely to satisfy an appetite for orderliness, but to achieve very practical purposes: to judge claims of community, to find out how they work and to see if we want them. Phillips argues that only when the definitional problem has been sorted out can we answer three types of question:

- *historical:* 'It is difficult to determine the prevalence of communities in the past without knowing what community *is*' [103] – important because of the constant harping back to times when it is claimed it did exist, against which claims of community in the present are judged;
- *sociological:* What are the conditions for the realization of community, and the mechanisms needed to maintain it?;
- *moral* and *political:* Is community an attractive possibility for us today?

From the answers to these, he wants to be 'able to offer an informed judgement about the crucial question concerning the viability of community in contemporary society'.[104] For Freie, definition is needed to identify counterfeit communities, to provide a basis for self-

---

[103] Phillips, 1993: 7-9, emphasis in original
[104] Phillips, 1993: 7-9

criticism and to provide a vision.[105] Doheny-Farina sees the necessity to differentiate between communities and lifestyle enclaves.[106] These three American writers (Phillips a 'liberal', the other two communitarians) are all too aware of how the symbols of community are used for the purposes of political manipulation, and call for definition as a tool against such manipulation. The questions and concerns they raise are important, and are applicable to Southmead – would community there 'help ameliorate injustice and alleviate human suffering?'.[107]

Phillips' definition, based on his reading of communitarian writers, reads:

> A *community* is a group of people who live in a common territory, have a common history and shared values, participate together in various activities, and have a high degree of solidarity.[108]

If this definition were applied to Southmead, the answer would be that Southmead is *not* a community[109]: while there are *ideas* of territory, history, values and solidarity, in *practice* these ideas never achieve a full consensus. There are numerous fragmented collective activities. There are disagreements over values and conflict between groups that undermine the idea of an all-encompassing Southmead solidarity.

Merely testing Southmead against this definition does not provide a social understanding of the importance of community-type activity in Southmead, and devalues the collective actions that people do take. It assumes that community exists only in a complete form, as opposed to the fragments I have shown, and shown as important. It assumes that an area can be judged against one set of criteria alone, not that there is conflict between a variety of forces, of which community is but one. Trying to simplify and clarify the words does not simplify and clarify the practice.

There are writers who voice doubts as to whether, in the face of the definitional problems they have encountered, community even exists, as if definition is necessary for existence. Bell and Newby discuss the matter in some depth. They come to the conclusion that: 'Whether

---

[105] Freie, 1998: 23

[106] Doheny-Farina, 1996: 50

[107] Phillips, 1993: 9

[108] Phillips, 1993: 14 (emphasis in original). This is not dissimilar to Freie's definition quoted on page 141 in Chapter Five.

[109] In fact, Phillips concludes that there are no examples, past or present, that live up to his definition.

community exists is a matter of some dispute'.[110] Their doubt would be compounded by the account that I have given of Southmead. For them, the problem arises from the issue of whether community is a normative or an empirical concept. In their approach, there is no place for the normative in sociological analysis, which should be concerned with what exists, not with what should be. An argument of this book is that people's view of what should be (for example, that Southmead should be clear of heroin) is part of what is (which is not that Southmead is clear of heroin, but that people act in certain ways that change the place). Existence and aspiration are not neatly separable. Bell and Newby want to be able to define objects in a neutral, objective and classifiable way, without value judgements, in order for them to be useful for their kind of sociological analysis and comparison. They accuse community studies of subjectivity, idiosyncrasy and eccentricity.[111] It is, however, ironic that, because there are difficulties in fitting communities into a taxonomy, community rather than taxonomy should be considered at fault, and because community does not fit with their idea of sociological definition the existence of community is questioned.[112] This is itself a normative and prescriptive approach to what counts as social truth, in which incomparability and uncertainty, ambiguity and multiple meanings play no part, an approach that treats social forms as quasi-material objects that conform to a very narrow idea of definition. It is particularly ironic in relation to community, which is one of the means by which people assert their own difference from others. Bhabha points out that: 'The difference in cultures cannot be something that can be accommodated within a universalist framework ... cultural practices construct their own meaning and social organisation'.[113] Difference cannot be listed within an objective taxonomy; as we have seen, people use the idea of community in order to escape such one-dimensional labelling.

This approach is illustrative of what Young describes as Western conceptualisation: 'a desire to think things together into a unity, to formulate a representation of the whole, a totality'. Her own criticism of the dream of community is because it itself is a dream of unity and totality, of a defined object that does not allow for heterogeneity and difference: 'The desire for community relies on the same desire for

---

[110] Bell and Newby, 1971: 250. See also Charsley, 1986: 173, who is sceptical of the 'ontological status' of community.

[111] Bell and Newby, 1971: 13

[112] As regards taxonomy, there is the oft-quoted attempt by Hillery, which ended up with 94 definitions, 16 elements and 22 combinations (Bell and Newby, 1971: 27).

[113] Bhabha, 1990: 209

social wholeness and identification that underlies racism and ethnic chauvinism on the one hand and political sectarianism on the other'.[114] So while others reject community for its non-existence as a solid object, she rejects it because of the possibility of it becoming an object, illustrative of the (incommensurable) difference between a positivist definitional approach and her deconstructionist approach.

The desire for definition, as well as presuming the solidity of social objects, has an expectation of words that is over-simple. Wittgenstein long ago rejected the idea that words stand for objects (for example, *word* community = *object* community).[115] Derrida puts the argument in a more complex way:

> The signified concept is never present in and of itself, in a sufficient presence that would refer only to itself ... every concept is inscribed in a chain or in a system within which it refers to the other, to other concepts, by means of the systematic play of differences.[116]

This approach leads to a much more elaborate basis for formulating the meaning of community. Community itself has been described as a way that people define or recognise themselves, the way they assert their distinctiveness.[117] This definition is always in relation to others, for example, the idea of an inside and outside of Southmead, the expulsion of those who are different, the recognition of the differences in language and so on. Community as a concept is concerned with definition, definition through difference, but differences that, as Derrida points out, 'have not fallen from the sky fully formed'.[118] Bauman makes this point strongly, attacking the communitarian idea of situatedness as a creator of difference: '"Situatedness" is socially, and *controversially*, produced; it is always an outcome of competitive struggle'.[119] Definitions of community are the result of a relationship of struggle, as shown throughout this book. Social difference and definition do not have an *a priori* existence, but are continually being created and struggled over.

---

[114] Young, 1990: 302
[115] Plant, 1974: 9
[116] Derrida, 1982: 11
[117] Cohen, 1985: 107; 1986b: ix. Castells, quoted earlier in this chapter, made a similar point, as did Bhabha.
[118] Derrida, 1982: 11
[119] Bauman, 1993: 46 (emphasis in original)

Even when words are formed, they are not singular expressions. Bakhtin states this baldly: 'no word relates to its object in a *singular* way'.[120] My own (simplified) understanding of Derrida shows at least three elements within any word: trace, 'impossible presence' and supplement, as follows:

- Trace is described by Derrida using this 'formula': it is a 'past that has never been present'.[121] The concept of community always seems to contain the idea of an imagined past, wholeness, nature and so on. This trace can also be a taint, with racism as a strong example within the idea of community. Trace, however, does not mean origin: 'there is above all no originary trace'.[122] Although always present, this trace does not *determine* meaning. However, it does *allow* meaning; the traces of vernacular struggle within the idea of community, for instance, give a kind of permission for people to act collectively and challenge powerful institutions.
- While the lack of empirical verification of community is bemoaned, in fact community never does exist in completeness – it is never all there. Solidarity and mutuality are concepts that can never be *fully* achieved; they are an impossible presence. Completion of them, final closure of the relationships, is always deferred. This idea of the impossible presence goes beyond the alternatives of either presence *or* absence, the idea that community either exists or it does not, which is the method of definitional strategies.[123]
- Any attempt to define presence through words, by supplying the 'thing' with a sign, is *adding* a supplement: 'The sign is always the supplement of the thing itself'.[124] Any definition of community is supplementing it, adding to, not clarifying, its meaning. This supplement is not imprisoned by previous definitions, which gives it a certain danger ('... *That dangerous supplement* ...' being the title of Derrida's chapter): danger of 'misuse' of the term, but possibilities too of its extension.[125] The idea of supplement applied to community emphasises that it is always incomplete, as more can always be added to it, but this possibility of addition also creates the possibility of

---

[120] Bakhtin, 1981: 276. Williams writes that it is the way words vary that is interesting (1983: 21).
[121] Derrida, 1982: 21
[122] Derrida, 1976: 61. See also Williams' description of origins (1983: 20-1). His entry on community (pp 75-6) describes many of the traces contained in the word.
[123] Derrida, 1976: 19
[124] Derrida, 1976: 145
[125] Derrida, 1976: 141

active involvement, the ability to change community by adding one's own activity.

In applying these three elements to Southmead, we can see that the usage of community will always be full of traces (the community play, old photographs), will never exist as an absolute presence and is continually being supplemented by new meanings.

Does this approach help at all in an understanding of community? Does it just obfuscate the very practical and humane politics espoused by Phillips and Freie? While tussling with the prolixity of deconstructivist writings can be a perfect excuse for inaction, basing action on definition leads to continual disappointment; the object defined never exists in practice, is not there to be worked either with or on. Definition precludes action, just as deconstruction allows it. In the next sections of this chapter, I want to show how pulling apart the idea of community can help us with an understanding that can inform involvement. I will look at the relationship between dreams, actions and materiality, a relationship that evades the definitional strategy, but without which the concept of community is impoverished. I will then look at certain characteristics of community (incompleteness, division, ambiguity and changeability) that make it an 'impossible presence'. This leads on to a discussion of the effects of community. Finally, I will look at how community is created.

Dreams, actions, materiality

Community is a combination of thoughts, dreams, actions and materiality. The issue of the relationship between the materiality of the world and the mental constructions of that same world is a major one within social thought, and one that exists not only in relation to community. For example, Keith and Cross write that the relationship between the imaginary and the empirical lies at the heart of racism[126], and the same could be said for class, gender and any number of other terms of social description. It is at the heart of Berger and Luckman's work on the social construction of reality[127], and in the major issues of the power of ideology and/or discourse in social life.[128]

---

[126] Keith and Cross, 1993: 11

[127] Berger and Luckman, 1967

[128] Foucault, 1972; Habermas, 1987; Zizek, 1991a; Parker, 1992; and, in specific relation to community, Plant 1974.

One of the advantages of using *bricolage* for this book is the possibilities it has given for a multi-perspectival view. I have been able to show evidence of the materiality of place and economic condition, official and media discourses, the alternative views of community expression and a variety of forms of community action. This approach has shown that community in Southmead does not exist just on one plane, in one mode.

The problem in writing about all this evidence, however, lies in bringing together the material, the psychic and the active, and not separating them out as being independent of each other by saying that community is all in the mind or that it is a subjective formation of thoughts and actions as opposed to the objectivity of material conditions. This view is articulated by Owen Kelly in his radical book on community art: 'The preconditions for the formation of community are of an objective nature, the formation of community, and its subsequent growth, are by nature subjective'.[129] One of the potential outcomes of separating the subjective from the material is that material conditions are conceived of as external and objective, and subjective responses as internal and psychological. I have shown, in the portrayal of poor places, the way material conditions excite a psychic response that leads to a distancing and creation of the 'other'.[130] *Phagic* and *emic* strategies are not the product of a community acting on its own, but exist in relation to psychic boundary marking of those others; the community psyche is affected by the way Southmead itself has been branded and expelled and is not an autonomous or internally created identity. I have shown the desire for community in Southmead to be contained in official discourses, and in the motivation of the coaxers of community. Desire is not simply internal, and psychic constructions of community are as much part of social relationships with others as material conditions are part of the relationships within an economic system.

Teasing out the relationship between the psychic and the material, and, within the psyche itself, the relationship between instrumental thoughts and affective desires can be confusing, as shown by the following statements by Maffesoli. First, he writes that: 'The community ideal of the neighbourhood or village acts more by permeating the collective imagination than by persuading the social reason'.[131] The imagination here is seen as separate to and different from a utilitarian

---

[129] Kelly, 1984: 49
[130] In Chapter Two
[131] Maffesoli, 1996: 18

response to social conditions. A few pages later, however, Maffesoli writes of neighbourhood as representing 'the overlapping of a certain functionality with an undeniable symbolic weight'.[132] It is that *overlap* that is the crucial part of the relationship. Without the overlap, any formation of collective identity becomes totally free-floating, merely aesthetic, confirming the criticism of community that it is illusory denial of the material. Lastly, 'Causality or utilitarianism alone are insufficient to explain the propensity for association'[133]; by inference neither are they unconnected with that propensity. So while I have been very aware of the aesthetic and non-utilitarian aspects of community, these are always also related to the material context. The processes of community consist both of dreams and desires, and a certain pragmatism. While the affective influence of narrative was a major part of the growth of community groups, they also had instrumental ends.

This picture of a material–psychic coupling is incomplete without the third element of community that has been strikingly apparent in Southmead: the element of action. Community is an active relationship, not merely a relationship created by material conditions or by dreams and desires. These actions have both those strong aesthetic elements of carnival, performance and narrative, and instrumental aims, both always related to the material context. It is tempting to conceptualise these collective actions as the keystone that holds together, as community only arises through action, but this would simplify the relationship. There is no simple separation of condition, thought and action.

Community, therefore, is a hybrid construction, a 'heterogeneous ensemble'.[134] However, its hybridity is not a neat holistic resolution to the divisions of social life that pervade community.

Community as incomplete, split, changeable and ambiguous

One of the dangers of the communitarian ideal, spelt out by Young earlier in this chapter, is that it proposes a total way of organising society. There are those who see community as a vision of wholeness, what Rachid Amirou calls 'a primordial unity'.[135] The evidence from Southmead is of division, movement and incompleteness of community, of community that is not a total social form.

---

[132] Maffesoli, 1996: 22
[133] Maffesoli, 1996: 41
[134] See Chapter Five for use of this term of Foucault's.
[135] Amirou, 1989: 119

As pointed out by Parker, all discourses refer to and relate to other discourses.[136] Poverty, class, gender, race and globalisation are some of the discursive forces that have been related to Southmead throughout this book. Community is not a total discourse into which these can be submerged, nor vice versa, as we saw in the discussion on globalisation. Not all the relationships that people are involved with in Southmead can be subsumed under the meaning of community. People are also involved in systemic relationships with economic, political and organisational systems; while the queue waiting to collect state benefits at the Post Office may contain its own camaraderie, the exchange when the counter is reached is financial and bureaucratic. Most of the food, energy, housing and work in Southmead are not provided through communal relationships, but are, as in the case of the supermarket, dependent on international capital.

One of the points made in Chapter Five is how very different relationships can take place in close proximity to each other, so both community-type and systemic relationships exist simultaneously in the same space. Community relationships are only one modality of all the relationships in Southmead.[137] Southmead even includes its own non-places, to which the surveillance cameras testify: 'the user of non-place is always required to prove his innocence'.[138] Their effect is illustrated by this short piece in the exhibition The Place We're In:

> I don't know what day it was. I live on Greystoke and decided to go down the chippy on the same street.... Went into the chippy and got myself a bag of chips.... Walking back towards my house, as I was approaching the telephone boxes, I looked up towards the camera, and seen it was following me.... They must have realised I'd spotted them, so they did a sort of routine turn check, making out it wasn't following me. I feel harassed by that.[139]

While community is not a total entity, and there are always these other forces that can undermine it, neither is it a totality within itself, in its own sphere of relationships. There is not one distinct community in Southmead, and people do not themselves belong to only one

---

[136] Parker, 1992: 12

[137] Compare Cohen, 1985: 117

[138] Augé, 1995: 102

[139] From one of the panels from The Place We're In, in which it was more powerfully presented, with photographs and computer graphics.

community or even, necessarily, to any at all. Sandel, one of the more prominent of the North American communitarians, writes that there is:

> ... no single 'ultimate' community whose pre-eminence just goes without argument or further description. Each of us moves in an indefinite number of communities, some more inclusive than others, each making different claims on our allegiance, and there is no saying in advance which is *the* society or community whose purpose should govern the disposition of any particular set of our attributes and endowments.[140]

The occasion of the Southmead Barbadan funeral showed clearly people's multiple membership of different communities.

Within Southmead, we have seen a number of different claims to community, with no single claim being able to encompass them all. What is claimed by some as their own communal space (Badocks Wood by joyriders) is seen by others as a frightening non-place taken over by the guilty. What is community to some is terror to others. Community action is not united in itself. Jean-Luc Nancy makes this incompleteness, this lack of an ultimate community, not a deficiency but a strength. In the place of entity, Nancy's view of community is that: 'Incompletion is its "principle"', taking the term 'incompletion in an active sense ... as designating not an insufficiency or lack, but the activity of sharing'.[141] Incompletion is to him a dynamic concept. But even as any community is never complete inside, achieved in itself, neither does it, nor can it, encompass all things. As Chantal Mouffe points out, there is always a constitutive outsider; there always is one, or a series of, external opposites[142], which can be other communities, or some other kind of relationship seen as external, such as crime, heroin or bureaucracy.

The lack of wholeness within community, what Ivy Baker calls 'the division', is deeply troubling to those who wish community to heal social conflict. However, intrinsic in all the ideas of community, particularly in those that seek a wholeness, is division – the idea of there being an 'inside' and an 'outside' itself is a division of the world. In the creation of collectivities in Southmead, different 'bad' parts of

---

[140] Sandel, 1982: 146
[141] Nancy, 1991: 35
[142] Mouffe, 1992. See also Young, 1990: 304

Southmead are split off, as Southmead itself has been split off as bad; in the examples given, young people, heroin users, the Iranian or those involved in what is considered to be sexual malpractice, are split off. This splitting to put *outside* is part of the organisational structure of community, and splitting to put out means splitting what is *within*.[143] I compare this communal identity development with Melanie Klein's view both of the importance of splitting in ego development, and of its effects: 'I believe that the ego is incapable of splitting the object – internal and external – without a corresponding splitting taking place within the ego'.[144] Splitting, however, is 'of vital importance for normal development'[145]; splitting is how we survive. It is also how people are effective. Voice of Southmead was severely criticised for splitting the community, for being disruptive[146], but was a powerful campaign. Much collective action is concerned with deciding who, and/or what behaviour, is acceptable within, and what has to be changed or excluded, for example, in the very different approaches to drug users and drug use. These decisions are controversial and contested, and themselves act to fragment Southmead, with differing views leading to those separate groups that each claim community legitimacy.

Claims of community to be a unified phenomenon overlook the changeability of community, the way it operates through time as well as over space, the way it veers between sociality and action. Community sociality is a passive relationship of people being able to rub along together, community action a more active idea of people doing things together. Sociality ignores difference in order to maintain existing normality; community action is about the assertion of difference in order to change it. Sociality is a tacit acceptance of the given conditions that community action is critical of.[147]

Community action is time-based, coalescing around certain moments of excitement and mobilisation. These moments are powerful, but temporary, as shown by the examples in the text. Any changes that they achieve come very quickly, and are then taken over by organisational forms, or incorporated into a new form of sociality. The most ephemeral bursts of community are those of young people, but in the adult examples too the first burst of participation was the defining point,

---

[143] Benjamin, 1998: 102

[144] Klein, cited in Mitchell, 1986: 180. See also Jessica Benjamin: 'The notion of splitting does not require that we posit a preexisting unity, or an ideal of unity to which splitting gives the lie' (1998: 89).

[145] Klein, cited in Mitchell, 1986: 184

[146] Diary notes, April 1997

[147] For ideas of tacit, given and critical community, see Rajchman, 1991: 101-2.

both in terms of the identity of the participants, and in the political changes they brought about.

Incompletion, division and changeability make community a far more ambiguous concept than allowed for in the claims of its champions and the accusations of its detractors. It provides no unambiguous answers to what are the best forms of social organisation. This should be no surprise; Bauman points out that 'ambivalence resides at the heart of the "primary scene" of human face-to-face'.[148] His own dislike of the communitarian ideal is the aspiration it contains to conquer this ambivalence, making it part of the ideology of modernity in which all conflict and difference is considered to be resolvable. Community in Southmead, however, is rather one of the domains in which conflict is staged and difference asserted, and as such is not a resolution.

Any idea of community being a substantive social form evaporates in the face of its incompletion, division, changeability and ambiguity. Community continually metamorphoses, undermining attempts at its morphology. However, community, for all its lack of what Derrida calls 'the authority of presence'[149], is still a *powerful insubstantiality*, creating a wide range of effects.

The effects of community

So far, this discussion has largely been concerned with the composition of community. Relationships from outside and relationships inside have been considered insofar as they affect that composition. This approach, however, does not show the salience of community: true, it is something that is heterogeneously constructed, but so what? In one of his lectures, Foucault says that it is best to refrain from posing 'labyrinthine and unanswerable' questions about the internal workings of power, or worry about the problem of its 'central spirit', but instead look at 'where it installs itself and produces its real effects'.[150] Parker, taking up the same theme, writes that what is 'real' about discursive formations is their effects:'Discourse constructs "representations" of the world which have a reality almost as coercive as gravity, and, like gravity, we know of the objects through the effects'.[151] Community's main import is the way it (as concept or ensemble) affects the relationships both of the people it has constructed as being within and the relationships they have with

---

[148] Bauman, 1993: 10
[149] Derrida, 1982: 10
[150] Foucault, 1980: 97–8
[151] Parker, 1992: 8

other people and social forces that, in this assemblage, are constituted as without. Community in Southmead may lack tangible substance, but it has a gravitational pull, a magnetic existence.

There is an argument that community is its own effect. Freie criticises the wide variety of perspectives that, as he puts it, viewed community as an independent variable. In that perspective, he writes: 'Community was not an end in itself, rather a means to achieve other ends – to solve the problems they had identified'.[152] I have shown how community has been thought of as a way of solving the problems that local government feels that it cannot itself solve. For Nancy, on the other hand, community is 'inoperative': it does not *do* anything.[153] It does not lead to political programmes, but confusingly is of itself anti-capitalist, anti-fascist and anti what he calls 'real' communism. This view of community as itself a good that is both anti-totalitarian and against the narcissism of untramelled capitalism is held by many of the North American communitarians.[154] I have my own questions of whether community is always good, and have shown examples of political and personal effects of community that are both good and bad. I want to briefly recapitulate some of these.

When I visited Badocks Wood in the spring of 1996, effects of the collective actions of young people were obvious: fires and destruction. I only knew of the actions from seeing their effects. These effects led to a police clampdown, another effect. Untargeted, unprogrammed collective activity like this shows possibilities of power, but with no vision or control over what that power can achieve other than the enjoyment of transgression. Such political emptiness frustrates Beatrix Campbell, for not carrying '*critiques of oppression in the present or a fantasy about the future*'.[155] The effect was upset, not change, and the assertion of powerful activity by young people was soon routed. Those young people are living in the world of uncertain flows, where, in Castells' words, 'there is no tangible oppression, no identifiable enemy, no center of power that can be held responsible to specific social issues'.[156] When there was a tangible cause, the cutting of youth facilities in the area, the same young people took part in an effective campaign. However, effects do not have to be purposeful or rational to exist. I suggest that

---

[152] Freie, 1998: x
[153] The inoperative community is the title of his book (1991).
[154] For example, Etzioni 1988, 1995b; Taylor 1991
[155] Campbell, 1993: 93 (emphasis in original)
[156] Castells, 1989: 349

for those involved the experience of being part of the carnival was sufficient reason, the enjoyment sufficient effect.

The various adult campaigns did have a greater political purpose. They brought about certain innovations and some resource redistribution, and made public what had previously been considered as private concerns. There was a public, communal discussion on an ethical position to take in relation to heroin use. This would not have been possible from individual action alone; morality is established by debate, which, up until the time of the actions, had not taken place. Previously subjugated stories became told through, and created, relationships of community, as with the community play; without some kind of community, they would remain silenced. These changes are important, if not revolutionary. The argument for community politics is put by Michael Walzer: 'Dominated and despised individuals are likely to be disorganized as well as impoverished, whereas people with strong families, churches, political parties and ethnic alliances are not likely to be dominated or despised for long'.[157] This presents a problem as to what happens with the organisations once that domination has been overcome; Alinsky's work was with Poles in Chicago, who grew to be a powerful group that were then seen as oppressive by African-Americans.[158] Fighting for one's own group brings communal conflict in Asia, 'in which each community recognizes only its betterment as legitimate'[159], and sectarian parochialism in West Belfast.[160] The effects of community may not be welcomed, but they certainly exist.

Collective activity in Southmead has had the effect for some people of change, and growth. Volosinov describes the importance of the collective life thus:

> The 'we-experience' is by no means a nebulous herd existence; it is differentiated. The stronger, the more organized, the more differentiated the collective in which an individual orients himself, the more vivid and complex his inner world will be.[161]

Examples of this could be seen in the community play, and changes to individuals brought about by community action. It is difficult to

---

[157] Walzer, 1992: 100
[158] Alinsky, 1969
[159] Gusfield, 1975: 69
[160] Gillespie et al, 1992: 3
[161] Volosinov, 1973: 88

underestimate the power of exclusion and inclusion, the phagic and emic strategies that have been discussed. The crime rate (especially for juvenile crime) in Southmead dropped dramatically during the period of growth of inclusive collective activity in Southmead, much faster than when individual 'at risk' young people were being targeted with exclusive special programmes.[162] One of the joys of youth work was seeing young people who had previously been labelled by such programmes taking part in sporting activities organised by Voice of Southmead as of right, as members of the collectivity, rather than because of their pathologising labels, and the enjoyment and feeling of value that this approach gave them.[163] Community has, of course, also affected individual lives by its practices of exclusion. The inclusionary and exclusionary forces of community change people's lives.

I want to look at one further effect of community: the effect that it has had on social and political thought. The persistence of small groupings and resistances has been reiterated throughout this book, and forms a major part of the thinking of A.P. Cohen, P. Cohen, Castells, Hall, Maffesoli and Sennett, among others; either as acceptance of these as empirical, celebration of them as liberatory, concern about their inevitable failure, or fear of their reactionary consequences. What their persistence does do, however, is change what is, in Castells' words, 'the sterile effort of reducing the social dynamic to that of direct contradiction between labour and capital'[164], into Foucault's much more polymorphous view of social process. In this view:

> ... there is no single locus of great Refusal, no soul of revolt, source of all rebellions, or pure law of the revolutionary. Instead there is a plurality of resistances.... resistances that are possible, necessary, improbable; others that are spontaneous, savage, solitary, concerted, rampant, or violent; still others that are quick to compromise, interested, or sacrificial; by definition, they can only exist in the strategic field of power relations.[165]

---

[162] Police crime figures reproduced in the Southmead Youth Sports Development Initiative Business Plan.

[163] In my professional notes, and in discussions with colleagues throughout 1998 and early 1999, there had been marked personal change with both N and D, previously labelled as trouble and excluded from school, but then involved in a range of activities and relationships. This improvement in their own personal lives probably contributed considerably to that drop in the crime rate as a side effect.

[164] Castells, 1978: 7

[165] Foucault, 1979: 95-6

What conclusions can be drawn from this plurality of resistances are not fixed or determined (Foucault's adjectives can easily be applied to my examples of community action), except for an indication of the importance of the small, of which local community is an example, as an important location of political, social and cultural meaning.

Community as creation

In this long discussion, I have kept on taking out and putting back all the bits and pieces that together make up the sheaf of meanings that reside in the concept of community. The holding together of these meanings, however, is still a problem. While for Nancy community is about being, all the evidence supports the fact that it does not just exist, without effort, by itself. It needs work to create it, and if this work is not carried out, community is overtaken by other types of social relationships or by a breakdown in relationships. All the examples of collective behaviour given have required tremendous effort and energy by the participants.[166]

To try to describe how that work creates community, I want to join together two ideas: that of discourse as described by Foucault and that of conjuration as described by Derrida.

Foucault writes that discourses are 'practices that systematically form the object of which they speak'.[167] People, through their practices and speech, discursively form the object that is called community. Part of that formation is in that naming itself, but this is not simply a matter of a free-floating choice: the meaning of the word carries traces, and the practices can only be what is possible in the prevailing conditions. There may be dreams of a utopia, but what can be created is severely constrained by already existing relationships (material, cultural, spatial, psychic), which may be challenged and changed, but cannot be escaped. As they confront these different relationships, any one community formation is different from any other.

The idea of discourses as being active ingredients of community, which in turn is also a discourse, does not, however, show how people become engaged. To say, for example, that Southmead is a discursive object produced by discourses of class, race, gender and place may be partly true, but gives no indication of how people enter into community action. I therefore want to add the idea of conjuration, which I have

---

[166] The essays in Cohen, 1986a make this point strongly.
[167] Foucault, 1972: 49

taken from Derrida[168], to describe what distinguishes collective action, and community in particular, as a social force. As usual with him, this one idea has several meanings, all of them active. Conjuration is people coming together for a purpose, conspiring, taking a common oath. This could be for any of a multitude of purposes, secret or illicit, political or open. Often this oath is publicly stated: at an early meeting of Voice of Southmead, the chair said: "Our sole aim is to stop drug dealers dealing in Southmead. All who attend must agree".[169] Conjuration is also an incantation, an evocation of something that is not there, conjuring: 'A first in Southmead history – a community play on such a scale, with an original script based on local true stories and memories'.[170] In other words, it is a creation brought into being by the acts of the participants: the conjuration of events, stories and structures that have arisen from community action. Finally, conjuration is an exorcism of threatening spectres: 'Rid Southmead Estate of Drug Dealers and Drug related crime'.[171] These need not be personal outsiders, but conflicting discourses or systems. The spectres that assail community in Southmead around the turn of the millennium have been drugs, poverty and crime. Other times and other places, other spectres, evocations and oaths ... and other community formations.

---

[168] Derrida, 1994: 40
[169] Diary notes, March 1997
[170] Life Lines publicity, 1994
[171] Voice of Southmead leaflet, June 1997

NINE

Engaging with community

Introduction

This thesis has not glossed over the complications and disorders of community, nor constructed unities or certainties where they cannot be found. It is what Plummer would call a late modernist story: 'Modernist tales largely provide [a] sense of order, whereas emerging late modernist stories are drenched in ambiguity'.[1] In this account, community as a claim to order has been replaced by community as a site of ambiguity. Ambiguity does not, however, reduce the imperative to engage with the issues raised: if anything, the imperative is increased. If young people take part in action that is both joyful and destructive, neither laissez-faire neglect nor disciplinarian policing can provide an effective response: a more serious engagement is necessary. Without certainty to rely on, engagement and action become more important, if more problematic, as facets of social life. This final chapter looks at some of the issues of engagement with community.

Engaging with, or for, some 'thing' as unattainable as community at first appears futile. If there is no achievable end, why make the effort? There is a persuasive argument, however, that it is because of the lack of a secure end that there exists such a strong desire for community and connectedness. Community illustrates what Zizek calls the 'very paradox of desire':

> We mistake for postponement of the 'thing itself' what is already the 'thing itself', we mistake for the searching and indecision proper to desire what is, in fact, the realization of desire. That is to say, the realization of desire does not consist in its being 'fulfilled', 'fully satisfied', it coincides rather with the reproduction of desire as such, with its circular movement.[2]

---

[1] Plummer, 1995: 177
[2] Zizek, 1991b: 7

It is the desire to overcome the lack, the adversity of social life, that is itself community, and it is the desire, not the thing, that commands engagement. The desire for community has manifested itself in a number of at times contradictory ways throughout the book, ways that appear both destructive and constructive, and lead to no unified form of relationships or direction of social action. The desires of the different groupings themselves vary: desire, Zizek points out, is itself something that has to be constructed, he says, through fantasy[3], and these fantasies differ in their relationship to different discourses, and to transgression, control or change. Community demonstrates the importance of desires and fantasies as an intrinsic part of social life.

Realising the roles of fantasy and desire in constructing community tempers the approaches of those whose own desire is to subject community to instrumental reason and instrumental ends alone. This chapter is not, however, an exercise in the analysis of desire; nor is it, as stated at the start of the book, a blueprint for Southmead or for community generally. Blueprints reduce political and relational issues to a technical level; they assume the possibility of resolution without recognising the aliveness and ambiguity of the situation. A reaction against this mechanistic approach is to proclaim community; the imposition of technical solutions produces community as a resistance to them. Blueprints are similar to community in that they are never achieved. Of themselves they do not possess sufficient powers of conjuration; none of the reports mentioned in this book has had all its recommendations acted on, let alone realised. Despite this, blueprints spawn more of themselves, in their own circle of desire; action plans and strategies abound, each with some effect, but each passing away before the next promise of a 'solution'. There are, of course, issues within community activity to which technical knowledge provides solutions (for example, book keeping, buildings, constitutions and so on), but these are always specific to particular situations. This book is about a wider approach to community *relationships* without which specific solutions are useless.

I have grouped the discussion under the following headings, which draw together some of the themes that have become apparent through the book:

- Complexity
- Representation
- Recognition and reflexivity

---

[3] Zizek, 1991b: 6

- Disunity and conflict
- Rights
- Young people
- Community as Social policy

There are two provisos that need to be made before tackling this list. The first is best expressed by Fowler:

> Community must always be approached, advanced, and limited by what I call *existential watchfulness*.
>
> Existential watchfulness welcomes community's potential joys, but insists that any community is fraught with paradox, including the paradox that it can end – and had ended – in tyranny.
>
> ... there are no guarantees, and those who offer them are enemies, not friends, of community.[4]

It would be difficult to argue that, in Southmead, or anywhere else, *any* community is better than none. The examples of community action in the book display the paradox. All claims to and promises of community have to be examined carefully to balance their joys against their dangers. The first task of engagement and becoming involved is, ironically, a watchfulness, which implies keeping separate.

The second proviso is as stated by Mayo:

> Community based initiatives cannot and should not be used to substitute for wider strategies for economic, social and political changes.[5]

To tackle the inequalities of health, income, education and social capital that plague Southmead by blaming them on the internal social relationships of the area is both devious, in masking these inequalities as difference rather than as asymmetries of power and resources, and insulting in imputing deficiency to the people who live in the

---

[4] Fowler, 1995: 94 (emphasis in original)
[5] Mayo, 1994: 207–8

area.[6] The engagement sought in this book is one that challenges those asymmetries. Community is not the only issue; engagement with community may be important, but is not enough to overcome inequity.

Complexity

After the evidence and argument of the previous chapters, it seems almost unnecessary to reiterate the point that community is complex, both in concept and practice. However, people do try to simplify community terribly. Dick Atkinson, for example, calls community simply a 'common sense', which has a 'practical relevance to solving everyday problems of life'. For him, families are the building blocks of community, and in their turn, 'neighbourhoods are the basic building blocks from which towns are constructed'. This 'new paradigm', as he calls it, is rooted in an extremely conservative view of the family, based on 'the love of the mother for the child and the duty of the father to protect and care for mother and child'.[7] Together with this patriarchal approach, Atkinson's view as to how society is made up of 'blocks' is simplistic in the extreme, and has no appreciation of the complexities and divisions of those 'blocks' as illustrated throughout this book. The dangers of such a simple idea of community with a global community have been pointed out by Thompson.[8] A different metaphor of community is given by Etzioni, who likens it to a nest: 'It is best to think about communities as nested, each within a more encompassing one'. This comfortable picture tallies with his view of the stabilising role of community: 'communitarians are in the business of defining and promoting societal balances'.[9] Space, both as Massey reminds us, and as shown in the discussions on globalisation and locality, is not a tidy hierarchy of scales[10], and conflict rather than balance is the basis of community construction; the active moments of community challenge the tranquillity of tacit sociality. Times of powerful community activity are times of change and disruption, of dynamic disequilibrium, not passive equilibrium. The views of such communitarians would be

---

[6] Virginia Morrow (1999) has shown the importance of social capital, but also how places get pathologised for their lack of it. She argues that its presence should be seen as a privilege, not its absence a deficiency.

[7] Atkinson, 1994: 2, 11, 46, 52. The pamphlet was published by Demos, proclaimed as a 'left-of-centre think-tank'.

[8] See Chapter Eight

[9] Etzioni, 1995a: 25, 20

[10] Massey, 1998: 124

laughable if they were not so influential[11], and if a similar simple approach to community were not common in the rhetoric of social policy. Time and again 'the community' is referred to as an existing and unified structure, there to be consulted and relied on, as shown by this small but typical example. One of the aims of the Bristol Community Safety Partnership is 'to identify with local communities those issues which affect the fear of crime in their area'.[12] Local communities are seen as both identifiable and good, with the certainty of their existence posing no problem, and as places where perpetrators of crime do not live. They have a unified and collective mind that identifies 'needs' (a word commonly used in connection with community[13]) that a benevolent authority (of course) can and does meet.

The view of community as this simple does nothing to help with any engagement in community policies or politics, as anyone trying to achieve that particular community safety aim would soon find out, as they meet with division, disagreement and silence in the communities they consult.

Representation

One of the principal themes of this book is that representation itself is a practice. The struggle for representation has always been a major part of community action in Southmead, a battle over what are the stories of Southmead, and who tells them, the relationship between knowledge and power. However, engagement with Southmead has to go further than reversing its representation as bad to one that is good. The discourses surrounding Southmead do not merely portray an already constituted object that they misunderstand, but are themselves part of its construction as a social object and as an object of social intervention. Simple reversal of itself does not change that construction, and can even reinforce it, in what Sennett calls the celebration of the ghetto.[14] Changing representation does not lead magically to a change in the facticity of Southmead. The discourses surrounding it are deeply embedded, and their effects cannot be easily willed away. Major changes would be needed for coverage in the media to change; areas of problems and low repute make for dramatic and easy

---

[11] For an antagonistic critique of the growth and influence of this US-style communitarianism in the 1990s, with its attacks both on women and the poor, see Campbell (1995).

[12] Bristol Community Safety Partnership, 1999b: 7

[13] For example, Lightfoot, 1990: 11; Burton, 1993: 45

[14] Sennett, 1986: 295

news stories. To make changes in social policy representations would demand a major change in the thinking of what social policy is about, and how it identifies areas of action; it means challenging the way it first pathologises people and areas, and then proposes its own cures.[15] Representation of Southmead, or other similar areas, is as much about the self-construction of the social identity of those outside (newspaper readers, policy makers) as it is about the construction of what is within, their own splitting off of the 'bad' to an elsewhere.[16]

The most damaging aspect of representation is when it is not aware of itself as representation, and considers that it is merely displaying the truth. As Derrida puts it: 'Writing is dangerous from the moment that representation there claims to be presence and the sign of the thing itself'.[17] This ultimately very simple idea is continually overlooked in all forms of social representations, whether they be travellers' tales, maps, community surveys, the community play or art exhibitions, all of which make claims to presence and objectivity, and disclaim the effects of their representations. Recognising that representation is both *only*, but also *importantly*, representation, is a major rule of engagement for anyone committed to change.

There is a major problem in the accepted representational forms used to depict poor areas. Pile and Thrift point out that extant maps fail 'to articulate a clear sense of exploitation and oppression', and neglect emotions.[18] The same can be said for community profiles: they are by nature static representations that reify social processes. Representing Southmead makes it into an object, and the simpler and more static the representation is, the simpler and more static an object Southmead seems. While the technique of *bricolage* helps give a more multi-perspectival view, it is cumbersome, and cannot be used in all circumstances, especially when quick explanations are needed. Unfortunately, there is no perfect method of representation to fall back on.

The biggest changes in representation of Southmead have occurred not through the presentation of an alternative standpoint, but when that standpoint is backed by political action. New portrayals of the area were created by the collective activity of Voice of Southmead. Its approach to political representation, in which the media was used

---

[15] The point gained from Melucci in Chapter Three.
[16] This point was discussed at length in Chapter Two.
[17] Derrida, 1976: 144
[18] Pile and Thrift, 1995: 371-2

rather than blamed, changed (in a small way) depictive representation. Representation does not only exist within texts.

All representations of Southmead, as of everywhere, are, in Derrida's term, supplements. I have experienced myself, from the act of writing this book, how much this has not so much described as added to my own relationship with the area: 'Representation regularly *supplements* presence'.[19] The realisation of the idea of representation as supplement can free people from the hegemony of dominant representations, as it deposes their claims of merely reflecting reality. The idea of the supplement thus provides greater possibilities to break away from old meanings, and to produce new ones; community art is far more exciting when it breaks from the mould of realism, and instead challenges and supplements reality, as shown by the exhibition Fresh Evidence. Once people involved in community art and expression realise that their productions provide new and additional meanings whether they intend them to or not, they are freer to create radical rather than conservative representations. While the word supplement may bear connotations of frivolous extra, its importance in the change and expansion of meaning is there to be realised, and used. 'A good community,' says Williams, 'will ... actively encourage all and any who can contribute to the advance in consciousness which is the common need.'[20]

The importance of representation underlines the fact that communities are not based merely on face-to-face relationships. It is Derrida who again makes the simple point that: 'One writes in order to communicate to those that are absent'.[21] There is a necessity to communicate with these absentees, as their representations and actions in turn affect Southmead, but this leads to the representation (text, picture, film or whatever) leaving the context from which it was produced, with all the issues of translation that this raises as it crosses contexts. Communication and translation between social worlds is a major part of any form of representation and action, whoever is involved – the activist calling for change, the police officer asking for help against crime, the community artist making a film – and requires an understanding of the strengths and weaknesses of recognition and reflexivity.

---

[19] Derrida, 1982: 313
[20] Williams, 1958: 320
[21] Williams, 1958: 320

Recognition and reflexivity

The crossing of social worlds, and the navigation of the relationships between them, are crucial factors in engagement with 'others' of any sort. Frazer and Lacey write that:

> Since diversity is a fact, learning to live without defining difference in terms of the 'otherness' which entails political marginalisation and voicelessness is one of the most pressing political problems confronting our societies.[22]

There have been plenty of examples in this book to show how Southmead has been defined as other, and how that otherness entails and maintains inequality. It is more than diversity that divides; it is asymmetries of power. Engagement with Southmead (or any other such 'other') across inequalities, however benevolent its intent, can be a form of welfare colonialism[23] that reinforces those inequalities. Those receiving welfare are reduced to a client status without rights. Youth provision, which sounds like the bestowal of resources on young people, has, Osgerby writes, 'ultimately amounted to a mechanism of social control'.[24] Engagement of itself is not necessarily a liberator; resource provision (as with all gift giving) can be used as a weapon of domination.

Here, then, is an enigma. Living in a divided society without making attempts to cross or challenge the boundaries of social division increases marginalisation, and acts to exclude the less powerful from the resources of the dominant community, class, gender or racial identity. Engagement across these boundaries necessitates interference, meddling in the communities and collectivities that they conjure for themselves, with the danger of appropriating and disrupting their own formations. Any attempted engagement reminds us of a double interpretation of community: does it encompass the possibility of communicating across difference, or is it about asserting difference and keeping it separate?

As Habermas says, however much we desire the ability to cross boundaries and enter into unconstrained communicative relationships, we have to accept the impurities of communication: 'As little as we can do without the supposition of purified discourse, we have equally to

---

[22] Frazer and Lacey, 1993: 206-7
[23] Alinsky, 1969: 212
[24] Osgerby, 1998: 141

make do with 'unpurified' discourse'.[25] The desire to cross boundaries and enter into relationships of dialogic recognition with others is fraught with problems of misrecognition.[26] This is especially true of relationships in which there is an imbalance of power. Claims of recognition depend on whose terms they are made, and may be divisive, as people demand to be heard. In turn: 'As we see in social movements that found new identities, demands for recognition have their problematic side – a kind of entitlement or moral absolutism which is always inextricable from and fuelled by the power it opposes'.[27] That power it opposes might well be that of the benevolent interventionist, as the new identity wants to change the basis on which it is recognised. Young people feel particularly vulnerable to 'dialogue' from adults, which is more often one-way instruction than two-way exchange. The first moments of community action are about assertion, not communication, a stage in establishing a position of power from which communication on a more equal footing is possible, challenging the power of authority while asserting their own authority to speak.[28]

In all this there has to be a realisation that boundary creation is an activity of *all* those engaged in relationships, not just that of the 'others'. Southmead is created from outside as much as from within.[29] The boundaries and social demarcations we encounter are not natural. In writing about national identities, Robin Cohen writes that: 'Boundaries are legitimated, not legitimate.... key political and social actors selectively construct the walls that separate, or selectively permit access through the turnstiles and gateways linking the inner and outer worlds'.[30] Reflection on boundary-building effects needs to be a central part of any engagement with community, as anyone involved in that engagement can be one of those key actors in boundary construction. Boundaries can consist of language, accent or methods of communication, and can be built in innocence, disingenuous or otherwise; use of the internet, claimed by some to increase communication and the possibilities of community, excludes those without the technology. This book, in the way it is written, the types of arguments used and its length, of itself creates a boundary between those who can read it and those who feel separate from it. Public services and private capital, with their own power and identity, do not play a neutral role in, nor are they separate

---

[25] Habermas, 1987: 323
[26] See Benjamin, 1998: 25, quoted in Chapter Five
[27] Benjamin, 1998: 7
[28] See Chapter Seven
[29] See Chapter Three
[30] Cohen, 1994: 200

from, constructions of the boundaries of community. The clearest example given was in the work of the Bristol Social Project, in which strong differentiation was made between the intelligent outsider and the Southmeaders to whom it was not possible to talk cool sense[31], an approach usually not so boldly stated, but often tacitly exercised.

Recognition and reflexivity does not, Parker points out, dissolve discourse.[32] Recognising and reflecting on inequalities does not release anybody from inequality; this is a relationship that all are a part of, and not apart from. Understandings of difference need to recognise power. While publicly paid community activists can recognise they are part of the discourse of community, they also occupy a different position, and so cannot necessarily take part in some of the conjurations and solidarities that take place. Recognition and reflexivity can lead communitarian public servants to understand that they are part of the forces from which community is created, but which also separate them from membership.

Disunity and conflict

With this talk of boundaries, the idea of communities as solid and united keeps creeping back into the argument. That social boundaries are powerful (even if fluid and negotiable) does not mean that behind them there is a necessary unity. In fact, the opposite is the case; splitting is part of the process of creating external boundaries.[33] One of the most upsetting factors of community life for community activists is the disunity and conflict that occurs within what they would like to define as communities.

An effect of recognition should be the realisation that 'members of the community' are not ciphers, and that it is patronising to expect them all to think the same and act together, as if totally determined by their circumstances. This would reduce them to being mere components of the simple blocks proposed by Atkinson. As we recognise the aliveness of the 'other', so we have to jettison any naive ideas of lack of conflict. Community does not mean uniformity, except in its most totalitarian guise.

Community is not the only organising idea within a neighbourhood, one that supersedes all other difference. There are divisions of race, gender, income, religion and generation. Any unity of community is

---

[31] Wilson, 1963: 8; see Chapter Three
[32] Parker, 1992: 21; see Chapter Five
[33] Discussed in Chapter Eight

temporary, usually because of a single overriding issue of a moment. Engagement with community must always remember that it is not a totalising social form, and exists in relationship to other social forces and configurations. Disunity displays the lack of absolutism of community.

While conflict within communities may upset some communitarians, it is the implied uniformity that concerns sceptics. For Sennett, in the ideal of a united community there is repression, 'a consequence of the feeling of coherence in the community: the repression of deviants'.[34] Coherent, singular views of community do not uphold the rights of their members. In the face of these concerns, and in the face of the evidence, we need to revise our idea of community in order to accommodate disunity. If it cannot cope with division, community either disintegrates or becomes totalitarian. Frazer and Lacey spell out what must be done: 'The revised conception of community ... must embrace rather than suppress diversity and fragmentation'.[35] To replace the dream of unity, engagement with community needs what Maffesoli calls '*unicity*: the adjustment of diverse elements'. The vital principle of this unicity is multiplicity.[36] This new dream, this revised conception of impure community, is very difficult for many community bodies to accommodate. A simple view of community leads to coordinating organisations being set up with aspirations to speak for the whole with one voice, and with no mechanisms to countenance disagreement. That there is impurity and disagreement is not the end of community. Structures are needed that can work with disagreement, that do not require unanimity and that accept diversity.

Splits tend to occur at the times of most vibrant change, at the time when engagement is at a premium, and efforts to harmonise them tend to be a waste of energy. 'Community with disunity' should be the rallying call of all community activists.

Rights

One of the arguments against disunity in community is that it undermines efforts to secure rights and resources for the community as a whole. One of the arguments against community itself is that its emphasis on the common good overrides the rights of individuals, and that the dominant groups within community override the rights of

---

[34] Sennett, 1970: 43
[35] Frazer and Lacey, 1993: 201
[36] Maffesoli, 1996: 105 (emphasis in original)

subordinate groups. I have shown examples of this relating to gender, race and generation, as well as concerning issues such as drug use and sexual practices that offend community sensibilities, in which 'the community' has been used as a moral authority to enforce standards of behaviour and exclude those that offend against them.

Individual rights are a problem for the establishment of any social and political unity, and affect both tacit and active community: tacit, because it can rely on practices that deny difference and oppression, and as such can be a form of institutional racism and sexism; active, because it demands commitment, common action and strong solidarity that privileges the voice of the whole over the voice of the members.

Community development work prides itself on being anti-oppressive, 'anti-sexist, anti-racist and non-discriminatory'[37], but in so doing is imposing its own standards on the communities it is working with, and can be met with the reaction that 'This is the way we do things round here'.[38] The problem is whether the more powerful bodies should lay down such ethical standards for those with less power, even if they in turn are acting in an oppressive manner, and what effects the laying down of standards has. Phil Cohen points out, for example, how teaching anti-racism in school can lead to resistance to the message (and therefore a reinforcement of racism) as part of a class-based resistance to the authority of the teacher.[39]

There have been attempts to resolve the conflict between community and individual rights; Bauman calls this squaring the circle, and his formula is that:'Community without freedom is a project as horrifying as freedom without community'.[40] John Tomasi similarly struggles with what he calls 'individual rights and community virtues', and has a similar solution: 'The moral quality of any intimate community is importantly connected to the capacity of each community member to conceive of herself as an independent holder of rights'.[41] The problem, as with Cohen's example, is converting these ideas from their verbal prescriptions into practice. The stuff of the abstract debate between liberals and communitarians is the stuff of everyday community practice.

One strategy is to show solidarity on the issues on which one can, and argue (rather than impose) those on which one cannot,

---

[37] Lightfoot, 1990: 5
[38] See examples in Chapters One and Six
[39] Cohen, 1988: 86
[40] Bauman, 1996: 89
[41] Tomasi, 1991: 522

showing recognition of the other point of view while still disagreeing. Recognition does not, however, overcome incommensurability. I have regular arguments on the rights of girls to have separate times in the youth centre, during which they can set their own programme that is not dominated by male activities. This can draw violent reaction from boys who see me allied with all the forces that dispossess them, and is not an easy stance. However, this is not only an issue of argument, but of the active protection of group and individual rights, sometimes in the teeth of community opposition. Once again there is no escaping ambiguity, which can be painful. I have illustrated the anguish felt by a youth worker hating the (im)moral behaviour of young people whom she otherwise supported; this anguish is a common experience of engagement with community.

Young people

Young people keep on recurring as a question of community in poor areas, with their delinquency seen as a major threat to community life, although its causes are also often seen as being the deficiency of community itself.[42] As illustration, here is an account that shows the difference that a community approach to young people can make, where an evening in which community values were to the fore is followed by an evening on which they had broken down. This last account is a reminder of the four settings around which the discussion has been based, and of the everyday, mundane relevance of the issues tackled by this book.[43]

Thursday 21 August, evening

A bit overcast, but pleasant. Various people from the Voice were doing the football training they had set up on the park.

In the centre of the park there was the under-14 football team squad training – dribbling around cones and having a game – with their adult trainers, three local men. Another local man was sat in his minibus, which he had used to fetch the goalposts and cones. To one side was a large group of younger children, including a sprinkling of girls, being trained and having a game with two other men. Quite a few of them were wearing full football kit, of their favourite teams. They were the best football-dressed group! Watching them were mothers and fathers, some with younger children in buggies. At the end of the park there was a whole group of older boys and men playing – some of them fathers of the children in the other two groups. There were other teenagers (mostly girls)

---

[42] See Chapter Six

[43] This is an edited version of my diary notes for August 1997.

hanging around, taking part in the occasion. The atmosphere was pleasant, relaxed. It was like a picture of community. All ages voluntarily doing something for each other, based on long-term friendships and networks, using local skills and resources.

Friday 22 August, evening

Hot, sultry, some rain. Disco night at the youth centre, run by two local young men. One is the singer in a local band that plays angry and uncompromising songs about being from Southmead: 'Aniseed ... From the Mead ...'. The arrangement with them was that they played free, in return for being able to borrow the youth centre speakers - a community, non-financial arrangement based on trust.

At the start of the evening it was mostly younger people (11-13). A group of young boys were all excited about drinking a large bottle of lager around the back of the youth centre. Two boys did dance, and obviously enjoyed it, but most people just sat around.

Another group of boys, 12- to 15-year-olds, visited. They spent their time in the porch pushing and throwing each other against staff, enjoying annoying them. One had a knife, and carved bits off the wooden windowsills. They bullied each other. Eventually (phew!) they left.

At around ten o'clock some older boys (16/17-year-olds) turned up. They marched past the staff at the door, refusing to pay. They barricaded themselves into the boys' toilet with some girls. Staff suspected that they were using the toilets for drug use. There were rows about this.

One of these boys, who is large, marched behind the coffee bar, pushing the woman member of staff in front of him into the kitchen, where he opened the fridge and started taking out ice pops. When she tried to stop him, he got abusive and threatening, filled a cup with water and threw it over her.

Police arrived. They had come in response to a call from a night watchman on a building site. Children had been throwing bricks at him. I told them that people had been in and out all night, but that I had enough on my plate inside. Some of the boys kept suspiciously out of the way.

In the girls' toilet there was a spray of blood on the wall of one of the cubicles.

The whole evening had a bored, destructive/self-destructive, depressing and unpleasant feel to it. It was a bad party, without enjoyment. One of the DJs said that he thought the kids had no morals.

Despite the pleasantness of the first evening (not to be undervalued), it was followed by the second troublesome evening, with many of the same people involved, so showing both the strengths and limitations of community. The first evening in its pleasantness did not challenge the tensions that came to the fore in the second evening, but provided a moment of enjoyment among the grimness of much of the experience of being young on a housing estate. A community approach is more than just being nice to young people, or just providing them with activities.

A major issue in a community response to young people is the question of their rights. Are they full members of the community, with full membership rights, or should they be treated as a separate category, or is even supporting these rights in itself deleterious to community? For instance, can they congregate in public areas, or should they be moved on? Young people have their own, often wild, assertions of community, even if they are not recognised as such, and the question posed by Brown – whose community is it, theirs, or the adults? – is consistently pertinent, although adults usually win: 'Policy continues to be about resolving the problems young people pose for adults, "about" youth, rather than "with", or "for", youth'.[44]

The evidence in this book shows that youth is created and treated as a separate category in social life. Does a communitarian youth worker accept this differentiation, or challenge it? Lightfoot feels that:

> The Youth Service has long responded to the view that young people see their own community and their needs as being different from local adults. However, it is important to avoid making assumptions about an automatic need for age segregation.[45]

But most segregation exists to keep young people out of adult places. The provision of places for young people is partly a response to that segregation; without them they would have no places to go. There are dangers to the interests of young people if they are merely allowed into adult spaces and have no separate place of their own. They could become submerged in any undifferentiated universal community space over which they have no control, which to them could become those non-places in which they have to behave to prove their innocence, or which they disrupt as they assert themselves; as with any minority group, the same provision as the dominant majority itself means domination. While community rhetoric that says that young people should be included in general provision can sound liberating for young people, it can also disguise a move of resources and independence away from them. There are plenty of good reasons as to why young people should

[44] Brown, 1995: 47
[45] Lightfoot, 1990: 4

be included in the wider community – 'they offer vitality, energy, enterprise and should be fostered, as a part of society, not as a separate entity'.[46] The issue is how best these attributes are to be fostered, and, unfortunately, as Brown puts it, 'projects directed at encouraging and training young people to take control of, and articulate, their own demands, are relatively rare'.[47] When they do articulate demands, as with the campaign to maintain the youth centre[48], it is usually for their own separate place, illustrating, yet again, how community ideals of unity have to encompass diversity of provision.

The joyfulness of the carnivalesque gatherings of young people that are so disruptive to sociality in poor areas can, in the words of Rajchman, lead one to 'identify with the passion of the delinquent'. He argues, however, that we need to go beyond this, and refuse to maintain the social order that creates that delinquency.[49] Williams' words that 'If people cannot have official democracy, they will have unofficial democracy', and that this *will* mean riot as a response to dominative organization[50], are useful to remember when thinking of the behaviour of young people: they get blamed as being a mob, but it is their way of reacting to that domination. Foucault's statement that 'The prison cannot fail to produce delinquents. It does so by the very type of existence that it imposes on its inmates'[51] equally well applies to poor housing estates.

This issue of the domination and control of young people is underlined by the argument that youth provision has always meant social control. Controlled outcomes continue to be the case in the arguments for such provision. In an article on approaches to youth work on 'social housing estates' in the late 1990s, the authors write that in 'the new climate of intervention' youth work 'must be willing to embrace new methodologies which can clearly demonstrate that it provided valued "outcomes" and value for money'.[52] Those outcomes are those chosen on behalf of young people by adults; the value for money is often a euphemism for conformity and value for adults. The trouble with such an instrumental approach to young people (and a reason for its regular failure) is that it both ignores the aesthetic component of young people's collective action, the joys of transgression and excess

---

[46] Power and Tunstall, 1995: 74
[47] Brown, 1995: 47
[48] See Chapter Six
[49] Rajchman, 1991: 106
[50] Williams, 1958: 303
[51] Foucault, 1977a: 266
[52] Coles et al, 1999: 54

that react against such manipulation, and does not include young people in decision making. The resolutionary approach of solving 'them' as a problem ignores the need for dialogue and mutual recognition, as the outcomes are laid down by adult authorities prior to any contact with young people, and continues to treat them as a subaltern group. Such approaches to young people, even if locally based, can be based on a denial of their rights as they become objectified into a problem to be solved.

Community does not provide an answer to the issues raised by young people, but several themes have emerged in this thesis that can provide some bases for engagement and community action with them.

- **Locality** Young people are attached to locality. Their own social networks tend to be local, particularly those of young people in poor areas, who have not the economic resources to travel out from their areas, and who feel lost, out of place and culturally marginalised when they do. In this world of uncertainty, local networks of support for young people can be crucial and can also provide a focus for the community activity of adults.
- **Connectedness** That yearning for connectedness among young people that leads to all those varieties of vibrant collective activity needs to be appreciated and accommodated, and certainly not ignored by community action and social policy.
- **Aesthetics** Young people need the opportunity for aesthetic activities and excitement, for that excess which is so different to the instrumental approaches of most policies to the 'problem' of youth.
- **Public space** Young people grab usage of the public space that exists, very little of which is designed with them in mind, which leads to conflict with other users. Young people should be involved in designing their own public spaces and places, and need to be recognised as major users of public space.
- **Recognition** Recognising the rights of young people means recognising that the stage of life called youth is not merely a deferral of real life, but is there to be lived for itself.
- **Voice and involvement** Without young people being involved in initiatives that involve them, they will react against their dominative nature. Initiatives that seek to control young people will set off their resistance to them.

Of particular relevance to poor areas, opportunities for poor young people need to be equalised with those who are wealthier, without forgetting that the distribution of resources is a social as well as a geographical factor.

Social policy

In drawing up that list of 'lessons' of community to be used in relationship to young people, the problem of using community as a solution becomes increasingly apparent, showing the difficulties of using community as a tool of social policy, although that social policy affects community has been shown in the thesis. Social policy is suffused with modernist ideas of rational management, here typified by Bauman: 'Modernity is about conflict-*resolution*, and about admitting of no contradictions except conflicts answerable to, and awaiting resolution'.[53] That community is conflictual, changeable, split and not to be taken for granted, and is based as much on dreams as on instrumental aspirations, poses great difficulties, even dangers, for social administration.

Using community as a way to achieving other desired results is its reduction to remunity[54], in which action requires repayment, for example, giving young people facilities so that they do not riot. This approach of remunity runs completely counter to the gift giving of community, in which there is no expectation of gain by the giver. Community is not based on a cost-benefit analysis: 'Collective action is never based solely on cost-benefit calculations, and a collective identity is never entirely negotiable'.[55] In opposition to these identities, social policy can be used as a form of control, even policies with the strongest sounding community credentials. Dominelli criticises much community work for being a soft approach to securing the consent of the governed, and Bauman pointed out that the rhetoric of self-management objectively means cooperation with the authorities, a criticism that can be made of many community initiatives.[56]

Social policy approaches to community tend to treat problems as spatial and ahistorical, as was shown by the way social problems are mapped and represented. In that forgetting of history in the synchronic surveys that are carried out, resources are wasted on unidimensional quick fixes that fail to recognise the time and continuing work

---

[53] Bauman, 1993: 8 (emphasis in original)
[54] See Corlett, 1989 for this idea
[55] Melucci, 1989: 35
[56] Dominelli, 1990: 17; Bauman, 1989: 136. Bauman was specifically referring to the Holocaust. In Claude Lanzmann's film, Shoah, there is an interview with a Nazi administrator of the Warsaw Ghetto. His benevolent-sounding language is chillingly similar to that of present-day community development (Lanzmann, 1995: 161).

needed in community creation.[57] Mere spatial solutions tend to push problems around.[58] Alinsky reminds us of the relationship of the local to wider issues, even as he champions local action: 'It should, thus, always be remembered that many apparently local problems are in reality microcosms of vast conflicts, pressures, stresses and strains of the entire social order'.[59] Many of the problems that confront people in Southmead are not local in origin, and social policy aimed at reducing poverty by redistribution through wage, benefit and tax systems would be of more use than local initiatives. An idea of community that is structurally unaware, says Elliott Currie, writing about community crime prevention, 'can slide into a sort of nostalgic voluntarism that exhorts shattered communities to pull themselves up by their own bootstraps, without help – and without money'.[60] Furthermore, schemes that are local may not of necessity be good, and may even further pathologise certain areas.[61]

Within these larger stresses and strains, however, there is a role for organisations that capture the flows of modern capital for the benefit of their own areas. Flows may not, in Castells' words, be able to be controlled or predicted, but like natural phenomena have to be accepted and managed.[62] Organisations like Southmead Development Trust, set up to catch these flows, are in an ambivalent position, straddling the aporia of dealing with flows to strengthen locality that may also be the flows undermining the community life that people want.

Community can be so awkward towards social policy: in its simple unreasonableness in the face of what appear to be logical forces, and in its challenge to the logic of the systems on which social policy is based as it tries to breach the system's limits through new demands and different value systems.[63]

However, community is not a natural phenomenon, and some of its component social processes can be helped by certain social policies. These are not that elusive blueprint of community, but give an idea as to how social policies can help in community construction, how it can (some would argue *must*) provide the conditions for community construction, if not the magic of conjuration. Castells paints a bleak picture of a world without such policies: 'Unless alternative, realistic

---

[57] Piper and Piper, 1999: 35; see also Chapter Three

[58] Saunders, 1985: 84

[59] Alinsky, 1969: 60

[60] Currie, 1988: 284

[61] Dominelli, 1990: 22

[62] Castells, 1989: 349

[63] Melucci, 1996b: 30

policies, fostered by new social movements, can be found to reconstruct the social meaning of localities within the space of flows, our societies will fracture into non-communicative segments whose reciprocal alienation will lead to destructive violence and a process of historical decline'.[64] Cornell West, in an argument aimed at black America, depicts a struggle of community versus a nihilist acceptance of despair.[65] In this struggle social policy can help build the institutions needed for communities to survive[66]; in Walzer's words, 'We have neglected the networks through which civility is produced and reproduced'[67], and these need rebuilding. In this book, the importance of public places in which networks were formed was seen as a major ingredient of later successful community action; Melucci calls 'public spaces independent of the institutions of government, the party system and state structures' a necessary condition of democracy that offers some guarantees that individual and collective identities are able to exist.[68] The provision of public places and resources of all kinds (clubs, meeting places, parks and so on) would be a major contribution that could be made by public policy towards creating the room that people use for their own creations of community.

However, that one practical suggestion goes nowhere near far enough as a suggestion as to how social policy would need to change in the way it and its agents represent, relate to and provide for community, and it is difficult to see how its instrumental approach matches with the desires for the aesthetic and spontaneous relationships of community connectedness.

Pursuing community

Community, throughout this book, has maintained its presence as an unattainable goal, whose pursuit is but 'the dream paradox of a continuous approach to an object that nevertheless preserves a common distance'.[69] Despite grounding the pursuit in the very material space of Southmead and the mundane practice of youth work, community maintains its unattainable existence – possibly a good thing too, as it keeps open a space to challenge the universal domination of otherwise dehumanising instrumental systems.

---

[64] Castells, 1989: 353
[65] West, 1992
[66] Currie, 1988: 283
[67] Walzer, 1992: 90
[68] Melucci, 1989: 173
[69] Zizek, 1991a: 4

Engagement with such an unattainable phenomenon as community is unending and inconclusive. As social ideal/practice/dream, community is laden with ambivalence, but is surely not alone in this. Throughout my thinking and writing about community, describing it in terms of metaphor and metonymy, is a growing realisation that no social forms fulfil their promises of certainty. Class, gender, race and sexuality are all a similar mixture of materiality, dreams and actions, indefinable but deconstructable, each with their own inexorable gravitational effects, but none providing fixed and static structures to social life.

An important part of the book has been the way it has approached its subjects – both the people involved, and the ideas of community. The essence of this approach has been akin to the essence of an intersubjective perspective as described by Jessica Benjamin: 'where objects were, subjects must be'.[70] People in Southmead are not objects to be packed into a larger object called community, but subjects engaging with their destiny. Ideas too are not inert, but are there to be used as part of engagement and action.

Although there is no finality, no simple solution to the questions raised by the book, these thoughts on the subject end the search for community – at least for now.

- Community is not a simple concept, and is dangerous if it is simplified.
- A recognition of both the significance and the difficulty of community is important, as collective experience, dreams and actions are of great significance, even (especially) in a modern globalised world. Community formations and aspirations will not go away.
- Community involves, and is not an answer to, conflict. In the interests of a diverse and humane society the ways of comprehending community and approaching this conflict are crucial.
- Community is not an answer to oppression, but is a form of resistance within asymmetrical relations of power.
- Young people are often excluded from adult-based communities, but strive for their own communities with great creativity. Their desires and yearnings for connectedness need to be recognised.
- An understanding of the complexity and aesthetic content of community eludes current social policy approaches.
- Engaging with community is a practice full of ambivalence, but always one full of hope.

---

[70] Benjamin 1998: xii

Unlike other writings, I do not conclude that community is what is needed to solve the problems of Southmead. I do, however, expect that both young people and adults there will continue to conjure up collective activity, and in their actions will continue to face issues of power and representation as they fight to express and enrich their lives.

TEN

Communicating what youth work achieves: the smile and the arch

As youth work becomes more managed and formalised, there is an instinctive reaction among youth workers against all ideas of targets, products and outcomes, in the struggle to maintain informal and non-managerial relationships with young people. Unfortunately, this reaction can be rather inarticulate. The language of both accreditation and so-called smart outcomes (specific, measurable, achievable, realistic, timed), with their promises of measurable and completed results, seems to have robbed youth work of its ability to express and explain itself on its own terms and in its own more subtle vocabulary.

However, in rejecting the current managerial vocabulary of an outcome-led approach, there is a danger of denying that good youth work actually does have very powerful achievements. The basis of youth work is the forward movement of young people, in a way that is chosen by young people, and not directed towards externally imposed targets. The process itself is valuable, but we believe in it because it also achieves more. We need to be able to describe this.

There is a constant concern that youth work should be directed towards process, as distinct from products. However, the 'products' of youth work should not be undervalued, as they can be intrinsic to the 'process'. One of the underlying intentions of youth work is to enable young people to do things for real, rather than postpone meaningful action until they reach adulthood. Young people attend youth projects because they enable them to live now, not wait for some deferred future. Youth work can, even should, result in products that are valuable for young people.

These arguments all bear great relevance to what the youth work relationship actually is; while valuing it, we need to be careful about claims made for this relationship. Too often youth workers claim that their relationship with young people is so special that it provides a complete justification of their work. However, the relationship is full of its own ambiguities and complexities, and we need to be sceptical of any assertions that somehow it is so pure and uncompromised that it is above scrutiny.

To illustrate my arguments, I will give two very recent examples of youth work practice that demonstrate the importance of outcomes and product to youth work. However, in using these examples, I immediately come up against major problems of claiming 'success' in youth work. Whose success is it, the youth worker's or the young person's? Can we lay claim to young people's growth and achievements? And then, in writing about young people there is a danger of betrayal; the act of writing turns them into objects of scrutiny, rather than the living subjects we value within the relationship. I was reminded of this when, taking a break from writing this article, I met my first 'example' in the street. We exchanged cheery greetings, each pleased to see the other – but here she is, transformed into an example of good practice. I hope she can forgive me.

The smile

My first example is deliberately a small, unspectacular, everyday example of youth work. In many ways, it is a paradigm of the youth work process. A 15-year-old girl starts attending the youth centre. She seems to come not in her own right, but as a shadowy appendage of her boyfriend. She looks miserable and unhappy, and takes no part in any of the activities available in a very active centre – no sport, no arts, no discussions, nothing. Staff note her presence, and are friendly and welcoming, but no plans or goals are made for her. Unlike most other professional work with young people, there is no initial interview, assessment procedure or plan.

Gradually she gets to talk a bit and we find out her name – we'll call her Kelly. Then she starts confiding to one staff member. It is Kelly who chooses to do this – the youth worker does not take it upon himself to 'intervene' with her, though he is ready and able to respond. Over a number of conversations, she tells him how miserable she is, how she feels her father dislikes her, how she has not been at school for years, how she wants to move out, how she has eating problems; problems for which we possess no solutions. We do organise a meeting for her with a housing worker. There is a serious discussion about getting a flat, with all the pitfalls explained, and questions as to whether this was really what she wants. There is no movement at all in getting a different place to live, and the matter seems to be dropped.

Then, one session after Kelly had been coming to the youth centre for about six months, she smiles. She even smiles at me, although my contact with her has been minimal.

Now Kelly throws herself into the life of the centre. She plans, but does not execute, a display of photos of all the youth club members. She is planning a trip to a theme park for 20 young people. She is active. She is articulate. She enters into social relations with young people and adults. She is part of something. She looks well.

How can we measure this success? There has been no product, no target met, no plan completed, yet all the evidence points to there being a profoundly important personal outcome for Kelly. It is the sort of episode that is the bread and butter of youth work, yet it is nothing we can give a certificate for, nothing to gain public recognition by. There may be outcomes for her in years to come – better relationships, better health, fewer drugs – but these we do not and cannot know. Still, that smile is so important; a real achievement, a triumph of good youth work.

The arch

Over the years, there have been a number of deaths of young people who have attended the youth centre: car and motorbike accidents, drug-related deaths, suicides, a collapsed trench on a building site, cystic fibrosis. Young death is particularly hard to deal with, and deaths that occurred 20 or 30 years ago still bear a great burden of grief. So the idea grew of converting a scrap of land outside the building into a garden of remembrance with, in its centre, some kind of monument.

No one knew how to make such a monument, so we employed a sculptor. He had a wide brief: to design and construct, with young people, something for the garden. He provided scraps of metal, sculpture books and a computer programme to experiment with designs. After much discussion, a young man whose brother had died on Christmas day from a drugs cocktail very carefully made a maquette of a double arch, which became the chosen design.

We wanted young people to be involved in the construction, but the main structure of the arch had to be made in a metalwork shop. Young people could not do this, but they were part of this adult process. When the completed frame was delivered, the young people were amazed at how the 15cm-high model had been turned into a 2.5m monument. The next stage was to embellish it with more steel. The room in which this was done throbbed with activity, as young people cut, shaped and welded metal. The project took on its own energy. When new young people came to the room to demand what was going on, it was not the staff or sculptor who explained what was happening, but young people who talked about the deaths and the purpose of the arch.

The project was very physical. One young man, whom I had seen self-anaesthetised with drink and drugs at the funeral of his brother (killed in a motorbike accident), was dripping sweat as he sawed through chunks of steel to give the arch the fruit of his effort. This was *doing* something, *creating* something, not just talking about it. It was the first time that I think he had properly grieved.

The arch, now installed, looks very splendid. People come to visit it, even though the garden around is as yet uncultivated mud.

This has been a powerful piece of youth work. The point of describing it for this article, however, was that it had a *product*. In fact, it *needed* a product. The process, the relationships with young people were immensely important – the fact, for example, that the arch was made by them, not just commissioned from the sculptor (and he, who had been unsure of the process, was bowled over by the power and creativity these relationships unleashed). The product did not get in the way of the process, and the project can partly be judged by its product.

The value of the arch far outweighs the value of any accreditation that could have been given to the young people for having taken part. In fact, accreditation in this context would have been demeaning. Certificates would have detracted from the importance of the arch as something worth doing for itself, and devalued the emotional depth of its content.

We could surmise the learning outcomes of the young people involved, but that feels almost sacrilegious. They were personal to them. I would not dream of asking them, let alone giving them a questionnaire to fill in. The project had, as so often in youth work, unrecordable outcomes, outcomes that cannot be encompassed by any evaluation form.

Our messy relationship

These examples show the type of successes that can be achieved using a youth work approach, based on a mode of relationship between adult worker and young people. They point to a number of conclusions:

- Youth work is not about delivering to predetermined targets. Both the examples show effective work that did not start off aiming for targets. There was no idea as to what the end result would be, or even, in the first example, that there would be a result at all. We must remember, and tell others, that targets are not necessary for outcomes. In both these cases, the lack of predetermined targets actually allowed powerful unplanned outcomes.

- The lack of targets helps young people themselves learn about creation and transformation. They are not merely following instructions. In the case of the arch, not having a predetermined end result enabled the young people to create one for themselves, and in doing so see the process unfold.
- Youth work is active and material as well as discursive and verbal – young people learn about themselves by physical action as much as by talking. The example was arts work, but the same holds for sport.
- Accreditation should not be confused with achievement. Better things can happen than gaining a certificate.
- Youth work is organised and professional. Neither of the examples would have happened without both strong organisation and professional sensitivity. Being untargeted does not mean being disorganised. Running a project in which the end result is not known requires greater organisation and strength than running a predetermined programme. When compared with more mechanistic approaches, youth work can seem to be less precise and organised, but in practice it is its flexibility and responsiveness that are valuable. Ironically, to be non-managerial with others takes a much greater depth of management of self.
- Youth work has effects that are valuable both to individual young people and to the public good – not just to Kelly and for the makers of the arch, but also to wider social relationships.

If, for the sake of argument, we compare these outcomes to the SMART model, we see that they are specific after the event, immeasurable (which gives the lie to the fallacy that what is immeasurable does not exist), achieved and real, but not completed within a strict time frame. In fact, the outcomes of both these examples have not ended – they will run on through those young people's lives.

Despite these upbeat conclusions, there is a danger of becoming pious about the nature of the youth work relationship, claiming rather romantic attributes of some kind of pure and unmediated understanding between youth workers and young people. These utopian claims are untenable. There have been plenty of thinkers, in philosophy, psychoanalysis, sociology, linguistics, cultural studies and other disciplines, who have argued convincingly against the possibility of having any form of relationship that does not contain within it a relationship of power, the possibility of misrecognition and the uncertainties of communication. It only needs a session working with young people to experience all of these complications.

Of course, our relationships with young people are based on the voluntary principle, so distinct from, say, teachers, social workers or youth justice workers, all of whom have statutory powers and responsibilities inherent in their roles. But this voluntarism does not and cannot exempt us from all responsibility and difficulties. As well as the optimistic examples given above, I could have given descriptions of much more difficult relationships with young people, full of conflict and struggle. The relationship that youth workers have with young people around substance use is, for me, a particular problem. Youth work is about young people exploring and making up their own minds, but I have seen too many young people that I have known and liked severely damaged by the substance use that they have chosen. My imperfect work with young people around substance use is a mixture of information, education, providing alternatives, supporting young people who do not want to use drugs, enforcing prohibition of use on the premises, and care of users – a confusing list that leads to almost irresolvable contradictions in practice. Youth work is messy, ambiguous and complex.

Youth workers are increasingly in the uncomfortable position of being squeezed between a managerialist approach that demands targeted results and certificated outcomes, and an awareness that transferring this type of directive relationship on to the young people we work with would undermine the value of what we do. It is a strain for youth workers to be on the receiving end of one kind of relationship that we do not pass on to others. We are a kind of kink in the chain of command. To counter that pressure, we have to continually articulate, for ourselves and others, why it is that our informal and non-managerial relationships with young people are so valuable. And we have plenty of examples.

Author's acknowledgements

I would like to thank the following for their help:

- the Kingswood Foundation Ltd, for providing generous financial assistance to cover the expenses of this research. Special thanks are due to John Westcott, who was Executive Director of the foundation when the research was started, and is Chair of Friends of Southmead Youth Centre;
- Meg Lovelock, for reading and commenting on the whole book, and support thoughout the process;
- Trevor Brent and Colin Brent, for their ideas, criticisms and encouragement;
- my supervisors, Jeffrey Weeks, Richard Johnson and John Bird, for their patience, criticisms, suggestions and unfailing support;
- all those who provided, unwittingly, the data on which this book is based.

Southmead eight years on

On a rainy evening in September 2006, around 600 people braved the weather to pile into Southmead Adventure Playground. This was a different crowd from the usual children who used the adventure playground (although some of them were there too). There were university lecturers, trade unionists, artists, old members of the youth centre and Jerry's relatives and friends, among others. They had all come together to take part in a celebration of Jerry's work in Southmead, with live music, displays of photos and art from over the years and speeches. Significantly, the two key organisers of this event were M and P, of the Southmead Project and the Voice of Southmead, respectively. However briefly, the different worlds that Jerry describes crossing between in Chapter Five of this volume shared this space, a tribute to his ability to bring together people of different backgrounds and opinions. Here we will try to update the reader on the developments in Southmead since Jerry completed his thesis in 2000. This is just one version of how Southmead is now, seen from inside the area. While it lacks the depth and complexity of Jerry's work, we hope it will be of some use to the reader.

First, an update of the two organisations mentioned above. The Southmead Project remains in a similar position to that in 2000. M's refusal to adapt the qualitative nature of the project's work to the box ticking required by many funders means that it continues to battle for short-term funding. This has restricted the organisation to its counselling activities, although it is looking to move towards more holistic prevention work with 'the addicts of tomorrow'. The project tries to maintain the pressure on funders and policy makers through publishing research into its work, with the view to changing the direction of current policy towards more long-term aims.

In many ways, the members of Voice of Southmead and M have put aside their differences. Both now value the nature of the other's work, while maintaining the validity of their own arguments. The Voice never registered as an organisation, and has been largely inactive for several years. Both P and T remain workers at the youth centre, and the focus of the Voice is firmly on young people. The members are still in contact, and there has on occasions been talk of using the Voice as a pressure group on certain issues. Most importantly, however, the

Voice has left a legacy in the area, a hope that if people come together things can change. Whether the members feel it necessary to reconvene the Voice, or indeed if it reappears in a different form, is down to the situation in Southmead.

In many ways, Southmead has changed significantly since 2000. To the casual observer, the area has undergone a renaissance. It is no longer such a common sight to see heroin addicts waiting to score. The dealers no longer openly flaunt the law, and far fewer young people are taking up the drug. The very public scars of the heroin epidemic of the mid-'90s seem to have healed somewhat. The area now is more prosperous than it has been for a long time. Whereas before people had to leave the area to do their shopping, now people from outside come to the shops in Southmead. The youth centre has seen large investment – including a new gym and a full refurbishment – and facilities for young people in the area are much better.

It would be a mistake, however, to portray the changes in Southmead as anywhere near complete. While the superficial, *communal*, face of heroin abuse may be less visible, private tragedies still abound in Southmead. The Southmead Project is over-subscribed. Many of the young people using the youth centre are the children of addicts – while the vast majority have not taken up the drug themselves, the youth workers deal daily with the psychological damage done to them. Many young people continue to search for *something* through destructive behaviour like that described in Chapter Seven, and cocaine has become the drug of choice.

None of this should undermine the importance of the work done to improve the area. However, it should warn us away from complacency. The need for long-term social change and investment to overcome deep-seated inequalities – both within Southmead and Britain as a whole – is starkly evident. Without this, the agencies in Southmead will continue to be restricted to crisis management, without the ability to tackle head on the underlying problems of domestic abuse, poverty, poor parenting, racism and so on. Southmead, as much as anywhere, is a victim of national and international structural inequalities. The momentum gained by the Voice of Southmead was followed by 10 years of economic stability and investment. Without this, it is hard to know if such dramatic changes would have occurred. If this stability is broken, or that investment withdrawn, it is similarly hard not to envision cracks in the fragile improvements to the area. When Jerry was writing his thesis, he noted that he wanted to write a work that 'can be used to push forward the boundaries of effective youth work'. Working alongside Jerry, we came to recognise the importance of this if we are to challenge the inequalities faced by young people in Southmead, and we will battle to build on the legacy Jerry left in the area and in his writing.

Patrick Dorney, Pauline Teddy, Mike Pierce, Colin Brent

Why Jeremy Brent's work is more relevant than ever

Unlike Richard Johnson, my acquaintance with Jeremy was tantalisingly brief. Some five years ago, I worked with a team of colleagues based at the University of the West of England, exploring the varying ways in which community and youth workers and related staff were identifying and addressing the dilemmas that were increasingly emerging in their professional roles. Jeremy agreed to participate in the research. This included individual interviews, action learning groups and a final workshop, bringing participants from each case study area together, to reflect on the emerging findings and their implications for policy and practice. I had been deeply impressed with the transcripts of Jeremy's interviews, so I was very much looking forward to meeting him in person, at this final session.

In the event, that final session was scheduled for 7 July 2005, an ill-fated date as it turned out, as the bombings disrupted travel to London – an ironic reminder of the wider context for community and youth work in contemporary Britain. But the meeting was rescheduled, and Jeremy contributed to the discussions in ways that were so evidently characteristic of his approach more generally: outstandingly reflective, constructively critical, gently humorous and personally modest. I remember that we remarked on this appreciatively as a team, afterwards, as we digested the session's implications for the conclusions to our research. It was precisely because Jeremy's own research had succeeded in being so reflective and yet so engaged, I think, that he was able to provide such valuable insights, linking the local with the wider material and cultural contexts, as Richard has already illustrated. While the research was rooted in Southmead, the issues and tensions that he explored had immediate relevance for the ethical dilemmas facing professionals with increasing intensity in the current policy framework.

Community and youth work has traditionally involved competing pressures and professional dilemmas. In the workshop, we had identified the continuing relevance of *In and against the state*[1], exploring the

---

[1] London Edinburgh Weekend Return Group, 1980

tensions inherent in the role some 30 years previously. Community and youth workers continue to play these balancing roles, needing to demonstrate flexibility while retaining their ethical principles, enabling subordinated groups to find their agency and voice while maintaining an appropriate degree of critical detachment, neither idealising young people and disadvantaged communities nor simply acting as the agent of an increasingly regulatory state.

As Jeremy's contributions demonstrated, these dilemmas have sharpened as the policy context has become more complex in recent years. As the Secretary of State for Communities and Local Government emphasised in her introduction to the government's recent policy proposals, 'Communities in control: real people, real power': 'Ours is a government committed to greater democracy, devolution and control for communities'.[2] Devolution and decentralisation should be the hallmark of the modern state, in her view 'with power diffused throughout our society'[3], giving control over local decisions and services to a wider pool of active citizens. Community empowerment has been central to government agendas for public service modernisation in Britain over the past decade, then, as well as being advocated as a means of promoting democratic renewal and active citizenship more generally – including active citizenship for young people.

Although widely welcomed, these strategies for community empowerment, capacity building and community development have also been the subject of fundamental criticism. As Pitchford has argued, while colleagues have suggested that 'community development has arrived at the policy table', in his view, in contrast, based on interviews with experienced practitioners, 'it is the importance of "community" to the New Labour government that has arrived and not that of community development'.[4] Government has been more concerned with agendas to promote self-help, in his view, than 'enabling communities to have control over resources and institutions' to a significant degree.[5] Community development was becoming increasingly incorporated into government agendas from the top down, he argued, with community engagement strategies stronger on the rhetoric than the reality of community empowerment from the bottom up. There have been parallel criticisms of government policies towards young people, promoting young people's participation on

---

[2] Blears, 2008: iii
[3] Blears, 2008: iii
[4] Pitchford, 2008: 93
[5] Pitchford, 2008: 93

---

the one hand while on the other enacting policy directives that have focused on the achievement of top-down targets, emphasising law and order and social control in ways that have effectively criminalised so many young people.

Our research identified both optimism and scepticism in response: optimism as these new spaces have been opened up, tempered with scepticism about the impacts of these policies in practice. As Jeremy and others demonstrated, as they reflected on their experiences over time, professionals face increasing dilemmas in this context. While there may well be spaces for new forms of professionalism, with greater accountability downwards, as Banks has argued, professionals are also engaging with new challenges to their professional ethics, fearing the dilution of their very professional identities.[6] Jeremy provided a range of examples from his work in Southmead to illustrate the possibility of working with these dilemmas constructively, however, containing the contradictions with sensitivity, patience and principles. After the first shock of Jeremy's loss, we decided to dedicate the book that draws on this research to his memory. This is with the hope that he would have appreciated the possibility that those who are currently grappling with these dilemmas might draw on his wisdom and commitment, reflected, albeit anonymously, in its pages.

Since the research was completed, I have drawn on Jeremy's work in other ways too. His writings have included a number of articles with particular relevance for theory as well as for practice. In particular, Jeremy's writings on the contested nature of community provide thought-provoking challenges, raising questions about the fundamental principles underpinning current policy initiatives.[7] As he argued, 'Community is constantly invoked as an "answer" to problems of power, voice and social peace, yet never arrives'.[8] While recognising the elusiveness of the concept, its ambiguity and its conservative potential, he was also sensitive to its potential as desire, continually replenishing itself 'as people seek the ever receding goals of voice, meaning and connectedness in all their imperfections'.[9] He so clearly recognised the centrality of ideas, ideologies and emotions, despite the present policy focus, based on notions of individuals as rational actors, pursuing their self-interest in accordance with the tenets of neoliberal economics. Jeremy's work has more relevance than ever, then, for those

---

[6] Banks, 2004
[7] Brent, 2004
[8] Brent, 2004: 213
[9] Brent, 2004: 222

committed to more transformative approaches, linking local initiatives with wider strategies, working towards agendas for social justice and equalities, building social solidarity within and between communities locally and beyond.

Marjorie Mayo
Professor of Community Development
Goldsmiths, University of London

Bibliography

Books, reports and articles

Abu-Lughod, J. (1994) 'Diversity, democracy and self-determination in an urban neighbourhood: the East Village of Manhattan', *Social Research*, Spring, pp 181-203.

Agnew, J. (1993) 'Representing space. Space, scale and culture in social science', in J. Duncan and D. Ley (eds) (1993) *Place/culture/representation*, London: Routledge.

Agnew, J.A. (1989) 'The devaluation of space in social science', in J.A Agnew and J.S Duncan (eds) (1989) *The power of place: Bringing together geographical and sociological imaginations*, London: Unwin Hyman.

Agnew, J.A. and Duncan, J.S. (eds) (1989) *The power of place: Bringing together geographical and sociological imaginations*, London: Unwin Hyman.

Alinsky, S.D. (1969) (first published 1946) *Reveille for radicals*, New York, NY: Vintage Books.

Amirou, R. (1989) 'Sociability/"sociality"', *Current Sociology*, vol 37, no 1, pp 115-20.

Anderson, B. (1991) *Imagined communities: Reflections on the origin and spread of nationalism* (revised edn), London: Verso.

Archibugi, D., Held, D. and Köhler, M. (1998) *Re-imagining political community: Studies in cosmopolitan democracy*, Cambridge: Polity Press.

Arts Council of Great Britain (1974) *Community arts. The report of the Community Arts Working Party*, London: Arts Council of Great Britain.

Atkinson, D. (1994) *The common sense of community*, London: Demos.

Atkinson, P. (1990) *The ethnographic imagination: Textual constructions of reality*, London: Routledge.

Atkinson, P. and Hammersley, M. (1994) 'Ethnography and participant observation', in N.K. Denzin and Y.S. Lincoln (eds) *Handbook of qualitative research*, London: Sage Publications.

Augé, M. (1995) *Non-places: Introduction to an anthropology of supermodernity*, London: Verso.

Auslander, P. (1995) '"Just be your self": logocentrism and difference in performance theory', in P.B. Zarilli (ed) *Acting (re)considered: Theories and practices*, London: Routledge.

Avineri, S. and de-Shalit, A. (eds) (1992) *Communitarianism and individualism*, Oxford: Oxford University Press.

Avon County Council (1983) *Social stress in Avon 1981: A preliminary analysis*.

Avon County Council (1984) *Report of the Joint Member/Officer Team for the Southmead area.*

Avon County Council (1993) *1991 Census: Selected statistics.*

Avon County Planning Department (1991) *Social stress in Avon 1991.*

Bagguley, P., Mark-Lawson, J., Shapiro, D., Urry, J., Walby, S. and Warde, A. (1990) *Restructuring: Place, class and gender,* London: Sage Publications.

Bakhtin, M.M. (1968) *Rabelais and his world,* Cambridge, MA: MIT Press.

Bakhtin, M.M. (1981) 'Discourse in the novel', in M Holquist (ed) (Translated by C. Emerson and M. Holquist) *The dialogic imagination,* Austin, TX: University of Texas Press.

Bakhtin, M.M. (1986) *Speech genres and other late essays,* in C. Emerson and M. Holquist (eds) (Translated by V.W. McGee) Austin, TX: University of Texas Press.

Bakhtin, M.M. (1994) *The Bakhtin reader,* P. Morris (ed), London: Edward Arnold.

Banks, S. (2004) *Ethics, accountability and the social professions,* Basingstoke: Palgrave Macmillan.

Barthes, R. (1973) *Mythologies,* London: Paladin.

Bauman, Z. (1989*) Modernity and the Holocaust,* Cambridge: Polity Press.

Bauman, Z. (1993) *Postmodern ethics,* Oxford: Blackwell.

Bauman, Z. (1996) 'On communitarianism and human freedom. Or, how to square the circle', *Theory, Culture and Society,* vol 13, no 2, pp 79-90.

Beddow, N. (1994) *Life Lines:The Southmead community play, remembered, devised and created by the people of Southmead,* Unpublished playscript.

Bell, C. and Newby, H. (1971) *Community studies:An introduction to the sociology of the local community,* London: Allen and Unwin.

Bell, C. and Roberts, H. (1984*) Social researching. Politics, problems, practice,* London: Routledge and Kegan Paul.

Bell, M.M. and Gardiner, M. (eds) (1998) *Bakhtin and the human sciences,* London: Sage Publications.

Bellah, R.N. (1997) 'The necessity of opportunity and community in a good society', *International Sociology,* vol 12, no 4, pp 387-93.

Benjamin, Jessica (1990) *The bonds of love: Psychoanalysis, feminism, and the problem of domination,* London:Virago.

Benjamin, Jessica (1998) *Shadow of the other: Intersubjectivity and gender in psychoanalysis,* London: Routledge.

Benjamin, Joe (1966) *In search of adventure:A study in play leadership* (new edn), London: National Council of Social Service.

Benjamin, Joe (1974) *Grounds for play,* London: Bedford Square Press.

Benjamin, W. (1969) *Illuminations,* New York, NY: Schocken Books.

Benjamin, W. (1973) 'The author as producer', in *Understanding Brecht,* London: New Left Books

Benjamin, W. (1997) *One-way street*, London: Verso.

Berdoulay, V. (1989) 'Place, meaning, and discourse in French language geography', in J.A. Agnew and J.S. Duncan (eds) (1989) *The power of place: Bringing together geographical and sociological imaginations*, London: Unwin Hyman.

Berger, P. and Luckman, T. (1967) *The social construction of reality: A treatise on the sociology of knowledge*, London: Penguin.

Berman, M. (1983) *All that is solid melts into air: The experience of modernity*, London: Verso.

Bertram, C. (1997) 'Political justification, theoretical complexity, and democratic community', in *Ethics*, 107, pp 563-83, vol 107, no 4.

Bhabha, H.K. (1990) 'The third space', in J. Rutherford (ed) (1990) *Identity, community, culture, difference*, London: Lawrence and Wishart.

Bhabha, H.K. (ed) (1991) *Nation and narration*, London: Routledge.

Bhabha, H.K. (1994) *The location of culture*, London: Routledge.

Blagg, H., Pearson, G., Sampson, A., Smith, D. and Stubbs, P. (1988) 'Inter-agency co-operation; rhetoric and reality', in T. Hope and M. Shaw (eds) (1988a) *Communities and crime reduction*, London: HMSO.

Blears, H. (2008) 'Introduction', in *Communities in control: Real people, real power*, Cm 7427, London: The Stationery Office (www.communities.gov.uk/documents/communities/pdf/886045.pdf).

Bornat, J. (1993) 'Representations of community', in J. Bornat, C. Pereira, D. Pilgrim and F. Williams (eds) (1993) *Community care: A reader*, Basingstoke: Macmillan.

Bornat, J., Pereira, C., Pilgrim, D. and Williams, F. (eds) (1993) *Community care: A reader*, Basingstoke: Macmillan.

Boswell, J. (1990) *Community and the economy: The theory of public co-operation*, London: Routledge.

Bourdieu, P. (1984) *Distinction: A social critique of the judgement of taste*, London: Routledge.

Bowlby, S., Lewis, J., McDowell, L. and Foord, J. (1989) 'The geography of gender', in R. Peet and N. Thrift (eds) (1989a) *New models in geography. Volume two The political economy perspective*, London: Unwin Hyman.

Braden, S. (1978) *Artists and people*, London: Routledge and Kegan Paul.

Breitbart, M.M. (1998) '"Dana's mystical tunnel". Young people's designs for survival and change in the city', in T. Skelton and G. Valentine (eds) *Cool places: Geographies of youth culture*, London: Routledge.

Brent, J. (1992) 'The battle of Golden Hill. Narrative, identity and community in middle-class protest', Unpublished Masters dissertation, University of Birmingham.

Brent, J. (1997) 'Community without unity', in P. Hoggett *Contested communities: Experiences, struggles, policies*, Bristol: The Policy Press.

Brent, J. (2004) 'The desire for community: illusion, confusion and paradox', *Community Development Journal*, vol 39, no 3, pp 213-23.

Bristol Broadsides (1980) *Corrugated iron works. Poems and stories by the Hut Writers*, Bristol: Bristol Broadsides.

Bristol Broadsides (1986) *A Southmead festival of words*, Bristol: Bristol Broadsides.

Bristol City Council (1983) *Southmead report – Report of Southmead Working Group.*

Bristol City Council (1985) *Poverty in Bristol: Final report.*

Bristol City Council (1988) *Poverty in Bristol: An update.*

Bristol City Council Housing Department (1989) *Key statistics for quarter ending 1989.*

Bristol City Council (1990) *Report to Housing Committee.*

Bristol City Council (1991) *1991 ward report.*

Bristol City Council (1994) *Poverty in Bristol 1994.*

Bristol City Council (1996a) *Poverty in Bristol 1996: An update.*

Bristol City Council (1996b) *North Area: A statistical profile of North Bristol 1996.*

Bristol City Council (1997a) *Indicators of quality of life in Bristol: Sustainability update 1997.*

Bristol City Council (1997b) *North Area 1997 profile: A statistical profile of North Bristol.*

Bristol City Council (1999) *Indicators of quality of life: Sustainability update 1998/1999.*

Bristol City Council Housing Services (1994) *Key statistics for the period 1 April 1994 – 30 September 1994.*

Bristol Community Safety Partnership (1999a) *Tackling crime and disorder in Bristol, 1999-2002.*

Bristol Community Safety Partnership (1999b) *Audit of crime and disorder in Bristol.*

Brown, S. (1995) 'Crime and safety in whose "community"?: age, everyday life, and problems for youth policy', *Youth and Policy*, no 48, pp 27-48.

Burton, P. (1993) *Community profiling. A guide to identifying local needs*, Bristol: SAUS Publications.

Callaghan, G. (1992) 'Locality and localism: the spatial orientation of young adults in Sunderland', *Youth and Policy*, no 39, pp 23-33.

Calvino, I. (1993) *Time and the hunter*, London: Picador.

Campbell, B. (1993) *Goliath: Britain's dangerous places*, London: Methuen.

Campbell, B. (1995) 'Old fogeys and angry young men', *Soundings*, 1, pp 47-64.

Castells, M. (1978) *City, class and power*, London, Macmillan.

Castells, M. (1989) *The informational city*, Oxford: Blackwell.

Castells, M. (1997) *The power of identity*, Oxford: Blackwell.

Centre for Contemporary Cultural Studies (1976) *A critique of 'community studies' and its role in social thought*, Birmingham: Centre for Contemporary Cultural Studies.

Chamoiseau, P. (1997) *Texaco*, London: Granta Books.

Chamoiseau, P. (1999) *Solibo Magnificent*, London: Granta Books.

Charsley, S.R. (1986) '"Glasgow's miles better": the symbolism of community and identity in the city', in A.P. Cohen (ed) (1986a) *Symbolising boundaries: Identity and diversity in British cultures*, Manchester: Manchester University Press.

Cohen, A.P. (1985) *The symbolic construction of community*, London: Ellis Horwood.

Cohen, A.P. (ed) (1986a) *Symbolising boundaries: Identity and diversity in British cultures*, Manchester: Manchester University Press.

Cohen, A.P. (1986b) 'Of symbols and boundaries, or does Ertie's greatcoat hold the key?', in A.P. Cohen (ed) (1986a) *Symbolising boundaries: Identity and diversity in British cultures*, Manchester: Manchester University Press.

Cohen, P. (1988) 'The perversions of inheritance: studies in the making of multi-racist Britain', in P. Cohen and H.S. Bains (eds) *Multi-racist Britain*, Basingstoke: Macmillan.

Cohen, P. (1997) 'Beyond the community romance', in *Soundings*, 5, pp 29-51.

Cohen, P. and Bains, H.S. (eds) (1988) *Multi-racist Britain*, Basingstoke: Macmillan.

Cohen, R. (1994) *Frontiers of identity. The British and the others*, Harlow: Longman.

Coles, B., England, J. and Rugg, J. (1999) 'Playing its part in "joined-up" solutions: youth work on social housing estates', *Youth and Policy*, no 46, pp 41-55.

Collins, P.H. (1990) *Black feminist thought: Knowledge, consciousness, and the politics of empowerment*, Boston, MA: Unwin Hyman.

Cooke, P. (ed) (1989) *Localities. The changing face of urban Britain*, London: Unwin Hyman.

Cooke, P. (1990) *Back to the future*, London: Unwin Hyman.

Corlett, W. (1989) *Community without unity: A politics of Derridian extravagance*, Durham, NC: Duke University Press.

Coward, R. (1994) 'Whipping boys', *The Guardian*, 3 September.

Crook, S. (1998) 'Minotaurs and other monsters: "everyday life" in recent social theory', *Sociology*, vol 32, no 3, pp 523-40.

Cross, M. and Keith, M. (eds) (1993) *Racism, the city and the state*, London: Routledge.

Currie, E. (1988) 'Two visions of community crime prevention', in T. Hope and M. Shaw (eds) (1988a) *Communities and crime reduction*, London: HMSO.

Danziger, N. (1997) *Danziger's Britain: A journey to the edge*, London: Flamingo.

Davies, N. (1998) *Dark heart: The shocking truth about hidden Britain*, London: Chatto and Windus.

de Certeau, M. (1984) *The practice of everyday life*, Berkeley, CA: University of California Press.

Della Porta, D. and Diani, M. (1999) *Social movements: An introduction*, Oxford: Blackwell.

Denzin, N.K. (1994) 'The art and politics of interpretation', in N.K. Denzin and Y.S. Lincoln (eds) *Handbook of qualitative research*, London: Sage Publications.

Denzin, N.K. and Lincoln, Y.S. (eds) (1994) *Handbook of qualitative research*, London: Sage Publications.

de Peuter, J. (1998) 'The dialogics of narrative identity', in M.M. Bell and M. Gardiner (eds) (1998) *Bakhtin and the human sciences*, London: Sage Publications.

Derrida, J. (1976) *Of grammatology*, Baltimore, MD: John Hopkins University Press.

Derrida, J. (1978) *Writing and difference*, London: Routledge.

Derrida, J. (1982) *Margins of philosophy*, Hemel Hempstead: Harvester Wheatsheaf.

Derrida, J. (1994) *Specters of Marx: The state of the debt, the work of mourning, and the New International*, New York, NY: Routledge.

Derrida, J. (1995) *On the name*, Stanford, CA: Stanford University Press.

DETR (Department of the Environment, Transport and the Regions) (1999) *Update*, May, London: DETR.

Dickson, M. (ed) (1995) *Art with people*, Sunderland: AN Publications.

Doheny-Farina, S. (1996) *The wired community*, New Haven, CT: Yale University Press.

Dominelli, L. (1990) *Women and community action*, Birmingham: Venture Press.

Dreyfus, H.L. and Rabinow, P. (1983) *Michel Foucault: Beyond structuralism and hermeneutics*, Hemel Hempstead: Harvester Press.

Duncan, J. and Ley, D. (eds) (1993) *Place/culture/representation*, London: Routledge.

Duncan, S. (1989) 'What is locality?', in R. Peet and N. Thrift (eds) (1989a) *New models in geography: Volume Two: The political economy perspective*, London: Unwin Hyman.

Entrikin, J.N. (1989) 'Place, region, and modernity', in J.A. Agnew and J.S. Duncan (eds) (1989) *The power of place. Bringing together geographical and sociological imaginations*, London: Unwin Hyman.

Etzioni, A. (1988) *The moral dimension: Towards a new economics*, New York, NY: The Free Press.

Etzioni, A. (1989) 'Towards an I and we paradigm', *Contemporary Sociology*, 18.

Etzioni, A. (ed) (1995a) *New communitarian thinking: Persons, virtues, institutions, and communities*, Charlottesville, VA: University of Virginia Press.

Etzioni, A. (1995b) 'Old chestnuts and new spurs', in A. Etzioni (ed) *New communitarian thinking: Persons, virtues, institutions, and communities*, Charlottesville, VA: University of Virginia Press.

Etzioni, A. (1995c) *The spirit of community: Rights, responsibilities and the communitarian agenda*, London: Fontana.

Fay, B. (1996) *Contemporary philosophy of social science: A multicultural approach*, Oxford: Blackwell.

Felshin, N. (ed) (1995) *But is it art? The spirit of art as activism*, Seattle, WA: Bay Press.

Ferguson, M. and Golding, P. (eds) (1997) *Cultural studies in question*, London: Sage Publications.

Ferrara, A. (1997) 'The paradox of community', *International Sociology*, vol 12, no 4, pp 395-408.

Finer, C.J. and Nellis, M. (eds) (1998) *Crime and social exclusion*, Oxford: Blackwell.

Foster, H. (1996) *The return of the real: The avant-garde at the end of the century*, Cambridge MA: MIT Press.

Foucault, M. (1972) *The archaeology of knowledge*, New York, NY: Pantheon Books.

Foucault, M. (1977a) *Discipline and punish: The birth of the prison*, London: Allen Lane.

Foucault, M. (1977b) *Language counter-memory, practice*, Ithaca, NY: Cornell University Press.

Foucault, M. (1979) *The history of sexuality: Volume 1: An introduction*, London: Allen Lane.

Foucault, M. (1980) *Power/knowledge: Selected interviews and other writings 1972-77*, ed C. Gordon, London: Harvester.

Foucault, M. (1986) *The Foucault reader*, ed. P. Rabinow, Harmondsworth: Penguin.

Fowler, R.B. (1995) 'Community. Reflection on definition', in A. Etzioni (ed) (1995a) *New communitarian thinking: Persons, virtues, institutions, and communities*, Charlottesville, VA: University of Virginia Press.

France, A and Wiles, P. (1998) 'Dangerous futures: social exclusion and youth work in late modernity', in C.J. Finer and M. Nellis (eds) *Crime and social exclusion*, Oxford: Blackwell.

Fraser, R. (1979) *Blood of Spain: The experience of civil war, 1936-1939*, Harmondsworth: Penguin.

Frazer, E. and Lacey, N. (1993) *The politics of community: A feminist critique of the liberal-communitarian debate*, Hemel Hempstead: Harvester Wheatsheaf.

Freie, J.F. (1998) *Counterfeit community: The exploitation of our longing for connectedness*, Lanham, MD/Oxford, UK: Rowman and Littlefield Publishers Inc.

Friedman. M. (1989) 'Feminism and modern friendship: dislocating the community', in S. Avineri and A. de-Shalit (eds) (1992) *Communitarianism and individualism*, Oxford: Oxford University Press.

Friends of Southmead Youth Centre: Annual Reports 1993-1999.

Furlong, A. and Cartmel, F. (1997) *Young people and social change: Individualisation and risk in late modernity*, Buckingham: Open University Press.

Gates, H.L. Jr. (1995) *Colored people*, London: Viking.

Giddens, A. (1992) *The transformation of intimacy: Sexuality, love and eroticism in modern societies*, Cambridge: Polity Press.

Gillespie, N., Lovett, T. and Garner, W. (1992) *Youth work and working class youth: Rules and resistance in West Belfast*, Buckingham: Open University Press.

Gilroy, P. (1987) *'There ain't no black in the Union Jack.': The cultural politics of race and nation*, London: Unwin Hyman.

Gilroy, P. (1993) *Small acts: Thoughts on the politics of black cultures*, London: Serpent's Tail.

Goldberg, D.T. (1993) *Racist culture: Philosophy and politics of meaning*, Oxford: Blackwell.

Goodwin, M. (1995) 'Poverty in the city: "you can raise your voice, but who is listening?"', in C. Philo (ed) *Off the map: The social geography of poverty in the UK*, London: Child Poverty Action Group.

Gourevitch, P. (1998) *We wish to inform you that tomorrow we will be killed with our families: Stories from Rwanda*, London: Picador.

Green, K. (1997) 'A community response to drug issues on a Bristol estate', *Community Health Action*, 43.

Gregory, D. and Urry, J. (eds) (1985) *Social relations and spatial structures*, Basingstoke: Macmillan.

Grunberger, R. (1974) *A social history of the Third Reich*, Harmondsworth: Penguin.

Gusfield, J.R. (1975) *Community: A critical response*, Oxford: Blackwell.

Habermas, J. (1987) *The philosophical discourse of modernity*, Cambridge: Polity Press.

Habermas, J. (1992) *Postmetaphysical thinking: Philosophical essays*, Cambridge: Polity Press.

Hall, J.K. (1995) '(Re)creating our worlds with words: a sociohistorical perspective of face-to-face interaction', *Applied Linguistics*, vol 16, no 2, pp 206-32.

Hall, S. (1991) 'The local and the global: globalization and ethnicity' and 'Old and new identities, old and new ethnicities', in A.D. King (ed) *Culture, globalization and the world system: Contemporary conditions for the representation of identity*, Basingstoke: Macmillan.

Hall, S. (1993) 'Culture, community, nation', *Cultural Studies*, vol 7, no 3, pp 349-63.

Hammersley, M. and Atkinson, P. (1995) *Ethnography: Principles in practice* (2nd edn), London: Routledge.

Harding, S. (1986) *The science question in feminism*, Milton Keynes: Open University Press.

Harloe, M., Pickvance, C. and Urry, J. (1990) *Place, policy and politics: Do localities matter?*, London: Unwin Hyman.

Harris, V. (1994) *Review of social action projects in Bradford*, Leicester: Centre for Social Action, De Montfort University.

Harvey, D. (1990) *The condition of postmodernity*, Oxford: Blackwell.

Harvey, D. (1996) *Justice, nature and the geography of difference*, Oxford: Blackwell.

Hertz, R. (ed) (1997) *Reflexivity and voice*, Thousand Oaks, CA: Sage Publications.

Hobsbawm, E.J. (1994) *Age of extremes. The short twentieth century 1914-1991*, London: Michael Joseph.

Hobsbawm, E.J. (1998) 'On history from below', in *On history*, London: Abacus.

Hodgson, G. (1995) *People's century*, London: BBC.

Hoggett, P. (1997) *Contested communities. Experiences, struggles, policies*, Bristol: The Policy Press.

hooks, b. (1991) *Yearning: Race, gender, and cultural politics*, London: Turnaround.

Hope, T. and Hough, M. (1988) 'Area, crime and incivilities: a profile from the British Crime Survey', in T. Hope and M. Shaw (eds) (1988a) *Communities and crime reduction*, London: HMSO.

Hope, T and Shaw, M. (eds) (1988a) *Communities and crime reduction*, London: HMSO.

Hope, T. and Shaw, M. (1988b) 'Community approaches to reducing crime', in T. Hope and M. Shaw (eds) (1988a) *Communities and crime reduction*, London: HMSO.

Hylton, R. (1995) 'I said, I am that I am. I am. I am. I am', Introduction to Imagined Communities exhibition catalogue, London: National Touring Exhibitions.

Jackson, P. (1989a) 'Geography, race, and racism', in R. Peet and N. Thrift (eds) (1989a) *New models in geography. Volume two. The political economy perspective*, London: Unwin Hyman.

Jackson, P. (1989b) *Maps of meaning: An introduction to cultural geography*, London: Routledge.

James, A. (1986) 'Learning to belong: the boundaries of adolescence', in A.P. Cohen (ed) (1986a) *Symbolising boundaries. Identity and diversity in British cultures*, Manchester: Manchester University Press.

Johnson, R. (nd) 'Two ways of remembering: exploring memory as identity', Unpublished paper.

Johnson, R. (1987) 'What is cultural studies anyway?', *Social Text*, no 16, pp 38-80

Keith, M. and Cross, M. (1993) 'Racism and the modern city', in M. Cross and M. Keith (eds) *Racism, the city and the state*, London: Routledge.

Kellner, D. (1997) 'Overcoming the divide: cultural studies and political economy', in M. Ferguson and P. Golding (eds) (1997) *Cultural studies in question*, London: Sage Publications.

Kelly, O. (1984) *Community, art and the state: Storming the citadels*, London: Comedia.

Kimberlee, R.H. (1998) *Young people's survey of Southmead 1998*, Bristol: Southmead Youth Centre.

Kimberlee, R. and Cassidy, M. (1999) 'Young people *really* owning urban regeneration', Unpublished.

King, A.D. (ed) (1991) *Culture, globalization and the world system. Contemporary conditions for the representation of identity*, Basingstoke: Macmillan.

Laclau, E. (1990) *New reflections on the revolution of our time*, London: Verso.

Laing, S. (1986) *Representations of working-class life 1957-1964*, Basingstoke: Macmillan.

Lanzmann, C. (1995) *Shoah: The complete text of the acclaimed Holocaust film*, New York, NY: Da Capo Press.

Lasch, C. (1986) 'The communitarian critique of liberalism', *Soundings*, 49.

Lash, S. (1996) 'Postmodern ethics. the missing ground', *Theory, Culture and Society*, vol 13, no 2, pp 91-104.

Lash, S. and Urry, J. (1994) *Economies of signs and space*, London: Sage Publications.

Lefebvre, H. (1991) *The production of space*, Oxford: Blackwell.

Lévi-Strauss, C. (1966) *The savage mind*, London: Weidenfeld and Nicholson.

Ley, D. (1989) 'Modernism, post-modernism and the struggle for place', in Agnew, J.A. and Duncan, J.S. (eds) (1989) *The power of place. Bringing together geographical and sociological imaginations*, London: Unwin Hyman.

Lightfoot, J. (1990) *Involving young people in their communities*, London: Community Development Foundation Publications.

London Edinburgh Weekend Return Group (1980) *In and against the state*, London: Pluto.

Maffesoli, M. (1988) 'Jeux de masques: postmodern tribalism', *Design Issues*, vol 4, nos 1/2, pp 141-51.

Maffesoli, M. (1989) 'The sociology of everyday life (epistemological element)', *Current Sociology*, vol 37, no 1, pp 1-16.

Maffesoli, M. (1991) 'The ethics of aesthetics', *Theory, Culture and Society*, vol 8, no 1, pp 7-20.

Maffesoli, M. (1996) *The time of the tribes: The decline of individualism in mass society*, London: Sage Publications.

Marquand, D. (1988) *The unprincipled society: New demands and old politics*, London: Fontana.

Marx, K. and Engels, F. (1967) *The communist manifesto*, Harmondsworth: Penguin.

Marx, K. and Engels, F. (1970) *The German ideology*, London: Lawrence and Wishart.

Massey, D. (1985) 'New directions in space', in D. Gregory and J. Urry (eds) (1985) *Social relations and spatial structures*, Basingstoke: Macmillan.

Massey, D. (1998) 'The spatial construction of youth culture', in T. Skelton and G. Valentine (1998) *Cool places: Geographies of youth culture*, London: Routledge.

Mayo, M. (1994) *Communities and caring: The mixed economy of welfare*, Basingstoke: Macmillan.

McCormick, J. and Philo, C. (1995) 'Where is poverty? The hidden geography of poverty in the United Kingdom', in C. Philo (ed) *Off the map: The social geography of poverty in the UK*, London: Child Poverty Action Group.

McRobbie, A. (1991) *Feminism and youth culture*, Basingstoke: Macmillan.

Meegan, R. (1989) 'Paradise postponed: the growth and decline of Merseyside's outer estates', in P. Cooke (ed) *Localities: The changing face of urban Britain*, London: Unwin Hyman.

Melucci, A. (1989) *Nomads of the present: Social movements and individual needs in contemporary society*, London: Hutchinson Radius.

Melucci, A. (1996a) *The playing self: Person and meaning in the planetary society*, Cambridge: Cambridge University Press.

Melucci, A. (1996b) *Challenging codes: Collective action in the information age*, Cambridge: Cambridge University Press.

Melville, J. (1994) 'The reactionary radicals', *Druglink*, Sept/Oct.

Mercer, K. (1995) 'Imagine all the people: constructing community culturally', in Imagined Communities exhibition catalogue, London: National Touring Exhibitions.

Mewett, P.G. (1986) 'Boundaries and discourse in a Lewis crofting community', in A.P. Cohen (ed) (1986a) *Symbolising boundaries. Identity and diversity in British cultures*, Manchester: Manchester University Press.

Mitchell, J. (ed) (1986) *The selected Melanie Klein*, Harmondsworth: Penguin.

Modood, T. (1988) '"Black" racial identity and Asian identity', *New Community*, vol 14, no 3, pp 397-404.

Monaghan, G. (1993) *Drug misuse on the Southmead estate*, Bristol: Bristol Drugs Prevention Team.

Morrow, V. (1999) 'Conceptualising social capital in relation to the well-being of children and young people: a critical review', *The Sociological Review*, vol 47, no 4, pp 744-65.

Mouffe, C. (ed) (1992) *Dimensions of radical democracy: Pluralism, citizenship, community*, London: Verso.

Mowlam, M. (1994) 'A broadcasting future for all – not just the powerful', *Airflash*, April, pp 12-13.

Murgatroyd, L., Savage, M., Shapiro, D., Urry, J., Walby, S., Warde. A. and Mark-Lawson, J. (1985) *Localities, class, and gender*, London: Pion.

Nancy, J.-L. (1991) *The inoperative community*, Minneapolis, MN: University of Minnesota Press.

Newman, G. (1999) *Drug misuse in the Northern Arc Area of Bristol*, Bristol:

Nietzsche, F. (1990) *Beyond good and evil*, London: Penguin.

Noble, C. (1999) 'Silence: absence and context', in Parker, I. and the Bolton Discourse Group (1999) *Critical textwork. An introduction to varieties of discourse and analysis*, Buckingham: Open University.

O'Neill, J. (1998) 'Rhetoric, science, and philosophy', *Philosophy of the Social Sciences*, vol 28, no 2, pp 205-25.

Osgerby, B. (1998) *Youth in Britain since 1945*, Oxford: Blackwell.

Papastergiadis, N. (ed) (1996) *Annotations 1. Mixed belongings and unspecified destinations*, London: Institute of International Visual Arts.

Parker, I. (1992) *Discourse dynamics. Critical analysis for social and individual psychology*, London: Routledge.

Parker, I. (1999) 'Introduction: varieties of discourse and analysis', in I. Parker and the Bolton Discourse Group (1999) *Critical textwork: An introduction to varieties of discourse and analysis*, Buckingham: Open University.

Parker, I. and the Bolton Discourse Group (1999) *Critical textwork. An introduction to varieties of discourse and analysis*, Buckingham: Open University.

Peet, R. and Thrift, N. (eds) (1989a) *New models in geography. Volume two. The political economy perspective*, London: Unwin Hyman.

Peet, R. and Thrift, N. (1989b) 'Political economy and human geography', in R. Peet and N. Thrift (eds) (1989a) *New models in geography. Volume two. The political economy perspective*, London: Unwin Hyman.

Phillips, D.L. (1993) *Looking backward: A critical appraisal of communitarian thought*, Princeton, NJ: Princeton University Press.

Philo, C. (ed) (1995) *Off the map: The social geography of poverty in the UK*, London: Child Poverty Action Group.

Pile, S. and Keith, M. (eds) (1997) *Geographies of resistance*, London: Routledge.

Pile, S. and Thrift, N. (eds) (1995) *Mapping the subject: Geographies of cultural transformation*, London: Routledge.

Piper, H. and Piper, J. (1999) '"Disaffected youth" – a wicked issue: a worse label', *Youth and Policy*, no 62, pp 32-43.

Pitchford, M. (2008) *Making spaces for community development*, Bristol: The Policy Press.

Pitts, J. and Hope, T. (1998) 'The local politics of inclusion: the state and community safety', in C.J. Finer and M. Nellis (eds) (1998) *Crime and social exclusion*, Oxford: Blackwell.

Piven, F.F. and Cloward, R.A. (1977) *Poor people's movements: Why they succeed, how they fail*, New York, NY: Pantheon Books.

Plant, R. (1974) *Community and ideology: An essay in applied social philosophy*, London: Routledge and Kegan Paul.

Plant, R. (1978) 'Community: concept, conception, and ideology', *Politics and Society*, vol 8, no 1, pp 79-107.

Plummer, K. (1995) *Telling sexual stories: Power, change and social worlds*, London: Routledge.

Potter, J. and Halliday, Q. (1990) 'Community leaders. A device for warranting versions of crowd events', *Journal of Pragmatics*, vol 14, no 6, pp 905-21.

Potter, J. and Reicher, S. (1987) 'Discourses of community and conflict: the organization of social categories in accounts of a "riot"', *British Journal of Social Psychology*, no 26, pp 25-40.

Potter, J. and Wetherall, M. (1987) *Discourse and social psychology. Beyond attitudes and behaviour*, London: Sage Publications.

Power, A. and Tunstall, R. (1995) *Swimming against the tide: Polarisation or progress on 20 unpopular council estates, 1980-95*, York: Joseph Rowntree Foundation.

Power, A. and Tunstall, R. (1997) *Dangerous disorders: Riots and violent disturbances in thirteen areas of Britain, 1991-2*, York: Joseph Rowntree Foundation.

Pratt, G. (1989) 'Reproduction, class, and the spatial structure of the city', in R. Peet and N. Thrift (eds) (1989a) *New models in geography. Volume two. The political economy perspective*, London: Unwin Hyman.

Rajan, V. (ed) (1993) *Rebuilding communities: Experiences and experiments in Europe*, Totnes: Green Books.

Rajchman, J. (1991) *Truth and Eros: Foucault, Lacan and the question of ethics*, New York, NY: Routledge.

Reason, P. (1994) 'Three approaches to participative inquiry', in N.K. Denzin and Y.S. Lincoln (eds) (1994) *Handbook of qualitative research*, London: Sage Publications.

Richardson, L. (1994) 'Writing. A method of inquiry', in N.K. Denzin, and Y.S. Lincoln (eds) *Handbook of qualitative research*, London: Sage Publications.

Ricoeur, P. (1981) *Hermeneutics and the social sciences. Essays on language, action and interpretation*, Cambridge: Cambridge University Press.

Ricoeur, P. (1991) *From text to action: Essays in hermeneutics, II*, London: The Athlone Press.

Rock, P. (1988) 'Crime reduction initiatives on problem estates', in T. Hope and M. Shaw (eds) (1988a) *Communities and crime reduction*, London: HMSO.

Rose, G. (1997) 'Performing inoperative community. The space and the resistance of some community arts projects', in S. Pile and M. Keith (eds) *Geographies of resistance*, London: Routledge.

Rose, N. (1996) 'The death of the social? Re-figuring the territory of government', *Economy and Society*, vol 25, no 3, pp 327-56.

Rutherford, J. (ed) (1990) *Identity, community, culture, difference*, London: Lawrence and Wishart.

Safe Neighbourhoods Unit (1991) *The Southmead Survey 1991*, Prepared for Bristol City Council and Bristol Safer Cities Project.

Said, E.W. (1978) *Orientalism*, London: Routledge and Kegan Paul.

Sandel, M.J. (1982) *Liberalism and the limits of justice*, Cambridge: Cambridge University Press.

Sandel, M. (1992) 'The procedural subject and the unencumbered self', in S. Avineri and A. de-Shalit (eds) (1992) *Communitarianism and individualism*, Oxford: Oxford University Press.

Saunders, P. (1985) 'Space, the city and urban sociology', in D. Gregory and J. Urry (eds) (1985) *Social relations and spatial structures*, Basingstoke: Macmillan.

Saunders, P. (1986) *Social theory and the urban question* (2nd edn), London: Unwin Hyman.

SCRiPT (Southmead Crime Reduction Project Team) (1996) *Community safety in Southmead*.

Sennett, R. (1970) *The uses of disorder: Personal identity and city life*, Harmondsworth: Penguin.

Sennett, R. (1986) *The fall of public man*, London: Faber and Faber.

Sennett, R. (1994) *Flesh and stone: The body and the city in Western civilization*, London: Faber and Faber.

Sennett, R. and Cobb, J. (1977) *The hidden injuries of class*, Cambridge: Cambridge University Press.

Shields, R. (1991) *Places on the margin: Alternative geographies of modernity*, London: Routledge.

Shields, R. (1992) 'The individual, consumption cultures and the fate of community', in R. Shields (ed) *Lifestyle shopping: The subject of consumption*, London,: Routledge.

Shotter, J. and Billig, M. (1998) 'Bakhtinian psychology: from out of the heads of individuals and into the dialogues between them', in Bell, M.M. and Gardiner, M. (eds) (1998) *Bakhtin and the human sciences*, London: Sage Publications.

Sibley, D. (1995) *Geographies of exclusion: Society and difference in the West*, London: Routledge.

Skelton, T. and Valentine, G. (1998) *Cool places. Geographies of youth culture*, London: Routledge.

Skogan, W.G. (1988) 'Disorder, crime and community decline', in T. Hope and M. Shaw (eds) (1988a) *Communities and crime reduction*, London: HMSO.

Smith, M.A. and Kollock P. (eds) (1999) *Communities in cyberspace*, London: Routledge.

Smith, M.K. (1994) *Local education. Community, conversation, praxis*, Buckingham: Open University Press.

Soja, E.J. (1989) *Postmodern geographies: The reassertion of space in critical social theory*, London: Verso.

Southmead Community Handbook (1997) Coordinated and produced by Working in Southmead for Health (WISH).

Southmead Project: Strategies and Annual Reports, 1995-1999.

Southmead Youth Sports Development Initiative: Business Plan 1999.

Spencer, J., Tuxford, J. and Dennis, N. (1964) *Stress and release in an urban estate: A study in action research*, London: Tavistock.

Spivak, G.C. (1988) 'Can the subaltern speak?', in L. Grossberg and C. Nelson (eds) *Marxism and the interpretation of culture*, Urbana, IL: University of Illinois Press.

St Stephen, Southmead (1988) *Church and community.*

Stallybrass, P. and White, A. (1986) *The politics and poetics of transgression*, London: Methuen.

Stanley, L. (ed) (1990) *Feminist praxis: Research, theory and epistemology in feminist sociology*, London: Routledge.

Stewart, J. (1995) *Saffron Young People's Project final report*, Leicester: Centre for Social Action, De Montfort University.

Stock, B. (1993) 'Reading, community and a sense of place', in J. Duncan and D. Ley (eds) (1993) *Place/culture/representation*, London: Routledge.

Strauss, A. and Corbin, J. (1994) 'Grounded theory methodology: an overview', in N.K. Denzin and Y.S. Lincoln (eds) *Handbook of qualitative research*, London: Sage Publications.

Taylor, C. (1991) *The ethics of authenticity*, Cambridge, MA: Harvard University Press.

Thompson, E.P. (1968) *The making of the English working class*, 2nd edn, Harmondsworth: Penguin.

Thompson, E.P. (1971) 'The moral economy of the English crowd in the eighteenth century', *Past and Present*, no 50, pp 76-136.

Thompson, J. (1998) 'Community identity and world citizenship', in D. Archibugi, D. Held and M. Köhler *Re-imagining political community: Studies in cosmopolitan democracy*, Cambridge: Polity Press.

Tomasi, J. (1991) 'Individual rights and community virtues', *Ethics*, vol 101, no 3, pp 521-36.

Touraine, A. (1988) *Return of the actor: Social theory in postindustrial society*, Minneapolis, MN: University of Minnesota Press.

Truman, J. and Brent, J. (1995) *Alive and kicking! The life and times of Southmead Youth Centre*, Bristol: Redcliffe.

Unger, R.M. (1976) *Law in modern society. Toward a criticism of social theory*, New York, NY: The Free Press.

Urry, J. (1985) 'Social relations, space and time', in D. Gregory and J. Urry (eds) *Social relations and spatial structures*, Basingstoke: Macmillan.

Urry, J. (1990) 'Conclusions: places and politics', in M. Harloe, C. Pickvance and J. Urry *Place, policy and politics. Do localities matter?*, London: Unwin Hyman.

Valentine, G., Skelton, T. and Chambers, D. (1998) 'Cool places: an introduction to youth and youth cultures', in T. Skelton and G. Valentine *Cool places: Geographies of youth culture*, London: Routledge.

Volosinov, V.N. (1973) *Marxism and the philosophy of language*, New York, NY: Seminar Press.

Walcott, D. (1984) *Midsummer*, London: Faber and Faber.

Walker, A. (1993) 'Community care policy: from consensus to conflict', in J. Bornat, C. Pereira, D. Pilgrim and F. Williams (eds) *Community care: A reader*, Basingstoke: Macmillan.

Walkerdine, V. (1997) *Daddy's girl: Young girls and popular culture*, Basingstoke: Macmillan.

Walzer, M. (1990) 'The communitarian critique of liberalism', *Political Theory*, vol 18, no 1, pp 6-23.

Walzer, M. (1992) 'The civil society argument', in C. Mouffe (ed) *Dimensions of radical democracy: Pluralism, citizenship, community*, London: Verso.

Warde, A. (1985) 'Comparable localities; some problems of method', in L. Murgatroyd, M. Savage, D. Shapiro, J. Urry, S, Walby, A. Warde and J. Mark-Lawson *Localities, class, and gender*, London: Pion.

Warner, B.D. and Rountree, P.W. (1997) 'Local social ties in a community and crime model: questioning the systemic nature of informal social control', *Social Problems*, vol 44, no 4, pp 520-36.

Webster, C. (1996) 'Local heroes. Violent racism, localism and spacism among Asian and white young people', *Youth and Policy*, 53, pp 15-27.

Weeks, J. (1991) *The sphere of the intimate*, Occasional Papers no 29, Manchester: Manchester Sociology Department.

Weeks, J. (1995) *Invented moralities. Sexual values in an age of uncertainty*, Cambridge: Polity Press.

Wellman, B. (1979) 'The community question: the intimate network of East Yorkers', *American Journal of Sociology*, vol 84, no 5, pp 1201-31.

West, C. (1992) 'Nihilism in black America', in G. Dent (ed) *Black popular culture*, Seattle, WA: Bay Press.

Whitt, L.A. and Slack, J.D. (1994) 'Communities, environment and cultural studies', *Cultural Studies*, vol 8, no 1.

Williams, F. (1993) 'Women and community', in J. Bornat, C. Pereira, D. Pilgrim and F. Williams (eds) (1993) *Community care: A reader*, Basingstoke: Macmillan.

Williams, L.O. (1988) *Partial surrender. Race and resistance in the youth service*, Lewes: The Falmer Press.

Williams, R. (1958) *Culture and society 1780-1950*, Harmondsworth: Penguin.

Williams, R. (1983) *Keywords: A vocabulary of culture and society* (revised edn), London: Fontana.

Willis, P. (1980) *Learning to labour*, Farnborough: Gower.

Wilson, R. (1963) *Difficult housing estates*, London: Tavistock.

Wittgenstein, L. (1976) *Philosophical investigations*, Oxford: Blackwell.

Young, E.D.K. (1986) 'Where the daffodils blow: elements of communal imagery in a northern suburb', in A.P. Cohen (ed) (1986a) *Symbolising boundaries. Identity and diversity in British cultures*, Manchester: Manchester University Press.

Young, I.M. (1990) 'The ideal of community and the politics of difference', in L.J. Nicholson (ed) *Feminism/postmodernism*, New York, NY: Routledge.

Zizek, S. (1991a) *Looking awry: An introduction to Jacques Lacan through popular culture*, Cambridge, MA: MIT Press.

Zizek, S. (1991b) *For they know not what they do: Enjoyment as a political factor*, London, Verso.

Zukin, S. (1991) *Landscapes of power: From Detroit to Disneyworld*, Berkeley, CA: University of California Press.

Zukin, S. (1995) *The cultures of cities*, Oxford: Blackwell.

Videos and films

(All these Southmead Youth Centre productions involved young people from Southmead, variously as actors, writers, interviewers and musicians.)
1989 24 Hours: 32 min. Video drama directed by John Podpadec.

1991 This is England: 6 min. Video documentary directed by John Podpadec.

1993 Hot and Twitchy: 3 min. Animated film directed by Debbie Collard.

1995 FIRE. A Summer of Dance at Southmead Youth Centre: 6 min. Directed by Mike Miller.

1999 Rush: 6 min. Film directed by Rob Mitchell.

1999 Southmead Slamming: An Excellent Centre: 12 min. Video documentary directed by Dave Greenhalgh.

Exhibitions

1986 Young People at Southmead Youth Centre: Photographic exhibition by John Podpadec.

1995 Southmead Photo Album: Photographs taken by young people from Southmead Youth Centre. Exhibited at Watershed Media Centre, Bristol.

1996 Fresh Evidence: Exhibition of paintings and installations by young people from Southmead, with Mike Miller and Alexei Thomson. Exhibited at Bristol City Museum and Art Gallery.

1997 The Place We're In: A multimedia exhibition by Southmeaders. Young people's work with Simon Poulter and Hannah Cox. First shown at Watershed Media Centre, Bristol.

1999 Distorted Stories and AlieNation: Digital printed images and CD ROM of digital animation and dance. Young people with Nick Kemp.

Other material

1991-93 *Say It!*: Southmead's community newspaper

1993- (bi-monthly) *Southmead writers*: a collection of poems and stories from local people in Southmead.

1994-96 *Southmead and Westbury-on-Trym Proclaimer/The Proclaimer/Southmead Community News*

1994 Fire It Up: music CD by Brabazon.

1994 Radio Southmead: broadcast from Southmead Youth Centre, August. Producer Heie Geilhaus.

1994 Life Lines: as well as the script (Beddow, 1994), there are posters, a souvenir programme, a video and a report. Performed at the Greenway Centre, Southmead, November/December 1994.

1998 kfs – Kids from Southmead: music CD produced by Dale Fry with The Vegas Kids and Magic Mix Music.

Index

Page references for footnotes are followed by n